Measuring Reading Abilities: concepts, sources and applications

Measuring Reading Abilities:
concepts, sources and applications

Peter D. Pumfrey
Senior Lecturer in Education
Department of Education
University of Manchester

HODDER AND STOUGHTON
LONDON SYDNEY AUCKLAND TORONTO

British Library Cataloguing in Publication Data

Pumfrey, Peter David
    Measuring reading abilities.
    1. Reading – Ability testing
    I. Title
    428'.4   LB1050.46

    ISBN 0–340–18797–2
    ISBN 0–340–18796–4   Pbk

ISBN 0 340 18797 2 Boards
ISBN 0 340 18796 4 Unibook

Printed in Great Britain for
Hodder and Stoughton Educational,
a division of Hodder and Stoughton Ltd,
Mill Road, Dunton Green, Sevenoaks, Kent,
by Cox & Wyman Ltd, London, Fakenham and Reading

Contents

Preface

I have been greatly helped in the preparation of this book by the comments on specific sections made by my colleagues in the Department of Education and the Colleges of Education Division of the Faculty of Education at the University of Manchester. In particular, I am indebted to Dr D. G. Lewis, Dr T. Fitzpatrick, Dr C. D. Elliott, Mr D. Murray and Mr J. Ryan.

Permission to reproduce copyright materials has been readily accorded me: The National Foundation for Educational Research has allowed me to use part of the conversion table for *Reading Test AD*; Harcourt, Brace, Jovanovich, Inc., gave permission for the use and adaptation of an extract from T. L. Kelley's work referred to in Adams, G. S. (1964) *Measurement and Evaluation in Education, Psychology and Guidance*, page 96; The University of Illinois Press allowed the reproduction of the results profile of the *Illinois Test of Psycholinguistic Abilities* (revised edition); The United Kingdom Reading Association and Ward Lock Educational agreed to my using an extract from Southgate, V. (Ed.) (1972) *Literacy at all Levels*, pages 140, 142 and 143; Professor T. C. Barrett has given permission for the use of the taxonomy of cognitive and affective dimensions of reading comprehension originally published in an article by Professor T. Clymer in the 67th Yearbook of the National Society for the Study of Education; Basic Books, Inc., allowed me to adapt Figure 3 'A paradigm for the analysis of influencing variables' from *The Search for Ability*, by David A. Goslin, © 1963 Russell Sage Foundation.

I have been fortunate in obtaining the cooperation of many practising Educational Psychologists and Remedial Education Organisers throughout England and Wales. They have enabled me to carry out a survey of the availability of in-service courses concerned with the uses of reading tests. I was also able to investigate the extent to which individual Local Educational Authority Schools' Psychological Services and Remedial Education Services have pertinent materials on tests and testing available to teachers. Reference to the findings is given briefly in the text.

While this work has been greatly facilitated by all of the above, I acknowledge especially the encouragement and help given to me by Professor John Merritt of the Faculty of Educational Studies at the Open University. The responsibility for the book as it is presented, however, is mine alone.

Peter D. Pumfrey
Department of Education
University of Manchester

1. Introduction: basic concepts

The appropriate use of reading tests can contribute towards improving the standards of literacy of our children, yet the uses of reading tests are frequently under- or over-valued by teachers. Often, this is a consequence of a restricted appreciation of the conceptual bases, sources and legitimate applications of reading tests. There is a vast variety of reading tests available. The most important British reading tests and some interesting overseas ones have been surveyed in a recent United Kingdom Reading Association (UKRA) monograph (Pumfrey 1976). While this book and the monograph have a related theme, each can be read independently.

To use reading tests effectively, it is essential that the user has considered the topics which form the titles of the chapters in this book. Teachers are the most frequent users of reading tests. This book has been written as an introduction to the field for the non-mathematician who is interested in the role of measurement in the teaching of reading. For those wishing to pursue the ideas presented here, ample references are provided.

It has been said that whatever exists, exists in some quantity and can in principle be measured. More important in so far as reading is concerned, measurement can usefully be undertaken in both the pupils' and their teachers' interests. The writer agrees with the principle stated by Lord Kelvin, who once said: 'When you can measure what you are speaking about and express it in numbers, you know something about it; but when you cannot measure it, when you cannot express it in numbers, your knowledge is of a meagre and unsatisfactory kind.'

Some twenty-three years ago Guilford, an eminent psychometrician, commented that 'No other contribution of psychology has had the social impact equal to that created by the psychological test. No other technique and no other body of theory in psychology has been so fully rationalised from the mathematical point of view.' Yet quantification by itself is not enough. Figures can be used as a smokescreen to obscure our lack of understanding and control of the reading process from ourselves and others, wittingly or otherwise, unless we are aware of the limitations both of mental measurement and of our conceptualisation of the reading process.

What is reading?

At a recent in-service course on the teaching of reading, one discussion centred on the question 'What is reading?' Considerable differences of definition were found within the group. In part these variations were related to the ages of the children taught (from nursery to secondary level) and to the teaching experience of the teachers, who ranged from first-year probationers to those with many years' experience.

Definitions of reading have changed markedly over the last fifty years as our knowledge of the reading process and of child development has increased. Yet an understanding of the nature of the reading process, and some attempt at definition, is essential if our teaching procedures and assessment techniques are to be adequate. The reading process is more than a simple mechanical skill whereby, say, the presentation of a flash card to an infant school child elicits the appropriate oral response from the child. It is more than the ability to understand the explicit meaning of the passage presented. It is, in essence, a constructive thinking process which includes comprehension of explicit and implicit meaning. It involves application, analysis, evaluation and imagination. *Reading is a process that requires thought.* It is one activity through which the child's cognitive development can be furthered (Stauffer 1969; Walker 1974).

The reading process is also characteristically developmental and the relative importance of component skills at a given stage in this process can vary considerably. In practice, it is sometimes assumed by junior school teachers that most children should have acquired the necessary basic competence in reading by the end of their infant school careers. The work of researchers such as Morris (1966), Goodacre (1967, 1968), Gardner (1968), Clark (1970), Davie *et al.* (1972) and many large-scale local surveys carried out by Schools' Psychological Services and Remedial Education Services throughout the UK have shown this assumption to be false (Vernon 1971; Moseley 1975). At a more fundamental level, if the teacher is faced with a typical first-year junior school class, the existence of children who find difficulty in mastering reading skills has a more striking impact than any research report.

We also know that at the top of the junior school, at the fifth year of secondary school education, and at all ages between, there are large numbers of children who have difficulty in reading at a level likely to be of any practical use or to give them any pleasure. A national survey carried out by the National Foundation for Educational Research (NFER) on behalf of the Department of Education and Science (DES) gives some indication of the extent of the problems (Start and Wells 1972). The secondary school teacher faced with a group of 'slow-learning' children needs no such survey to convince her of the nature and extent of the problem and its urgency.

There is evidence that a *laissez-faire* attitude towards the aims, methods and assessment of the reading programmes in many schools disregards what is known about the developmental nature of reading abilities and sound teaching practice. This results in a failure to maximise for many children the opportunity of achieving literacy by the end of their formal education.

The setting up by the DES of the Bullock Committee on 'Reading and the uses of English' was a recognition of concern in this area. Of the 333 recommendations made in the Bullock Report, seventeen are picked out for special mention (DES 1975). Of these, at least four stress the importance of the use of tests in the monitoring of standards of literacy and in the diagnosis and treatment of reading difficulties. Quoting from the recommendations:

'1. A system of monitoring should be introduced which will employ new instruments to assess a wider range of attainments than has been attempted in the past and allow new criteria to be established for the definition of literacy.'

'6. There should be close consultation between schools, and the transmission of effective records, to ensure continuity in the teaching of reading and in the language development of every pupil.'

'9. LEAs and schools should introduce early screening procedures to prevent cumulative language deficit and reading failure and to guarantee individual diagnosis and treatment.'

'11. There should be a reading clinic or remedial centre in every LEA, giving access to a comprehensive diagnostic service and expert medical, psychological and teaching help. In addition to its provision for children with severe reading difficulties the centre should offer an advisory service to schools in association with the LEA's specialist adviser.'

In chapters on 'Standards of Reading', 'Monitoring', 'Screening,

Diagnosis and Recording' and 'Children with Reading Difficulties' the vital role of tests as important sources of information for the teacher is stressed. The many constructive suggestions for helping teachers acquire the necessary competence to use this information are welcomed.

That much still remains to be done to implement even the above recommendations can be gathered from the findings of a survey carried out one year after the publication of the Bullock Report and to which ninety-six of the one hundred and eight LEAs in England and Wales replied. Of these authorities, only fifty-one claimed to have a formal system for screening all primary school children for language and reading difficulties. Seventy-five had either reading clinics or remedial centres for the diagnosis and teaching of children with language and reading difficulties (Makins 1976).

What is a reading test?

A reading test is a public means of collecting and quantifying information concerning the extent to which a child has mastered a given skill in, or acquired a particular attitude towards, some aspect of reading. The judicious selection and organisation of the material comprising a test enables the tester to obtain this information economically in terms of both his and the pupil's time. Reading tests are efficient means of obtaining reliable assessments that are valid for particular purposes. As we shall see, such information is potentially of great value to the teacher.

Measurement

Teachers generally are aware that the instruments used in the measurement of mental abilities have distinctive characteristics. The process involved is not the same as, say, measuring the height of a table with a ruler. To appreciate the import of this difference, we must briefly consider the nature of measurement: the assignation of numerals to objects or events according to rules.

For our purpose, four different levels of measurement can usefully be distinguished. In ascending order of the amount of information they can carry, these are: (i) the classificatory or nominal scale, (ii) the ranking or ordinal scale, (iii) the interval scale, and (iv) the ratio scale. Each scale has different formal properties and these determine the ways in which data at a given level of measurement can be manipulated (Siegel 1956).

The lowest level of measurement exists when categories such as numbers or other symbols are simply used to classify people, events or observations. For example, ethnic group classification is a nominal categorisation. The grouping of children in an unstreamed school according to their class teacher's initials is another. In each example, the classification of observations indicates the set of mutually exclusive sub-classes to which an observation belongs. Classifying readers as being, or not being, library users is a further example of measurement at this relatively weak level.

At a higher level, the ordinal scale of measurement is one much favoured by teachers. Children are still frequently ranked according to their reading attainments. Each observation at this level implies more than just being the same as, or different from, others and thus goes beyond what is required to classify on a nominal scale. Each stands in a hierarchical relationship to the others, being greater than, preferred, superior (or equal) to them (or the reverse). The distance or amount between rankings is not, however, known. For example, we merely know that John reads given material more accurately than Mary. The extent of the superiority cannot be assessed from their rankings. Despite this limitation, teachers find rank orders of considerable use in discussing the relative reading attainments of their pupils.

The interval scale has all the characteristics of the ordinal scale, but in addition the distances between any two numbers are of a known size. Such a scale is typified by a constant and common unit of measurement and accords a real number to all pairs of observations in the ordered set. At this level the ratio of any two intervals is independent of the unit of measurement and of the zero point. Commonly temperature is measured on an interval scale. Whether we use the centigrade or Fahrenheit scale is entirely a matter of choice. Each contains the same information. Although the scales have different zeros and different units of measurement, the *ratio of the differences between two pairs* of readings on the one scale is identical to the ratio between equivalent differences on the other. In such scales the zero point and the unit of measurement are arbitrary.

On the assumption that reading abilities are normally distributed in the individuals being tested (see p. 97), the distances between the frequencies of any two observations are known theoretically. The reading test constructor, then, is able to select test items until the presupposed normal distribution appears in the distribution of children's scores on the reading test. He thus obtains an interval scale. The interval scale is the first really quantitative level of measurement.

At a higher level, the ratio scale has all the characteristics of the interval scale, but also has a true zero. Thus length is an example. The ratio between any two lengths is independent of the unit of measurement. If we measure the lengths of two different pieces of wood in inches and then in centimetres, we would find that the ratio of the two measurements in inches would be identical to the ratio of the two measurements in centimetres.

The majority of standardised tests of reading claim to achieve measurement at the interval scale level. No conventionally standardised reading test achieves measurement at the level of a ratio scale. This is, in part, because of the theoretical and practical difficulty in specifying zero ability.

Objectives, assessment and teaching

The main functions of the teaching of reading are to bring about changes in the child's level of competence in, and attitudes towards, reading. It is accepted that this cannot be done in isolation from the rest of the educational programme (Merritt 1971). However, the focus of this book is deliberately narrowed to reading only. The types of change which the teacher expects to achieve constitute the goals of the reading programme arranged for her pupils. Thus the teacher at any level is concerned with the following related tasks in the teaching of reading:

1. the *assessment* of the child's current reading skills;
2. the *specification of reading objectives* which it is anticipated will be achieved by the child;
3. the *arrangement* of a pattern of learning experiences which will facilitate the child's achievement of the objectives;
4. the *assessment* of the degree to which the objectives of the reading programme have been achieved; and,
5. dependent upon the teacher's interpretation and evaluation of the results obtained, repetition of the cycle.

It is a legitimate concern for the teacher to use methods of assessing reading abilities that can provide a sound basis for describing, interpreting and evaluating the outcomes of her reading programme. Reading tests of markedly different types, designed to meet very different purposes, offer ways of meeting the teacher's needs in this respect. They also further the teacher's understanding of the reading process (McLaughlin 1966; Pumfrey 1976).

The teacher as tester

Reading is one aspect of the language arts or skills. Its teaching is recognised as an important function of the staff of schools in our society. The efficiency with which teachers can help children acquire the many inter-related skills involved in reading varies greatly. It is to a large extent dependent upon the individual teacher's knowledge of child development, the clarity with which the goals of the reading programme are expressed, teaching techniques, and her ability to use and interpret the results of various types of testing procedure. The testing of children's reading skills and attainments is not an end in itself, but is one means of promoting better reading.

'I've never needed to use a reading test in all my years of teaching reading.' So said a teacher who was patently competent at helping children learn to read. In fact, anyone observing her at work would realise that with individual children she was constantly applying highly effective *informal* tests of the child's mastery of reading skills. As a result of the information obtained in this way, she modified the content and sequence of learning experiences to which the child was exposed. This teacher mistakenly identified the process of testing solely with the administration of a particular type of standardised reading test. *Teaching and testing are complementary functions in efficient education.* They cannot be divorced.

The testing of reading is no more than the careful sampling of one important aspect of a child's behaviour related to language and thinking. This sampling can be done intuitively or formally. Both approaches are important, although this book is primarily concerned with the second, formal approach. The systematic testing of reading enables the teacher to assess whether or not a child's progress is appropriate in terms of accepted educational goals in this area. If it is not, the teacher needs to generate ideas as to the reasons why a child is failing. She must then decide what educational intervention or experience is likely to facilitate the child's progress. Even the exceptionally competent teacher of reading is likely to become more effective if she is aware of the time that can be saved in identifying a child's weaknesses and/or strengths in reading skills through the use of formal and systematic rather than intuitive testing.

Many teachers are unaware of the different types of reading tests that are available and of their possible uses and limitations. The restricted aims of this book are five-fold. Firstly, to present a rationale for the systematic use by the teacher of various types of reading tests, particularly standardised ones. This applies to reading programmes at any level from the infant school upwards. Secondly, to discuss some of the important concepts related to the effective use of reading tests. Thirdly, to describe some of the major sources of reading test information currently available. Fourthly, to discuss the principles of reading test administration and the nature of the results obtained. Fifthly, to consider some important dimensions of reading test interpretation and applications.

To this end the titles of the eight chapters of the book are topics which any potential user of reading tests needs to consider if she is to use tests effectively.

References

CLARK, M. M. (1970) *Reading Difficulties in Schools*. Harmondsworth, Penguin.

DAVIE, R., BUTLER, N. and GOLDSTEIN, H (1972) *From Birth to Seven*. London, Longman in association with the National Children's Bureau.

Department of Education and Science (1975) *A Language for Life* (The Bullock Report). London, HMSO.

GARDNER, K. (1968) A Study of Reading Standards in a Midland Borough. Paper read at the 1968 Annual Conference of the Education Section of the British Psychological Society. *Abstracts*, 7–10.

GOODACRE, E. J. (1967) *Teaching Beginners to Read. Reading in Infant Classes*. Slough, NFER.

GOODACRE, E. J. (1968) *Teaching Beginners to Read. Teachers and Their Pupils' Home Background*. Slough, NFER.

MAKINS, V. (1976) Bullock plus one. *Times Educational Supplement*, no. 3166, 6 February 1976.

MCLAUGHLIN, K. F. (Ed.) (1966) *Understanding Testing: Purposes and Interpretations for Pupil Development*. Washington, D.C., US Government Printing Office.

MERRITT, J. (Ed.) (1971) *Reading and the Curriculum*. London, Ward Lock.

MORRIS, J. M. (1966) *Standards and Progress in Reading*. Slough, NFER.

MOSELEY, D. (1975) Special Provision for Readers: When will they ever learn? Slough, NFER.

PUMFREY, P. D. (1976) *Reading: Tests and Assessment Techniques*. London, Hodder and Stoughton.

SIEGEL, S. (1956) *Nonparametric Statistics for the Behavioral Sciences*. New York, McGraw-Hill.

START, K. B. and WELLS, B. K. (1972) *The Trend of Reading Standards*. Slough, NFER.

STAUFFER, R. G. (1969) *Directing Reading Maturity as a Cognitive Process*. New York, Harper and Row.

VERNON, M. D. (1971) *Reading and its Difficulties*. London, Cambridge University Press.

WALKER, C. (1974) *Reading Development and Extension*. London, Ward Lock Educational.

2. Why test reading?

The teacher's view

From the point of view of the teacher, the testing of reading must help her to maintain and improve standards of attainment in and attitudes towards reading of the children for whom she has professional responsibility (Farr 1970). Such attainments and attitudes can be measured with known degrees of precision. The information from reading tests can contribute towards the attainment of the objectives of reading instruction by helping the teacher in the following seven ways:

1. *To maintain and improve standards in reading*

Testing children's reading attainments and attitudes focuses the teacher's attention on standards both within the class from year to year and also between schools. Using tests, it is possible to know whether or not reading standards in a given situation are rising, falling or stationary. To do this, it is essential that appropriate records are kept.

2. *To compare the reading skills and attitudes of pupils within a class*

Objective tests of reading skills and attainments can discriminate reliably between the abilities of children within a class. If it is considered educationally desirable to group children for reading instruction so that a group has either a very narrow or a very wide range of reading ability, reading test results can provide the necessary information. Though tests of attitudes towards reading are less refined, there are some promising approaches (Pumfrey and Dixon 1970).

3. *To measure progress in reading*

Reading tests enable a teacher to establish a baseline from which
the progress of the individual or the group can be measured and
evaluated. Most teachers think of improvement as the difference
between test scores at the start of reading teaching and those at the
end. This is but *one* way of assessing progress, and it has some
advantages. But there are at least *five* different ways in which
progress in reading can be estimated. All have varying strengths
and weaknesses (Davis 1970).

4. *To evaluate various approaches to the teaching of reading*

Reading tests can be used to examine the effects of any innovation
in the teaching of reading that the teacher may make. For example,
many schools were concerned in the various Initial Teaching
Alphabet investigations. The teachers involved will be aware of the
use of reading tests in comparing the short-term and long-term
effects on children's acquisition of reading skills using either i.t.a.
or traditional orthography (t.o.).

5. *To diagnose reading difficulties*

The aim of the diagnosis of reading difficulties is to determine the
nature of the process by looking carefully at the functional relationships between its different aspects. Diagnostic reading tests enable
the teacher to locate the child's particular skill deficiencies. This is an
essential first step in alleviating the adverse effects of such deficiencies on his reading attainments. For the teacher, the major focus
in the use of diagnostic reading tests is to gather information that
will help in planning a reading programme for the child. Such a
programme will capitalise on strengths and also help to improve
skills found to be weak (Tansley 1967; Della-Piana 1968; Harris
1970; Dechant 1971; Pumfrey 1974).

The *Concise Oxford English Dictionary* defines diagnosis as
'Identification of disease by means of patient's symptoms'. Drever
(1964) extends this to 'Determination of the nature of an abnormality, disorder or disease'. The use of the concept of 'diagnosis'
in the context of the investigation of children's reading difficulties
is controversial. This is, in part, due to disagreement as to whether
the medical model implicit in the term is appropriate to education.
It is feasible that inter-individual differences in reading skills or

sub-skills are normally distributed in a population. Thus we might reasonably expect a wide range of attainments in and attitudes towards these skills at any age level.

Teachers are expected to respect the individuality of the child whilst at the same time ensuring that each child conforms to certain patterns of behaviour; for example, that he learns to read. Often, those children falling at the lower ends of the hypothesised normal distributions are categorised as children with reading difficulties. To some extent the difficulties in reading that such children experience are generated by a social desire for a conformity that is possibly at variance with the nature of human beings. In contrast, relatively little is heard of those children at the upper end of the normal distribution who are extremely competent readers. Margaret Clark's work in Scotland sets out to redress this imbalance (Clark 1975, 1976).

The above should not be taken as indicating a belief that the improvement of standards of reading skills generally and the alleviation of reading difficulties in particular cannot be achieved. The complexity of the reading process makes it possible for a wide range of poor reading habits and attitudes to be learned by the child.

In some cases a child's reading difficulties may be directly attributable to a physical abnormality, disorder or disease. For example, vision or hearing may be impaired. If the nature of such disorders can be identified and treatment given, this may enable the child to overcome his reading difficulty. However, in the majority of cases of difficulties in reading, highly specific causes cannot be identified. It is possible to calculate the relationships between a variety of reading difficulties and a host of physical, social, educational, emotional and motivational variables. Merely because a highly significant correlation is found between, say, poor auditory-visual integration (can the child match sound patterns and visual patterns?) and failure in reading, it cannot be assumed that the poor integration *causes* the reading difficulty. Teachers and researchers are well aware that for almost every child with a specific handicap who has reading difficulties, there are others with the same handicap who can read competently. This points to our incomplete understanding of and control over the development of the ability to read. It highlights limitations in our ability to diagnose difficulties adequately (Farr 1969).

Diagnosis of reading difficulties is not an esoteric exercise carried out solely by highly trained experts. It can be carried out at many levels (Wilson 1967; Kennedy 1971; Reid 1972; Schell and Burns

1972; DES 1975). The class teacher is constantly engaged in the informal diagnosis of children's reading difficulties and in making modifications to the experiences that the child encounters. These interventions are intended to ease the child's progressive acquisition of more complex skills (Gagné and Briggs 1974; Gagné 1977). Should this informal approach fail, the teacher may initiate a more formal examination of a child's difficulties, still within the classroom. If the child continues to experience difficulties, referral may be made to someone with more specialised knowledge and expertise, such as an educational psychologist or a remedial teacher.

At any level, the diagnosis of reading difficulties is perhaps most usually and most profitably seen as a process of hypothesis generation followed by an intervention, the result of which leads to a further modification of the hypothesis and thus of the intervention. More prosaically, 'Johnny can't synthesise phonically regular words; why not? Perhaps it is because . . ., so I will arrange for him to . . . and see if it helps. If it doesn't, I'll have to think again.' The testing of the hypotheses generated implies the use of an appropriate measure of the reading skill it is hoped to modify.

All teachers concerned with facilitating the learning of reading skills need to be aware of the principles of educational diagnosis. A comprehensive discussion of the topic can be found in Bond and Tinker (1967) and Sheldon (1970). The following list is adapted from their work:

Principles underlying the diagnosis of reading difficulties :
(i) Diagnosis is an integral part of effective teaching.
(ii) Diagnosis is intended to facilitate the child's acquisition of specified skills or attitudes.
(iii) Diagnosis is a continuous process in education.
(iv) Diagnosis is centred on the particular individual's reading difficulty.
(v) Diagnosis of reading difficulties often requires more than an assessment of reading skills because reading difficulties may be symptomatic of a wide range of causative factors.
(vi) Diagnosis of reading difficulties implies that the teacher is aware of the importance of the other language arts of listening, speaking and writing.
(vii) Diagnosis should involve the use of standardised test procedures, but the teacher needs to be aware of the limitations of currently available instruments in this field and be able to use other types of tests, i.e. criterion-referenced tests (see pp. 44, 138 and 142.

(viii) As our knowledge of the reading process is incomplete, any decision made in diagnosing a difficulty should be based on a pattern of scores.

(ix) The heart of diagnosis is the intelligent interpretation of a series of observations coupled with the ability to relate the interpretation to a plan for remedial teaching.

(x) Only by developing and refining diagnostic procedures can our understanding of the reading process be furthered and our ability to prevent and alleviate reading difficulties advanced.

6. *Aids in matching materials and methods to the child*

If a teacher knows the level of a child's reading attainment as measured by a reading test, she will be in a better position to select and prepare reading materials suited to the child. Knowledge of the reading levels of books means that their selection for a given child or class of children can be much more systematic, with less chance of inappropriate purchases (Gilliland and Merritt 1972). Three of the most useful British publications giving information concerning the reading and interest levels of children's reading materials are those by Lawson (1968), Atkinson and Gains (1973) and Kelly (1973). The UKRA periodical *Books in Schools* provides reviews and readability ratings of new books.

7. *To increase the teacher's professional competence*

The information provided by reading test results can help the teacher to obtain a better understanding of the reading process. The teaching and testing of reading go hand in hand. If either is neglected, the other suffers. The careful, controlled observation and analysis of the reading skills of the child is the essence of testing. The information obtained can help the teacher become more effective in helping her pupils achieve literacy (Pidgeon and Yates 1968; DES 1975).

Other viewpoints

Whilst the above considerations are of major concern to the teacher of reading, other people are also interested. For example, local education authorities require some means of assessing how effectively children are being helped to become competent readers. It should be possible to identify schools where all is not well and to take appropriate action on the basis of objective information rather than opinion. An objective test of reading attainment is one ready means by which the educational system can be monitored. Indeed, there are good reasons for expecting the regular assessment of basic skills such as literacy and numeracy to become far more general, regular and systematic than is currently the case (DES 1972, para. 34; 1975, paras 3.1–3.3).

The establishment by the Department of Education and Science of an 'Assessment of Performance Unit' in 1974 gives some indication of future policy in this respect. The terms of reference of the Unit are 'To promote the development of methods of assessing and monitoring the achievement of children at school, and to seek to identify the incidence of under-achievement'. A Consultative Committee responsible for advising and making suggestions for the Unit's programme has been set up under the chairmanship of Professor Barry Supple. The Committee includes representatives of local authorities and of educational associations plus twelve members representative of parents, employers and unions.

In 1976, the head of the Assessment of Performance Unit described the progress made by the Unit during the first two years of its operation. He discussed reasons why developments had been rather slow: 'First, a model of the curriculum had to be devised that would match the goals of schools, both primary and secondary, and serve as the framework for assessment. To create this, to discuss it widely, to modify it and to embody it in a form of organisation all took time. That task is now completed, and a set of working groups is being formed to examine the assessment implications for the different areas covered by the model.' The work of the Bullock Committee provided an excellent starting point for certain of the groups. In relation to the field of writing '. . . a point has almost been reached when a research team can be called upon to develop the appropriate assessment techniques in accordance with specifications laid down by the working group'. Later in the same article, we are informed that 'similar work has gone on in the analysis of reading, especially in relation to the ways of categorising the different types of material pupils read, both in school and outside, and the different purposes for which they read them, with a view to sampling both of these for testing purposes' (Kay 1976). It may be coincidence that the three UKRA monographs prescribed for the extremely popular Open University course on Reading, the second version of which started in January 1977, are *Reading, Writing and Relevance* (Hoffman 1976), *Print and Prejudice* (Zimet 1976) and *Reading and the Consumer* (Williams 1976).

The concept of 'accountability' in education is one of which teachers are likely to become increasingly conscious in their professional capacity. Despite current spending of 6 per cent of the gross national product on education compared with about half that in the 1930s, a significant increase in the length of teacher training and a marked reduction in class size, there exists a widespread suspicion that standards of reading are not as high as might be expected. From the preceding comments concerning the Assessment of Performance Unit, it appears that there is a demand for more precise knowledge concerning reading standards than has hitherto been available. In England and Wales, the effects of an earlier attempt to improve standards in certain subjects including reading, and simultaneously to increase the efficiency of schools, has already been tried and found wanting. The 'Payment by Results' system introduced during the last century in the Revised Code of 1862 and disposed of in the Code of 1897 has left emotional scars on the teaching profession and a deep suspicion of methods of monitoring reading attainments by central authority. There are also lessons to be learned from the recent American experience of 'Educational Performance Contracting' under which commercial firms accepted, for example, the responsibility of providing instruction in reading. The arrangement was that the firms concerned would receive no payment unless the children made a specified amount of progress in a given period.

The entire question of *what* should be assessed in the field of language in general and reading in particular and *how* it should be done must be under continuous review. A narrow concept of the objectives of a reading curriculum can have a negative and restricting washback effect: 'However, performance contracting also develops a marked emphasis on the individual pupil and his reading attainments as an index of the programme's efficiency. It facilitates the introduction of radical changes in teaching by encouraging learning system contractors to contribute to the education of pupils. A danger is that the teacher of reading may not make her voice heard because the profession's knowledge and understanding of the technicalities of mental measurement is relatively undeveloped. Our interest in all aspects of development should ensure that the notion of a simplistic view of accountability should be questioned. Being teachers of reading is secondary to being teachers of children' (Pumfrey 1976).

There is considerable difficulty in assessing at either a regional or a national level whether or not reading standards of pupils at school are increasing, decreasing or static. This point was well made in a recent examination of six large British studies reported between 1966 and 1973 (Burke and Lewis 1975). All six studies were normative in that they were designed to establish reading standards. Some were additionally concerned with identifying psychological or organisational variables related to relative success or failure in reading. Most of the studies used either a single criterion or two of the same type. Burke and Lewis conclude that due attention must be paid by commentators to the restrictions in sampling both of reading skills and of pupils if overgeneralisation is to be avoided. The authors argue that the national survey reported by Start and Wells (1972), and which was widely interpreted as indicating a decline in reading standards, does not in fact justify such a conclusion. Recent developments in test construction techniques coupled with the formation of the Assessment of Performance Unit hold out hope that in the future more valid estimates of regional and national reading standards will be available.

From the parents' point of view, the testing of reading is an assurance that the school is concerned with its effectiveness in helping its pupils to become fluent and enthusiastic readers. These two educational objectives are generally accepted as being of considerable importance in Western society.

To the child, the informal and formal testing of reading can help to give a sense of direction. There is considerable evidence that children and adults learn more effectively when they are able to quantify and record their individual progress. Where the child is concerned in recording his own progress against his own previous performances, self-testing can help in maintaining a child's motivation. For example, individual records are contained in the nine SRA *Reading Laboratories* (Parker 1972), the Ward Lock *Reading Workshops* (Conochie *et al.* 1969, 1971) and the Stott *Programmed Reading Kit* (Stott 1971). Such records use the motivation provided by immediate feedback of reading test results (often obtained in situations using games) to encourage children's reading progress.

This is not to argue that *all* children should immediately be informed of their results on *all* reading tests, but merely to indicate that there are a number of circumstances in which such knowledge can help the child.

Finally, the testing of reading and its related skills plays an important part in educational research. Contrary to some teachers' belief, a great deal of further research into the nature of the reading process is essential if we are to be able to provide the informed professional help that will maximise children's chances of achieving literacy (Blanton *et al.* 1974).

Testing and the teaching of reading

A constructive way of viewing the relationships between the teaching, testing and evaluation of reading is for the teacher to consider the teaching of reading as a continuous series of experiments. These involve the interaction of educational experiences and the development of the child's reading skills. Teachers of reading are usually interested in new methods and materials, mainly because they are well aware that there is no one method of reading instruction that is the best for all children. Hence, a knowledge of the range of materials available and of innovations is professionally important. The value of new methods and materials can be established by asking such questions as 'Was it effective in helping the child overcome the particular difficulty?' and 'Has the anticipated improvement taken place?'. *At this point measurement becomes important.* Tests of reading will enable an objective assessment of the merits of a particular intervention to be measured more adequately than by relying on the teacher's subjective impressions. This is not to say that test results are the *only* component in the evaluation of the effectiveness of materials.

Because of the nature of reading tests and of reading abilities, a teacher can never know with complete certainty that one given method or approach is better than another. The teacher's acceptance of this uncertainty, the abandonment of a dogmatic assurance in her own approach to the teaching of reading, *whatever it may be*, is vital. It can help the teacher to be more aware of and responsive to the individual instructional needs of the children she teaches. In many cases the appreciation of this inherent uncertainty is only achieved by the teacher through her teaching experience and through reading about the use of tests. Both these experiences indicate the importance of ideas such as individual differences. The latter formalises an intuitive understanding of sampling error, the variability of human behaviour, and the weaknesses of unsystematic observation and subjective assessments.

The teacher of reading is in a key position in the education of our children. Tests are *one* tool in her professional training that has frequently been neglected. If the following three principles are embodied in the use of reading tests in school, there is every chance that the results of using them will benefit both the pupil and the teacher:

1. The reading test result should give information indicating the extent to which the teacher's instructional objectives in reading are being achieved.
2. The data obtained should be utilised in the improvement of the reading programme.
3. The testing of reading should be an integral part of the regular testing programme within the school.

References

ATKINSON, E. J. and GAINS, C. W. (1973) *An A–Z List of Reading and Subject Books.* Norwich, National Association for Remedial Education.
BLANTON, W. E., FARR, R. and TUINMAN, J. J. (Eds.) (1974) *Measuring Reading Performance.* Newark, Delaware, International Reading Association.
BOND, G. L. and TINKER, M. A. (1967) *Reading Difficulties, Their Diagnosis and Correction* (second edition). New York, Appleton-Century-Crofts.
BURKE, E. and LEWIS, D. G. (1975) Standards of reading: a critical review of some recent studies. *Educational Research,* 7, 3, 163–74.
CLARK, M. (1975) Language and reading: a study of early reading. In LATHAM, W. (Ed.) *The Road to Effective Reading.* London, Ward Lock Educational.
CLARK, M. (1976) *Young Fluent Readers.* London, Heinemann Educational.
CONOCHIE. D., MILNE, H., SPENCE, J. and WRENCH, S. (1969) *Reading Workshop 9–12.* London, Ward Lock Educational.
CONOCHIE, D., MILNE, H., SPENCE, J. and WRENCH, S. (1971) *Reading Workshop 6–10.* London, Ward Lock Educational.
DAVIS, F. B. (1970) The Assessment of Change. In FARR, R. (Ed.) *Measurement and Evaluation of Reading.* New York, Harcourt, Brace and World.
DECHANT, E. (Ed.) (1971) *Detection and Correction of Reading Difficulties.* New York, Appleton-Century-Crofts.
DELA-PIANA, G. M. (1968) *Reading Diagnosis and Prescription: An Introduction.* New York, Holt, Rinehart and Winston.
Department of Education and Science (1972) *Education: A Framework for Expansion.* London, HMSO.
Department of Education and Science (1975) *A Language for Life.* London, HMSO.
DREVER, J. (1964) *A Dictionary of Psychology.* Harmondsworth, Penguin.
FARR, R. (1969) *Reading: What can be Measured?* Newark, International Reading Association.
FARR, R. (Ed.) (1970) *Measurement and Evaluation of Reading.* New York, Harcourt, Brace and World.
GAGNÉ, R. M. (1977) *The Conditions of Learning* (third edition). New York, Holt, Rinehart and Winston.
GAGNÉ, R. M. and BRIGGS, L. J. (1974) *The Principles of Instructional Design.* London, Holt, Rinehart and Winston.
GILLILAND, J. and MERRITT, J. E. (1972) *Readability.* London, Hodder and Stoughton.

HARRIS, A. J. (1970) *How to Increase Reading Ability* (fifth edition). New York, McKay.

HOFFMAN, M. (1976) *Reading, Writing and Relevance.* London, Hodder and Stoughton.

KAY, B. (1976) Justified Impatience: Brian Kay describes the progress made by the Assessment of Performance Unit in its first two years. *Times Educational Supplement*, no. 3200, 1st October.

KELLY, T. A. (Ed.) (1973) *Teacher's Guide to Reading Schemes for Slow Learners.* Sandwell, Sandwell Educational Committee Child Psychology Service.

KENNEDY, E. C. (1971) *Classroom Approaches to Remedial Reading.* New York, Peacock.

LAWSON, K. S. (1968) *Children's Reading.* University of Leeds Institute of Education Paper No. 8.

PARKER, D. H. (1972) *The Science Research Associates Reading Laboratory Series—Infant to University Level.* Described in the SRA Educational Catalogue.

PIDGEON, D. and YATES, A. (1968) *An Introduction to Educational Measurement.* London, Routledge and Kegan Paul.

PUMFREY, P. D. (1974) The diagnosis and remediation of psycholinguistic deficits. Paper read at the 1974 UKRA Annual Conference.

PUMFREY, P. D. (1976) Reading measurement and evaluation: some current concerns and promising developments. Paper read at the 1976 UKRA Annual Conference.

PUMFREY, P. D. and DIXON, E. (1970) Junior Children's attitudes to reading: comments on three measuring instruments. *Reading*, 4, 2, 19–26.

REID, J. F. (Ed.) (1972) *Reading: Problems and Practices.* London, Ward Lock Educational.

SCHELL, L. M. and BURNS, P. C. (Eds.) (1972) *Remedial Reading: Classroom and Clinic.* New York, Allyn and Bacon.

SHELDON, W. D. (1970) Specific Principles Essential to Classroom Diagnosis. In FARR, R. (Ed.) *Measurement and Evaluation of Reading.* New York, Harcourt, Brace and World.

START, K. B. and WELLS, B. K. (1972) *The Trend of Reading Standards.* Slough, NFER.

STOTT, D. H. (1971) *Programmed Reading Kit and Manual* (second edition). Edinburgh, Holmes McDougall.

TANSLEY, A. E. (1967) *Reading and Remedial Reading.* London, Routledge and Kegan Paul.

WILLIAMS, A. (1976) *Reading and the Consumer: a practical guide.* London, Hodder and Stoughton.

WILSON, R. M. (1967) *Diagnostic and Remedial Reading for Classroom and Clinic.* Columbus, Merrill.

ZIMET, S. G. (1976) *Print and Prejudice.* London, Hodder and Stoughton.

3. What are we looking for?

The skills comprising reading ability

In recent years there has been a tremendous amount of research activity in the field of reading. A great deal of this has been devoted to analysing the skills that make up the reading process and to devising tests to measure these skills. There are three major approaches to deciding which aspects of reading are crucial. These are the factor-analytic, the logical skill-analysis and the psycholinguistic approaches, respectively. In order to select reading tests likely to provide information pertinent to the development of children's reading abilities, a teacher requires knowledge of the importance of the skills and attitudes that underlie and comprise reading at various stages (Cane and Smithers 1971; Levin and Williams 1971; Smith 1971; Melnik and Merritt 1972; DES 1975).

Factor-analytic findings

Faith in the *name* of a reading test which may *seem* to give an unambiguous indication of what the test actually measures, is often misplaced. Reading tests that examine the same type of skill may have very different names. Conversely, tests with the same name may measure different skills. One approach to establishing which skills are most important in reading at a particular age level is to apply a statistical sorting technique known as factor analysis. The approach is based on the assumption that most of the cognitive abilities listed in almost any analysis of the reading process will be inter-related and that the names of the tests themselves may be misleading. The aim of factor analysis is to clarify a complex set of inter-relationships. Thus one potentially profitable approach to the identification of the most important skills comprising reading is to administer a large number of reading tests to a large number of children and to look at the most important factors derived from a factor analysis of the results. This simplifies the situation in that the number of factors required to account for the relationships between the test scores will usually be less than the number of tests used in the battery. The analysis tells us which tests fall into closely related groups. The factor-analytic approach has shown that the following four major components of reading ability *can* be recognised and measured reliably (Lennon 1970, p. 29):

1. a general verbal factor
2. the comprehension of explicitly expressed content
3. the comprehension of implicit meaning
4. appreciation

Taking each in turn, the general verbal factor concerns the extent of the child's vocabulary. Clearly this is related to many other measures of reading ability and to attainments in language-skills in general. The second factor, comprehension of explicitly expressed content, to a large extent comprises reading for the literal meaning of a written passage. The third factor, comprehension of implicit meaning, measures many of the advanced skills of reasoning with the content of written material. Appreciation, the fourth factor, is less well established, but is related to the reader's ability to be aware of the author's intentions, feelings and thoughts. According to Lennon, the first three of these factors can be reliably measured at *all* stages of reading development. Hence we have some empirical evidence supporting the contention made earlier that reading is essentially a thinking process in which the pupil is actively engaged. But is such a broad categorisation of the skills which comprise reading of value to the practising teacher?

An extremely useful survey of some important problems concerning the measurement of reading abilities has been produced by the International Reading Association in their series 'Reading Review' (Farr 1969). Entitled *Reading: What can be Measured?*, it describes the skills underlying and related to reading ability in considerable detail. The problems involved in measuring reading sub-skills are considered, together with the psychometric and psychological difficulties in assessing reading attainments and progress. While spelling out clearly many of the limitations in our ability to use measurement, the book contains a great deal of practical advice concerning the above matters.

Logical skill-analyses of reading

An alternative approach is based on an analysis of the process of reading by specialists in the teaching and learning of reading. This can yield a bewildering range of skills deemed to be relevant to reading attainments. In one survey of twenty-eight tests based on such analyses, it was noted that forty-nine differently named aspects of reading were identified (Traxler 1970). In some instances different names were given to tests which measured identical skills (as judged by the test's content and form). If these forty-nine sub-tests were administered to a group of children and the results factor-analysed, it would probably be found that a very much smaller number of factors than tests would be capable of accounting for the test results obtained. Some of the skills considered important by experts might be seen as being redundant after such an analysis.

Thus the components of reading identified as significant by the logical skill-analyses of reading specialists often appear to differ from the results of factor-analyses. This difference is of considerable practical importance to the teacher of reading.

It should not, however, be thought that the two approaches are incompatible. After all, both are looking at the same phenomena, but in different ways. Largely because of differences in approach, the differing results concerning the importance of certain abilities are more apparent than real. Indeed, when it is realised that there is no single factor-analytic solution to such a problem, but literally an infinite number of solutions, one's viewpoint may change. The psychological insights into the reading process by experts favouring the logical skill-analysis approach can be fruitful in terms of throwing up ideas concerning ways in which the teaching of reading might be improved. So can the insights derived from factor-analysis. However, the latter, because of their esoteric nature, are often viewed with suspicion by teachers.

Logical analyses usually indicate that vocabulary, speed of reading and comprehension are important and related components of the reading process. But what of the skills *underlying* these three aspects? Although there can as yet be no definitive statement concerning the relative importance of the component skills involved in the complex, unified and continuous process of reading acquisition, even at given age levels, there are helpful guidelines available from specialists in reading (Gardner 1970; Goodacre 1971; Merritt 1969, 1972; DES 1975). Both the factor-analytic and the logical skill-analysis approaches give some guidance concerning possibly significant sub-skills at particular ages. Clearly, what is of prime importance at an early stage in the acquisition of reading competencies is likely to be of reduced importance at a later stage. None the less, as the later stages are built on the earlier ones, their interdependence must not be overlooked.

A number of valuable diagnostic reading tests are based on their authors' logical analyses of the reading process. The skills assessed in a wide variety of such tests are listed in a recent United Kingdom Reading Association monograph (Pumfrey 1976).

Many teachers would agree with Stott that a central problem in the teaching of reading is to get the child to operate the phonic code with ease. Thus the sequence of skills built into his *Programmed Reading Kit* (Stott 1971) on the basis of a logical task-analysis provides a very helpful guideline in specifying operationally defined goals of reading instruction for children. These goals cover stages of reading development ranging from the child being unaware that words are made of sounds, up to a reading level of about nine years. The materials in Stott's kit also provide ready criteria by which the teacher can assess whether or not a child has mastered a particular skill. Stott has recently extended this approach to the pre-reading instructional needs of younger children (Stott 1972). As a further example, Stephen Jackson has produced a series of tests of phonic abilities based on an analysis of reading (Jackson 1972).

Under the auspices of the National Association for Remedial Education, a manual has been produced which lists fifty-eight phonic skills. Any of these might present difficulties to a child learning to read. For each of these skills the authors give details of materials and books that will provide activities specifically intended to help the pupil master a particular skill (Herbert and Davies-Jones 1975). A section on testing and recording is given. It links, in part, four well-known reading tests with some of the phonic skills considered. The manual is likely to be popular with teachers because of its pragmatic approach, in which testing and teaching are closely linked, albeit at an intuitive level in respect of certain skills. What is lacking in it is a theoretical structure indicating the function of phonic skills in the development of reading, and, even more important, the inter-relationship of the phonic skills at various stages of reading development. With reference to the first point, if linked to the work of Dean and Nichols described below, the *Index of Phonic Resources* is likely to be of greater value to the teacher. The second point is important particularly in relation to the discussion of profile analysis given in Chapter 8. The conceptual and practical problems involved will only be resolved when the necessary basic research into the reading process is carried out (see pp. 30–3).

An interesting developmental analysis of the skills and knowledge necessary for the acquisition of reading and writing skills has been produced, called *Framework for Reading* (Dean and Nichols 1974). The authors provide a series of checklists of the skills they consider essential. It is claimed that these provide a structure that will enable the teacher to identify the skills with which the pupil requires help. Guidance is given as to how children can be encouraged to master those in which they display weaknesses. The checklists can also be used as a cumulative record of the child's progress. Although no satisfactory evidence is given concerning the theoretical basis on which the checklists have been developed, their face validity, coupled with the appeal of the book to practising teachers, has resulted in its receiving considerable attention.

The *Reading Laboratories* produced by Science Research Associates (Parker 1972) and the *Reading Workshops* by Ward Lock Educational (Conochie *et al.* 1969, 1971) also provide guidance for the teacher. They help in considering the skills comprising reading ability at various stages by providing materials through which these skills can be learned, as well as criteria by which the teacher can assess whether mastery has been achieved by the pupils.

The following books are also worthy of note. They contain logical analyses of the reading process at different levels and in varying degrees of complexity. Most of them specify how the presence or absence of reading-related skills can be tested and taught: Cohen 1969; DES 1975; Duffy and Sherman 1972; Franklin and Naidoo 1970; Guszak 1972; Harp and Wallen 1972; Hughes 1973, 1975; Moyle and Moyle 1972; Tansley 1972; Wallen 1972.

Such approaches (and there are many of them) bring together authors' stated *goals* of reading instruction, the *methods and materials* pertinent to their attainment and *means of evaluating* the extent to which the goals are achieved. These three considerations are at the core of any reading programme at any level. However, for the teacher to abdicate the responsibility for the decisions involved in drawing up a school's reading programme by solely adopting available commercial material would be unthinkable, unless she were convinced that the commercially produced materials were in all instances better suited to her pupils' educational needs than anything she might produce herself. The development of more effective reading programmes in our schools depends largely on the innovations introduced and developed by teachers. Such considerations demand that schools take what they see to be of value for their pupils from commercially available materials, but continue to make their own important contribution to improving current practices. In practice, the major publishing companies are interested in promising developments initiated by teachers, and the mutual interests of the learner, teacher and publisher can be furthered through cooperation. CTB/McGraw-Hill has published a *Prescriptive Reading Inventory* (PRI) which represents a major attempt to meet the teacher's requirements in reading for children aged between $7\frac{1}{2}$ and 12 years, and provides an assessment of children's mastery of ninety clearly defined objectives. These objectives describe specifically the reading behaviour expected to result from instruction. The tests are of the criterion-referenced type and results are already keyed to thirty-two reading schemes. Programme Reference Guides have been produced for each of the reading programmes linked to the PRI. The system claims to provide diagnostic and prescriptive information from which the teacher can construct individualised reading programmes for her pupils (CTB/McGraw-Hill 1974).

Such an apparently comprehensive scheme has some disadvantages. Although a hand-scoring device will be available for use with the PRI, the essence of the system is that the publishers will provide a scoring service for the inventory. Unfortunately, the hand-scoring procedure is a lengthy one and *not* recommended for schools short of time and staff. None the less, the PRI is a development that cannot be ignored.

Psycholinguistic analyses

Psychologists and linguists have independently and jointly analysed the abilities underlying the reading process. Workers such as Bloomfield and Barnhart (1961), Fries (1963), Gibson (1965), Stauffer (1970), Haas (1970), Mackay *et al.* (1970), Wilkinson (1971), Smith (1973) and Wilkinson *et al.* (1974) have analysed the reading process and produced materials and ideas intended to help the teacher of reading and children learning to read. However, our focus is on *tests* pertinent to reading. In this context the *Illinois Test of Psycholinguistic Abilities* (ITPA) developed by Kirk *et al.* (1968) is of both theoretical and practical importance. This test is a systematic diagnostic device which aims to tap different aspects of the cognitive abilities involved in *communication*. Its purpose is to identify the strengths and weaknesses of children in various aspects of communication so that remediation can be carried out. The skills tested by the ITPA are in part similar to skills tested in various pre-reading tests. The strength of the ITPA is that its sub-tests are designed on the basis of a psycholinguistic model of communication. The sub-tests are concerned with the senses through which the content of communication travels and the level of mental organisation required to cope with the content. Thus children's abilities to cope with visually or aurally received material and to respond either orally or by gesture can be examined. It enables the tester to see whether the child can receive a message in one modality and express it in another. Further details of the test are provided on pages 136–41.

Kirk and his co-workers have provided a series of publications which are intended to enable the teacher to interpret the results of the ITPA and suggest activities likely to improve those aspects of psycholinguistic proficiency which appear particularly weak. Currently work is being carried out at the University of Manchester into the efficacy of some of these suggestions. From the point of view of the teacher, nothing is more important than linking a diagnostic procedure with a programme likely to improve the skills investigated (Kirk et al. 1968; Kirk and Kirk 1971; Naylor 1973; Pumfrey 1975). The ITPA has weaknesses, both conceptual and psychometric, that limit its usefulness, and recently there has been considerable comment on this (Hammill and Larsen 1974; Newcomer and Hammill 1975). Despite the reservations indicated, the instrument has much to commend it provided that the user is aware of its limitations (Kirk and Elkins 1974; DES 1975).

Goodman (1973) starts from the position that reading is a form of information processing involving simultaneously three distinct but related categories of data, namely, grapho-phonic, syntactic and semantic. A child who makes a mistake in oral reading is probably attending more to the semantic and syntactic aspects of the material than to grapho-phonic information. Goodman prefers to call such mistakes 'miscues' on the assumption that they are caused rather than accidental. He suggests that the teacher compares the child's observed oral reading response with the expected oral reading response and notes the discrepancies which occur. Goodman has devised a taxonomy of cues and miscues in reading that helps the teacher to categorise the miscues noted and to develop hypotheses concerning why they have occurred and, if necessary, how they might be minimised. For Goodman, the semantic aspect of reading is the most important: understanding is everything. His taxonomy

forms a basis on which the individual child's reading can be profitably tested in a diagnostic sense.

The importance of both the psychological and linguistic principles that underlie the development of reading, with reading
defined as the extraction of information from a text, has been
experimentally studied and discussed in relation to a theory of
perceptual learning (Gibson and Levin 1975). It is argued that in
learning the distinctive features of objects and of coded symbolic
materials such as written text the child becomes increasingly efficient
in picking up information. The contrasting reading behaviours of
the learner and the skilled reader respectively underline this point.
The notion that learning to read is in essence the formation of
stimulus-response associations that are strengthened by external
reinforcements is seriously questioned. The process is seen as the
child's learning a system of rules and strategies that enable him to
extract meaning from the text and to reduce his uncertainty concerning the messages contained therein. This type of learning is to
a large extent intrinsically reinforcing, the child's curiosity being
one of the most potent sources of motivation. In this respect the
approach is in line with that advocated by Walker and referred to in
Chapter 1. It is also consonant with the language-experience approach advocated by Stauffer. Gibson and Levin argue that the
teaching and learning of a complex task such as reading is best begun
by the child working either on the reading task itself or on a close
approximation to that task. This is considered preferable to training
the child to master what from a different theoretical position can be
seen as a number of discrete component skills and then integrating
these into the overall skill of competent reading. According to
Gibson and Levin, all instruction should be multi-level; this allows
the learner opportunity to make use of sentences, words, syllables,
letter clusters and other cues. Particular attention should be paid to
the levels with which the child finds difficulty, but the instruction
provided should be placed within a context that encourages and
enables the learner to use available redundant information. The
child's reading should, from the very start, be an attempt to approximate the model of the competent reader. Doubtless Skinner from
his operant conditioning position would agree with this point whilst
disagreeing with much of the theorising concerning the nature of
the learning involved. Despite such a comment, the work of Gibson
and Levin is well supported by experimental studies. It also provides
a coherent integration of theory, research and practice in relation
to the child's acquisition of reading skills.

Reading as a complex developmental process

In the mastery of *any* complex skill the individual's focus of attention varies with the level of competence reached. For example, when learning to drive a car, the necessary sequences of movement and action initially demand considerable concentration. At this stage of learning, when on the road, one is usually not *primarily* concerned with the view! Later on, the component skills require virtually no conscious effort for their efficient execution. In learning to read there are many skills which require application before they are so mastered that attention to them becomes less necessary. Perhaps the use of letter sounds to decode words would be an example of a reading skill initially requiring considerable effort (even if the teacher arranged for the child to acquire the necessary knowledge inductively through a game approach as in the first item of Stott's *Programmed Reading Kit*). At a later stage of competence in reading, conscious focusing on this skill becomes virtually nil. Competent adult readers rarely use such a skill, their focus of attention invariably being on the meaning of the writing. Argument by analogy has many weaknesses and it is not suggested that meaning is relatively unimportant in the early stages of reading, merely that different aspects of the reading process are accorded different emphasis, dependent upon the stage of mastery the child has reached.

In the main, children come to school able to communicate thoughts, opinions, ideas and feelings if given the opportunity. Their mode of thinking is, however, limited in certain respects. For example, the child in the infant school has great difficulty in appreciating points of view other than his own. Reading is *one* means by which the child's ability to communicate is developed. Thus reading *builds* on thinking processes of considerable complexity.

An appreciation of the links between experiences meaningful to the child, his spoken language and the printed symbol are the bases on which the child's reading ability is constructed, hence the importance of a language-experience approach (Stauffer 1970). At this early stage, reading for many children and teachers is very much concerned with the child learning the conventional printed symbols (words, phrases, sentences) corresponding to speech. It is frequently said that the child is reading when he is able to say aloud correctly the printed symbol presented to him (a measure of word-recognition attainment), or to respond appropriately to a printed instruction without necessarily saying the word aloud (a measure of word-recognition and understanding).

As the child extends his word-recognition skills, these become increasingly automatic. Simultaneously, the written material presented to him and produced by him increases in both grammatical and syntactical complexity. The emphasis on the *meaning* of what is written becomes increasingly dominant (Francis 1972). It is precisely because the reading process is a thinking process that proponents of the language-experience approach emphasise the importance of meaning at all stages in the teaching of reading (Goddard 1974). Fortunately there is a high relationship between the child's ability to recognise words and to understand them. 'Barking at print', a level of reading attainment implying absence of understanding, is deplored by most teachers and, in the writer's experience, is *not* frequently found in normal children.

During the junior school period, reading increasingly becomes a tool used by the child to explore a wide range of new concepts and imaginative ideas. He becomes aware of the differing purposes which reading can fulfil, ranging from the excitement of fact-finding and discovery-work to the delight afforded by stories giving reign to fantasy and imagination.

Throughout the secondary school stage of education, the process of differentiation in the functions of reading is continued. In so far as the adolescent becomes able to reflect on his own thought to a greater extent, an appreciation of implicit meaning and aesthetic appreciation develops more rapidly than during earlier years. This is continued in tertiary education. The development of reading ability is one facet of cognitive development in general. It is both a contributor to, and a result of, that development.

Harris (1970) has helpfully conceptualised the situation by suggesting that there are three major types of reading: Developmental, Functional and Recreational. The first refers to the skills in which the teacher's major role is to help the child increase his proficiency. In this situation, learning to read is dominant. The second indicates a type of reading the major function of which is to obtain information. Here, reading to learn is dominant. The third type of reading is that voluntarily engaged in because of the satisfaction that it affords the reader. Clearly, the three types of reading are not mutually exclusive. One need not be completely mastered before the others can be engaged in. All three are valid aspects of reading at all stages of reading development. The relative emphasis given them in a particular reading programme will depend upon the importance accorded to each by the individual teacher for the child with whom she is concerned.

Reading research and the teacher

A further important source of information concerning the skills underpinning attainment in reading lies in two related groups of experimental studies. The first of these centres on the effectiveness of different methods in improving some aspect of a child's reading attainments. Unfortunately, our knowledge of which methods to use with which children so as to optimise acquisition of reading skills is still fragmentary. Teachers often complain that the findings of research into reading have little practical value for them or their pupils and that researchers are divorced from the reality of the teaching situation. The situation would be improved if the assessment of children's attainment of operationally defined objectives were evaluated systematically by teachers using appropriate tests as part of normal school procedures. We would then have the beginnings of important school- and teacher-based applied research into an area in which most teachers claim concern, interest and involvement. The Schools' Council Research Projects 'Extending Beginning Reading', 'Effective Use of Reading' and 'Children as Readers' point the way in such a direction.

Being aware of the pressures on the teacher's time and the restrictions in the availability of research reports, the Schools Council commissioned an experienced teacher of English to review post-war research in the teaching of reading. The author writes: 'My chief concern has been to provide some information about major research investigations (most of them conducted over the past decade) relevant to reading activities in school; to sketch in a spectrum of aims and opinions about the teaching of reading within which practising teachers might find—and possibly reconsider—their own position; and most important of all, to raise many questions to which as yet there can be no firm answers, but which we cannot ignore for that reason.' The work is not intended to be comprehensive, but to highlight the findings of those studies the author considered significant. In 1973, a two-volume publication appeared. The first volume examines work related to the pre-reading stage and to the concept of reading readiness. Various teaching methods and media are also described and contrasting ways of planning a reading programme discussed. Volume two is in two distinct sections. The first concentrates on the teaching of literature and on children's reading interests and preferences; the second discusses techniques for analysing and assessing the reader's response to various types of material (D'Arcy 1973).

A second important group of studies is that concerned with identifying the differences in specific reading skills of children who, at a later stage, are seen either to succeed or to fail to achieve literacy; and with the extent to which these specific skills can be modified (De Hirsch *et al.* 1966). For example, what differences in specific reading-related skills exist between nursery school children who will be reading by the age of seven years and those who will not? Or, what are the differences in specific reading skills between eleven-year-old non-readers who leave school illiterate and those who will have mastered reading to a certain extent? Can the children who have been identified as likely not to succeed in acquiring competence in reading be helped by suitable experiences to improve their deficient skills?

Answers to questions of this type begin the breakdown of the reading process into more specific skills and contribute to our understanding of the reading process. Clearly, both groups of researches are related and will help to systematise our understanding of, and control over, the processes whereby children learn to read.

The early identification of very young children likely at a later date to show reading difficulties is predicated on the assumption that such identification enhances the possibility of constructive intervention. This area has been well considered in an IRA publication which outlines some promising approaches as well as indicating the complexity of the problems involved (Aukerman 1972). In contrast, an earlier extensive examination of the uses of reading readiness tests for prediction and diagnosis concluded on a rather pessimistic note (Dykstra 1969). As a consequence of interest in this field, encouraged in the UK by certain of the recommendations of the Bullock Committee, some interesting developments are likely to take place (Marshall and Gilliland 1976).

The early identification of educationally 'at risk' children was the concern of an international symposium organised by the University of Birmingham School of Education. The report of the symposium is essential reading for any educationist involved in early screening to identify educational difficulties, current or impending (Wedell and Raybould 1976). The conceptual, psychometric, theoretical and practical problems involved in screening are described and discussed, and the book makes one aware of the complexity of any such screening system. While there are dangers in screening, the alternative of not screening was considered by the Bullock Committee to present even greater dangers to those children in need of special help who could be overlooked.

In Britain it has been suggested that our pragmatic orientation and empiricist tradition often results in a denigration of theory. One consequence may be a suspicion by teachers of reading of theories of reading. Yet advances in the teaching of reading skills must be integrated into a theoretical framework if our professional knowledge and competence is to be enhanced. Only if we have such a theoretical basis can we deduce predictions, test them and thereby refine our model. The fact that there is no one theory of reading to which all teachers subscribe merely underlines the complexity and lack of knowledge that characterises this frontier of psychological and educational research and practice. All too often the teacher's theoretical formulation of the nature of the reading process is intuitive, vague and implicit; one which she would be hard put to elaborate in public. Logical, specific and explicit models, admittedly inadequate in some respects, do exist. A knowledge of some of these is essential.

A very helpful review of relationships between theories of language development and reading has been reported in *Reading Research Quarterly* (Athey 1971). In the same year a less extensive but none the less interesting review of some models relating language and beginning reading was carried out by another worker (Wardhaugh 1971). A consideration of some current theories of mental abilities, structures and processes involved in reading has been edited by Singer and Ruddell. Certain of the contributors also discuss the implications of the models for both the teaching of reading and for future research (Singer and Ruddell 1975). In 1971 Mackworth wrote an article in which he spelled out his schematic model of the reading process which enabled him to account for known differences between children learning to read and those considered to be skilled readers. Mackworth's model suggests how the visual, auditory and motor sub-systems are related both to one another and to short- and long-term memory. Feedback loops are hypothesised. The model is complex, as are the processes it purports to represent. Thus, for example, the visual input which occurs during a fixation pause, involves selection, attention, expectation and prediction. Mackworth is able to suggest why auditory memories are vital in learning to read but less important in skilled reading (Mackworth 1971). Models similar to that of Mackworth have been described by Samuels (1973) and by one of his co-workers (La Berge and Samuels 1975). Models of the reading process based on information processing notions appear to have much promise. Farnham-Diggory and Gregg have put forward a model in which the relationships between modality integration and memory are dealt with in a manner which clearly indicates theoretical reasons for the differences in performance of poor and competent readers (Farnham-Diggory and Gregg 1975). Work in Britain on the relationships between reading ability and temporal order perception in six-year-old boys has been related to their model (Combes 1975).

For the teacher to be ignorant of reading research and to rely on her own experience alone is as myopic as an uncritical acceptance of the findings of reading research. Involvement by teachers in the systematic evaluation of the effectiveness of materials and systems used in the teaching of reading would do more to increase our ability to help children than any other single measure. It is also a proposal that is economically viable!

What can the teacher do?

Teachers of reading are usually very interested in the question 'What experiences can I arrange for John in order to help him to read better?' Indeed, it is precisely this question that the use of suitable tests can help answer. One of the most profitable approaches in this situation is via the instructional objectives of the reading programme. When teachers concerned with the teaching of reading are asked to specify their instructional objectives, there is often a tendency for them to produce the type of global statement given earlier (p. 6), e.g. 'to help my pupils to become fluent and enthusiastic readers'. Such a general statement of the instructional aims of a reading programme can be broken down into operationally defined sub-goals. Only then can the teacher begin to see possible links between the level of skill development the child has, the level to which she might reasonably expect to be able to help John achieve given the available resources, and the level of the ultimate objective. In other words, to use tests of reading as a means of improving children's reading abilities implies that the teacher is willing to devote a considerable amount of thinking to the organisation of the reading programme around a coherent set of operationally defined objectives (see Chapters 4 and 8).

Neither the factor-analytic, the logical-analysis, the psycholinguistic nor the experimental approaches give, or can be expected to give, definitive descriptions of the skills comprising reading ability at the various stages of the development of reading competence. In practice, the teacher selects the 'best' plan she can in the particular situation. Frequently this plan is related to a basal

34 MEASURING READING ABILITIES

reading scheme at the primary school level. At the secondary stage, equally systematic and ordered materials are available, but having a rather different structure and content.

The skills required by a child to progress through published reading materials are often listed by the authors. Teachers can thus work initially within the framework of the skill development sequence inherent in the material, developing additional materials and methods to help children to acquire these skills. A skill development check-list for each child can be used by the teacher as a diagnostic instrument, indicating areas where help is needed. Helpful examples of the use of skill development sequences in the systematic assessment of reading can be found in Della-Piana (1968), (1968), in Jackson's *Phonic Skill Record Sheets* and the booklet *Get Reading Right* (1972) and in the materials indicated earlier in this chapter. The teacher's manual of most established graded reading schemes contains a detailed analysis of the reading skills that the particular scheme is intended to help its users acquire.

Children's attitudes towards reading

Teachers generally expect their pupils to become literate. It is also frequently assumed that the feelings of success associated with mastery of reading skills will lead to the child developing positive attitudes towards reading. Teachers deliberately engineer situations in which children's chances of being successful are high. This is but an application of the general principle that 'Nothing succeeds like success'. Whilst there is a considerable amount of truth in this, there are some situations in which children's reading attainments may be satisfactory but their attitudes towards the reading programme poor. For example, drilling and practice can increase word-recognition skills up to a point, but these activities could be disliked by the children if carried to excess. Similarly, there are other situations in which children's reading attainments are poor, but they are keen about their reading programme. For example, immigrants from underdeveloped countries may have very low reading attainment yet be extremely keen to learn to read. Children's reading attainments and attitudes towards reading are intimately related, each affecting the other and consequently producing further changes in both attainment and attitude. It is essential for the teacher intent on helping children to progress in reading to consider both the cognitive and affective aspects of this process (Georgiades 1967; Shaw and Wright 1967; Ravenette 1968, 1970; Williams 1976).

Children's attitudes towards reading can be measured, although there is doubt as to the stability of children's attitudes towards skills such as reading during the primary school years (Sharples 1969). In addition, the instruments commonly available for measuring children's attitudes towards reading are not as well developed as those for assessing reading attainments. There are, however, a small number of interesting approaches to the measurement of attitude currently being developed. Details of some of these are given in the UKRA monograph *Reading: Tests and Assessment Techniques* (Pumfrey 1976) referred to earlier.

The teacher will probably be more interested in the assessment of children's attitudes by the extent and enthusiasm with which the children engage in activities involving reading. This is no more than an interest in affective aspects of the goals of the reading programme. These goals can be expressed operationally and the extent to which they are achieved can be assessed. In practical terms, if one of the teacher's general objectives is to help children develop 'a love of books and reading', this very general aim can be operationally defined by specifying component behaviours of the aim. For example, the teacher can encourage children to keep a record of the books borrowed spontaneously from the class or school library and of their reactions to them. She then has available one index of the children's liking for reading as a self-initiated activity. The teacher can then consider these results and decide whether the goal has been achieved. If not, what can she do to increase the frequency of children's self-initiated borrowing of books and their enjoyment of expressing their opinions concerning the content?

Children experiencing failure in reading often develop self-denigrating attitudes towards their own abilities. Lawrence (1973) has shown that such children in junior schools can benefit from individual client-centred counselling. The consequences appear to be positive changes in the treated pupils' self-concepts *and* in their reading attainments greater than those found in control groups. This work is extremely interesting to any teacher concerned with the relationship between the orectic and cognitive aspects of failure in reading, but Lawrence's work has been criticised for raising teachers' expectations of what can be achieved by individual counselling (Pumfrey 1974). The efficacy of the approach advocated by Lawrence is being studied in a large group of junior school children with reading difficulties who live in a northern industrial conurbation (Coles 1975). What needs to be spelled out is precisely *which* pupils the approach will help, as no single method of helping children failing in reading will be equally successful with all. The considerable interest aroused by Lawrence's book has drawn attention to the all too frequently neglected affective aspect of reading failure. For this he is to be congratulated.

It has also been shown at the secondary school stage that children's attitudes towards the activities intended to promote literacy are important determinants of progress (Ablewhite 1967).

References

ABLEWHITE, R. C. (1967) *The Slow Reader*. London, Heinemann.

ATHEY, I. J. (1971) Language models and reading. *Reading Research Quarterley*, 7, 10–110.

AUKERMAN, R. C. (Ed.) (1972) *Some Persistent Questions on Beginning Reading*. Newark, Delaware, International Reading Association.

BLOOMFIELD, L. and BARNHART, C. L. (1961) *Let's Read: A Linguistic Approach*. Detroit, Wayne State University Press.

CANE, B. and SMITHERS, J. (1971) *The Roots of Reading*. Slough, NFER.

COHEN, S. A. (1969) *Teach Them All to Read*. New York, Random House.

COLES, C. (1975) A replication and extension of Lawrence's work on the use of counselling with retarded readers. Unpublished research, University of Manchester Department of Education.

COMBES, M. D. (1975) Reading ability and some relationships with temporal order perception in six-year-old boys. Unpublished M.Sc. thesis, University of Manchester Department of Education.

CONOCHIE, D., MILNE, H., SPENCE, J. and WRENCH, S. (1969 and 1971) *Reading Workshops 9–12 and 6–10*. London, Ward Lock.

CTB/MCGRAW-HILL (1974) *Prescriptive Reading Inventory*. Monterey, California, CTB/McGraw-Hill.

D'ARCY, P. (1973) *Reading for Meaning. Vol. 1: Learning to Read. Vol. 2: The Reader's Response*. London, Hutchinson Educational.

DEAN, J. and NICHOLS, R. (1974) *Framework for Reading*. London, Evans.

DE HIRSCH, K., JANSKY, J. J. and LANGFORD, W. S. (1966) *Predicting Reading Failure*. London, Harper and Row.

DELA-PIANA, G. M. (1968) *Reading Diagnosis and Prescription: An Introduction*. New York, Holt, Rinehart and Winston.

Department of Education and Science (1975) *Educational Priority: Vol. 3: Curriculum Innovation in London's EPAs*. London, HMSO.

DUFFY, G. G. and SHERMAN, G. B. (1972) *Systematic Reading Instruction*. New York, Harper and Row.

DYKSTRA, R. (1969) The Use of Reading Readiness Tests for Prediction and Diagnosis: a critique. In BARRETT, T. C. (Ed.) *The Evaluation of Children's Reading Achievement*. Newark, Delaware, International Reading Association.

FARNHAM-DIGGORY, S. and GREGG, L. W. (1975) Short-term memory function in young readers. *Journal of Experimental Child Psychology*, 19, 279–98.

FARR, R. (1969) *Reading : What can be Measured?* ERIC/CRIER Reading Review Series, Newark, Delaware, International Reading Association.

FRANCIS, H. (1972) Sentence structure and learning to read. *British Journal of Educational Psychology,* 42, 2, 113–19.

FRANKLIN, A. W. and NAIDOO, S. (1970) *Assessment and Teaching of Dyslexic Children.* London, Invalid Children's Aid Association.

FRIES, C. C. (1963) *Linguistics and Reading.* New York, Holt, Rinehart and Winston.

GARDNER, K. (Ed.) (1970) *Reading Skills : Theory and Practice.* London, Ward Lock Educational.

GEORGIADES, N. J. (1967) A report of a pilot study on the development of an instrument to investigate young children's attitude to reading. In DOWNING, J. and BROWN, A. L. (Eds.) *The Second International Reading Symposium.* London, Cassell.

GIBSON, E. (1965) Learning to Read. *Science,* 148, 1066–72.

GIBSON, E. J. and LEVIN, H. (1975) *The Psychology of Reading.* Massachusetts, MIT Press.

GODDARD, N. (1974) *Literacy : Language-experience Approaches.* London, Macmillan Education.

GOODACRE, E. (1971) *Children and Learning to Read.* London, Routledge and Kegan Paul.

GOODMAN, K. S. (1973) Analysis of Oral Reading Miscues. In SMITH, F. (Ed.), *Psycholinguistics and Reading.* New York, Holt, Rinehart and Winston.

GUSZAK, F. J. (1972) *Diagnostic Reading Instruction in the Elementary School.* New York, Harper and Row.

HAAS, W. (1970) *Phonographic Translation.* Manchester, Manchester University Press.

HAMMILL, D. D. and LARSEN, S. C. (1974) The effectiveness of psycholinguistic training. *Exceptional Children,* September, 1974.

HARP, W. and WALLEN, C. J. (1972) *Instructor's Guide to 'Competency in Teaching Reading' and 'The First R : Readings on Teaching Reading'.* Henley-on-Thames, Science Research Associates.

HARRIS, A. J. (1970) *How to Increase Reading Ability* (fifth edition). New York, McKay.

HERBERT, D. and DAVIES-JONES, G. (1975) *A Classroom Index of Phonic Resources* (second edition). Stafford, National Association for Remedial Education.

HUGHES, J. M. (1973) *Aids to Reading.* London, Evans.

HUGHES, J. M. (1975) *Reading and Reading Failure.* London, Evans.

JACKSON, S. (1972) *Get Reading Right.* Glasgow, Gibson.

KIRK, S. A. and ELKINS, J. (1974) *Summaries of research on the revised Illinois Test of psycholinguistic Abilities : Final Report on Project No. H 12-7145B.* Washington, D.C., US Department of Health, Education and Welfare, Office of Education, Bureau of Education for the Handicapped.

KIRK, S. A. and KIRK, W. D. (1971) *Psycholinguistic Learning Disabilities : diagnosis and remediation.* Urbana, University of Illinois Press.

KIRK, S. A., MCCARTHY, J. J. and KIRK, W. D. (1968) *Illinois Test of Psycholinguistic Abilities* (revised edition). Urbana, University of Illinois Press.

LABERGE, D. and SAMUELS, S. J. (1975) Towards a theory of automatic information processing in reading. *Cognitive Psychology,* 6, 293–323.

LAWRENCE, D. (1973) *Improved Reading Through Counselling*. London, Ward Lock Educational.

LENNON, R. T. (1970) 'What can be measured?' In FARR, R. (Ed.) *Measurement and Evaluation of Reading*. New York, Harcourt, Brace and World.

LEVIN, H. and WILLIAMS, J. B. (Eds.) (1971) *Basic Studies on Reading*. New York, Basic Books.

MACKAY, D., THOMPSON, B. and SCHAUB, P. (1970) *Breakthrough to Literacy*. London, Longman.

MACKWORTH, J. F. (1971) Some models of the reading process: learners and skilled readers. In DAVIS, F. B. (Ed.) *The Literature of Research in Reading with Emphasis on Models*. New Brunswick, N.J., Graduate School of Education, Rutgers University, pp. 8-67 to 8-100.

MARSHALL, C. P. and GILLILAND, J. (1976) A screening procedure for the early identification of children in need of help. *Division of Educational and Child Psychology of the British Psychological Society Occasional Papers, 9*, 392–400.

MELNIK, A. and MERRITT, J (Eds.) (1972) *Reading : Today and Tomorrow*. London, Hodder and Stoughton.

MERRITT, J. E. (1969) Reading skills re-examined. *Special Education, 58*, 1.

MERRITT, J. E. (1972) The intermediate skills. In MORRIS, J. M. (Ed.) *The First R*. London, Ward Lock Educational.

MOYLE, D. and MOYLE, L. (1972) *Modern Innovations in the Teaching of Reading*. London, Hodder and Stoughton.

NAYLOR, J. G. (1973) Some psycholinguistic disabilities of poor readers: their diagnosis and remediation. Unpublished M.Ed. thesis, Department of Education, University of Manchester.

NEWCOMER, P. and HAMMILL, D. D. (1975) The ITPA and academic achievement: a survey of the literature. *The Reading Teacher, 28*, 8, 731–41.

PARKER, D. H. (1972) *The Science Research Associates Reading Laboratory Series*. Henley-on-Thames, Science Research Associates.

PUMFREY, P. D. (1974) Review of 'Improved Reading through Counselling'. *Reading, 8*, 2, 40–2.

PUMFREY, P. D. (1975) The Illinois Test of Psycholinguistic Abilities in the diagnosis and treatment of reading failure. In MOYLE, D. (Ed.) *Reading : What of the Future?* London, Ward Lock Educational.

PUMFREY, P. D. (1976) *Reading : Tests and Assessment Techniques*. London, Hodder and Stoughton.

RAVENETTE, A. T. (1968) *Dimensions of Reading Difficulties*. Oxford, Pergamon.

RAVENETTE, A. T. (1970) Reading difficulties—and what else? In GARDNER, K. (Ed.) *Reading Skills : Theory and Practice*. London, Ward Lock.

SAMUELS, S. J. (1973) Learning to read: success or failure. *Reading Research Quarterly, 8*, 2, 202–39.

SHARPLES, D. (1969) Children's attitudes towards junior school activities. *British Journal of Educational Psychology, 39*, 1, 72–7.

SHAW, M. E. and WRIGHT, J. M. (1967) *Scales for the Measurement of Attitudes*. New York, McGraw-Hill.

SINGER, H. and RUDDELL, R. (Eds.) (1975) *Theoretical Models and Processes of Reading* (2nd edn). Newark, Delaware, International Reading Association.

SMITH, F. (1971) *Understanding Reading.* New York, Holt, Rinehart and Winston.

SMITH, F. (1973) *Psycholinguistics and Reading.* New York, Holt, Rinehart and Winston.

STAUFFER, R. G. (1970) *The Language-Experience Approach to the Teaching of Reading.* London, Harper and Row.

STOTT, D. H. (1971) *Programmed Reading Kit, Manual.* Edinburgh, Holmes McDougal.

STOTT, D. H. (1972) *Flying Start—Learning to Learn Kit.* Edinburgh, Holmes McDougal.

TANSLEY, A. E. (1972) *Reading and Remedial Reading.* London, Routledge and Kegan Paul.

TRAXLER, A. E. (1970) Values and limitations of standardised reading tests. In FARR, R. (Ed.) *Measurement and Evaluation of Reading.* New York, Harcourt, Brace and World.

WALLEN, C. J. (1972) *Competency in Teaching Reading.* Henley-on-Thames, Science Research Associates.

WARDHAUGH, R. (1971) Language and beginning reading. *Reading Research Quarterly, 2,* 1, 168–94.

WEDELL, K. and RAYBOULD, E. C. (1976) The early identification of educationally 'at risk' children. *Educational Review,* Occasional Publications No. 6, University of Birmingham.

WILKINSON, A. (1971) *The Foundations of Language: Talking and Reading in Young Children.* London, Oxford University Press.

WILKINSON, A., STRATTA, L. and DUDLEY, P (1974) *The Quality of Listening.* London, Macmillan Education.

WILLIAMS, B. (1976) The attitudes and reading attainments of primary school children. Unpublished M.Ed. (Ed. Psych.) dissertation, University of Manchester Department of Education.

4. Selecting a reading test

Reading objectives, methods and tests

It is generally helpful to know one's destination before setting out on a journey. This knowledge can guide one in deciding precisely *how* to reach one's goal. The degree of precision with which the destination can be specified is reflected in the precision with which plans can be laid. This should, in turn, result in more effective travelling than if arrangements are left to chance.

To a certain extent the same applies to the teaching of reading. The teacher *can* improve the chances of her pupils attaining literacy with positive attitudes towards reading (i.e. travelling successfully) if she specifies precisely the reading skills that it is reasonable to expect the children to acquire under her reading programme. 'All children shall read as well as they are able' is a laudable sentiment and an acceptable educational goal in principle, *but* it is so imprecise that almost any activity can be justified as helping the children to achieve it. Such statements can lead to sterile considerations such as 'Should I use a phonic or a "look and say" approach to the teaching of reading?'. The vagueness of the goal can lead to confusion on the part of the teacher as to how she should help children attain it. The definition of objectives of reading instruction must be thought through by the teacher so that some *observable* aspect of the child's reading behaviour becomes the instructional objective. This is known as the operational specification of an objective of reading instruction. For example, 'To read with understanding' is *not* an operational specification. Teaching children 'Individually to read with understanding sentences which require completion from a five-choice option' is *one* objective that could readily be related to the abilities of any group of children at any level by choosing appropriate content for the sentences. Achievement of the goal could also be assessed by administering an appropriate test.

It follows that, if testing and teaching are complementary to the pupils' attainment of the goals of reading instruction, only when these goals are adequately described can the teacher select a reading test likely to be of maximum use. This specification is more easily advocated than carried out because we do not, as yet, fully understand the nature of the reading process. Nevertheless, there is a wealth of knowledge and experience available on the developmental nature of reading skills and their inter-relationships (e.g. see Chapter 3), and of the contents and uses of various diagnostic tests of reading abilities.

Equally important are two guides to the specification of educational objectives. These are the books by Bloom and Krathwohl in which they give a system for the classification of educational objectives at various levels. Both cognitive and affective goals are described in the two volumes (Bloom *et al.* 1956; Krathwohl *et al.* 1964).

One of the most helpful taxonomies of reading skills, developed from the work of Bloom and his colleagues, is that devised by Barrett.* A readily accessible description of it is given by Clymer in one of the major texts used in the Open University Post-Experience Course 'Reading Development' (Melnik and Merritt 1972). The Barrett taxonomy of cognitive and affective aspects of reading comprehension helps the teacher appreciate a hierarchy of differing skills that comprise reading comprehension. The teaching of these skills can then form some of the objectives of the reading programme.

The teacher who wishes to use reading tests to their fullest advantage must be prepared to carry out the concentrated thinking necessary to make the instructional objectives of her reading programme observable. Having done this, the process of test selection is greatly simplified. It is also easy to record the children's progress towards their educational destinations. This does not imply that all children will reach literacy via the same 'route'. There is considerable evidence to show that the *same* objective of reading instruction can be reached in many ways. No one method suits all children equally. Recognition of individual strengths and weaknesses at least makes possible their matching to material whose structure will facilitate the mastery of a prescribed skill. There *are* aptitude × instruction interactions and these are likely to be vital. For example, given deaf children and blind children and a phonic and a 'look and say' approach, it is clear that only one method is appropriate to each group. Less marked, but still important, aptitude × instruction

* See also Chapter 8, pp. 131–4.

interactions exist for the individual child. Appropriate reading tests can help in identifying these.

Some basic points about reading tests

The importance of reading tests in helping the teacher ensure the child's acquisition of reading skills is frequently either over- or under-emphasised. One extreme considers the results obtained from standardised tests of reading to be unimpeachable indices of a child's abilities and indicators of necessary interventions. Possible limitations are overlooked and tests are considered superior to any other source of information concerning the reading process. Alternatively, some teachers consider the testing of reading to be a waste of valuable teaching time and possibly a source of harm to their pupils. Fortunately, most teachers are not extremists in this matter. The facts concerning the positive contribution that different types of reading tests can make to improving the teaching of reading show that the value of reading tests lies between the two extremes quoted. The teaching and testing of reading are closely related aspects of helping the child to acquire reading skills.

For tests of reading to make their maximum positive contribution to the children's acquisition of successively more complex reading skills, the following points should be borne in mind by the teacher:

1. All tests of reading contain a margin of error. They are *not* perfect measuring instruments. A child's score can vary from day to day on the same or parallel tests. The teacher needs to be aware of a given test's limitations in this respect.
2. The child's attitude and motivation can affect the results of reading tests to a marked extent.
3. The physical conditions under which a reading test is administered can affect the results. As an extreme example, who can read in pitch blackness, other than a user of Braille?
4. The value of reading tests lies in the relationship which their interpretation has with the reading programme arranged by the teacher for the child.
5. There are many skills in reading, not merely one. Because of this there is a wide range of tests of reading skills. Each test has usually been devised to be used for clearly stated purposes. The selection of a reading test by a teacher must be appropriate to the operationally defined instructional objective of reading in which she is interested. For example, is she concerned with a child's

relative reading comprehension attainment as measured by the child's ability to complete multiple-choice objective test items? Or is the focus of her concern with his ability to blend specified phonemes, etc.?

6. No *one* test of reading can be used as an overall estimate of a child's entire range of reading-related abilities. However, batteries of reading tests that measure a number of major dimensions of reading ability are available.

7. Most standardised reading tests are well designed, constructed and validated. If used for their intended purpose, where this is consonant with the teacher's, they can be of value to both teacher and child. For the former, the relationship between test results and methods of instruction can help the teacher to understand more fully the nature of the reading process. For the child, increase in a teacher's professional competence in the teaching of reading can only be beneficial.

8. The norms of reading tests vary over time. Some are so outdated as to give misleading results if used normatively (Bookbinder 1970; Shearer 1974). This does *not* mean that the test is of no value. The normative use of reading tests is only one aspect of their possible uses, albeit an important one. There are other uses, as will be indicated later.

9. The testing of reading should not be restricted to measuring cognitive abilities, for example, accuracy, comprehension and speed of reading. Children's attitudes towards reading are equally important. Although satisfactory progress in reading attainment and a positive attitude towards the skill usually go together, the teacher should be conscious of the two aspects. If a class of children scoring relatively highly on a reading test appear disinterested in using the class, school and local library facilities for no apparent reason, cause for concern about their attitudes towards reading might exist. Given time, poor attitudes towards reading can adversely affect a child's reading attainment. It is equally true that many children whose cultural background does not value literacy (i.e. their attitudes towards reading are likely to be poor) have greater difficulty in acquiring competence in reading than might be expected on the basis of their general mental abilities.

As was mentioned earlier, when thinking of the testing of reading many teachers consider only standardised reading tests such as those produced by the NFER or commercial publishers. On reflection, this can be seen to be a very restricted viewpoint. Testing is a means of collecting information in an economical and systematic manner. It involves careful observation under standard conditions. But how standard is standard?

In the writer's opinion, it is useful to distinguish between three approaches to the testing of reading: (i) the informal testing of reading, (ii) the use of standardised reading tests, and (iii) criterion-referenced testing. These are dealt with in more detail in Chapter 8 in connection with test interpretation, but are touched on briefly here in order to help the reader gain perspective in this matter.

The competent teacher of reading is continually observing the reading-related behaviours of her pupils. Her methods of teaching and record-keeping tend to determine the behaviours to which her attention is directed. In that she is working within a classroom or school situation, it could be claimed that, to some extent, the conditions of observation are standard. Such informal observations of individual children are a vital component of the diagnostic teaching of reading, and a relatively informal approach of this nature may be highly valid for the individual teacher. It helps her to become effective in maintaining children's progress in reading.

The standardised test of reading differs from the informal test in that what is to be tested, and how, is stated clearly. Its results are also usually related to a particular group of children, representative of many schools. It emphasises individual differences between children; while in a standardised diagnostic reading test giving a profile, the relative levels of various reading skills of an individual child are specified.

The third approach to the testing of reading is through criterion-referenced testing. These tests are so constructed that they provide measurements that can be directly interpreted in terms of specified performance standards. There are two major types (Cronbach 1970). The first provides a 'content-referenced scale'. Thus the child's attainment in some aspect of reading can be measured against a specified content. For example, a child might be expected to read a primer aloud without making any errors of word recognition before moving to the next reader. In this instance the child's word-recognition skill is tested against the criterion of the book's word content. In essence, mastery of the content represents the criterion of performance that the teacher might consider necessary for *any* pupil before he proceeds to more difficult material. If this did form the teacher's performance criterion, there would be *no* individual differences between children attaining the prescribed level of performance. This contrasts markedly with the standardised reading test which is designed to *maximise* individual differences in children's performance and in the construction of which any item passed by all children would be rejected.

The second type of criterion-referenced test focuses on predicting, for example, the pupil's reading performance in situations outside the test. Of the two types of criterion-referenced test, the former is by far the more common at present.

In practice, individual differences in children's reading attainments do not disappear if we choose to use criterion-referenced reading tests. It is important to remember that every criterion-referenced reading test has a normative aspect and, reciprocally, every standardised, norm-referenced reading test has a criterion-referenced component. Despite this, the distinction between these two approaches to the testing of reading is an important one.

Types of reading tests

A wide variety of reading tests is available. Because of this it is useful for the teacher who either uses or is considering using them to have a practical framework within which any particular test can be allocated to a given category. But what characteristics of a reading test shall we use as the basis of a comprehensive classification? Is it helpful to classify tests as, for example, individual or group, timed or untimed, multiple-choice or constructed response, power or speed? Although such considerations are important in the choice of a test for a particular purpose, other aspects are perhaps of more value in helping the teacher think about the use of reading tests as a component of effective teaching.

The following way of considering reading tests has proved useful in this respect. Three aspects of a test, shown diagrammatically in Figure 4.1 (p. 46), need be considered initially. These are:

A. Which *goal* of reading instruction is it to test? (*Ability*)
B. How is the information *collected*? (*Source*)
C. To what *use* will the information be put? (*Purpose*)

Thus, for example, the teacher may be interested in assessing her pupils' reading comprehension (instructional goal), using a standardised test (source of information) for the purpose of grouping children for a particular reading activity (use). This classification is dealt with in more detail in Chapter 8, where the definition of each dimension is expanded and illustrated in relation to the task of interpreting the results of reading tests.

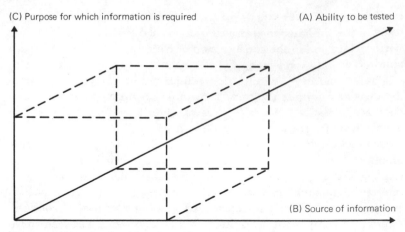

Figure 4.1   A classification of reading tests

The construction of a standardised objective test of reading

Teachers use informal tests of reading as an integral part of the effective teaching of reading, but do not always realise that the use of these informal tests is limited to the particular school situation. Application of an informal teacher-made reading test in a different school would lead to results that it would be difficult to interpret. For example, a teacher could make up her own word-recognition test based on an idiosyncratic selection of words from a particular reading scheme used by her pupils. Such a test would probably not be suitable for children from another school working on a very different reading scheme or approach. Similarly, an informal test of children's ability to read with understanding which is devised by a teacher in one school could easily be based on a content or have a structural emphasis so unfamiliar to children in another school that they would be unable to cope with the test. In each of the situations outlined, the reading test is *not* psychologically the same for all children and hence results obtained from it would be difficult to interpret.

The reader will perhaps have considered that the early stages of many reading schemes give *criterion tests* for the teacher's use with pupils. It could be found, for example, in the form of a complete list of the vocabulary used in a reader, the idea being that all these words should be mastered before the child proceeds to the next book. But even in this case, the criterion suitable for a child having used the 'Janet and John' series is not the same as that appropriate to children using, say, either a language-experience approach or the 'Royal Road' series. None the less, such a criterion test could be a valid means of comparison between schools using the *same* basal reading series.

If a teacher wishes to test her pupils' reading attainments *and* to compare these, for example, with national standards, then a nationally standardised test of reading attainment is necessary.

Reading tests are concerned with attainment. An objective of reading instruction can be defined in terms of children's relative competence in a reading skill. Let us assume that we are interested in assessing children's ability to read silently a series of sentences and, from the meaning, select from one of five alternatives the word that correctly completes the sentence. This could be considered as the operational definition of an index of *one* of the intermediate skills comprising reading comprehension. Examples are given below:

1. GO AND BUY SOME STAMPS FROM THE POST (COUNTER/ LETTER/SHOP/OFFICE/HOUSE).
2. THE VOLCANO CAUSED EXTENSIVE (EXPLOSION/DESTRUC- TION/INFUSION/SUSPICION/ILLUSION) IN THE VILLAGE.

It would be impossible to construct a test of this aspect of reading comprehension that, in one school period, covered the complete field for all children in all schools. As complete coverage is impossible, a sample of the subject matter must be taken and, as far as is possible, it must be fair to all children. In constructing a standardised reading test, ideally a team of teachers experienced in the teaching of reading would work in cooperation with a test construction expert. There is no reason other than pressure of other activities why teachers should not acquire the necessary skills (e.g. Macintosh and Morrison 1969; Marshall and Hales 1971; Schofield 1972; Thyne 1974). The Educational Testing Service (1964, 1969a) provide a series of very helpful pamphlets for teachers who are interested in developing skills in this area.

Initially a table of test specifications is drawn up to determine the content of the test in the light of the goals of the reading programme and the age range for which it is intended. The time that the final version must take to administer is decided right at the start, as is the number and type of items to be used. There are many different ways in which objective test items suitable for a standardised test can be written. In the national surveys carried out in England and Wales by the DES, and more recently by the NFER, tests made up of multiple-choice type items similar to those given above have been used. This type of reading test is rather like a high jump in that the earlier items are easier than the later ones. Thus the higher the child's raw score, the more competent he is at this particular aspect of reading for meaning. Such tests are known as 'power' tests in contrast with 'speed' reading tests where the items are of equal difficulty and children are differentiated by the number of words they read correctly in a given standard time (e.g. the *Ballard One Minute Reading Test*).

After the table of specifications has been drawn up, the teachers of reading then write a series of items in the appropriate style or styles that have been agreed. The teachers read each other's contributions to the pool of items, watching out for unintentional ambiguities, double negatives and other syntactic structures known to be undesirable. After this screening, there must remain many more items than are required to make up the final test of reading comprehension. At this stage, several parallel forms of the proposed test may be drawn up.

The next stage is for all the forms of the test to be tried out on a group of children selected to be representative of the children for whom the test is intended. When the completed reading tests in their try-out form have been administered and marked, *each individual item* is analysed in two ways. Firstly, the difficulty of each item is calculated by finding the percentage of children who mark it correctly. Items which all children either fail or pass are rejected as these have no effect on the rank order of pupils' total scores. Items which all pass might be used as 'lead in' items to encourage poor readers, but would not be scored. Secondly, after placing the children's scripts in rank order, two groups of scripts are chosen; for example, the top third and the bottom third in terms of total raw scores correct on the tests. This is done in order to look at what is called the discriminative power of each item in the test. In other words, one needs to discover which items best differentiate between children scoring low and children scoring high on the test. If an item discriminates satisfactorily, more pupils represented in the high-scoring upper third group of scripts will mark the correct response than children in the low-scoring group. For example, if on a given item all the children whose scripts were in the high-scoring group marked it correctly and none of the children in the low-scoring group marked it correctly, the item would be considered an excellent discriminator. On the other hand, if 70 per cent of the children in the top-scoring group and 65 per cent in the low-scoring group marked the same item correctly, that item would not be a good discriminator between the groups, and would be rejected.

If the test is of the multiple-choice type, the children's responses to the incorrect alternative answers to each item would be analysed. Where necessary, new 'distractors' would be written for use in a further try-out of items.

The teachers and the test constructor then select the most suitable items according to their difficulty level and their discriminative power. The 'try-out' version of the reading comprehension test is then assembled. It is administered to a *different* group of children selected from the population for whom the test is intended. The previous cycle of processes is repeated until an acceptable final version of the test is obtained.

When the final version of the test is available, norms for the test can be established. These could be on the basis of a nationally representative group of children of a given age range. If it is considered necessary by the committee responsible for the test, they can arrange for the production of separate norms for boys and girls respectively. Similarly, norms can be obtained for children from different socio-economic backgrounds or ethnic groups, or on the basis of geographical district areas such as 'rural' and 'urban'. Steps are also taken to test the test; that is, to see that it does what its makers intended. In test language, the reading comprehension test's various validities and reliabilities are calculated (see below).

This simplified account of *one* approach to the construction of an objective standardised test of reading comprehension of a prescribed type is given so that readers might appreciate the care and effort that goes into constructing such a measuring instrument. It is vital that anyone wishing to use such a test should read the test manual carefully and not rely on word-of-mouth instructions from a colleague as to the test's administration, scoring and interpretation. Without such care, the considerable strengths of a standardised test are lost.

Validity, reliability and practicability

Reliability and validity are two important concepts that must be employed in deciding whether or not a reading test is an adequate instrument for the function one wishes it to fulfil. The terms are related and *both* must be considered together.

In one sense, a reading test is like a gun aimed at a target. If a number of bullets from a gun fixed in a stand hit the target area, we know that the gun is directing its missiles in the intended direction. By analogy, if the reading test items are pertinent to the purpose we have in mind, the reading test is 'on target'. However, by itself this is *not* enough. Despite being aimed at the centre of a target, the bullets from a gun can produce a pattern of bullet holes ranging from a close cluster to a wide scatter. This spread of shots is mainly a function of the characteristics of the gun and the bullets. If it produces a very close cluster of bullet holes in the target, this close cluster indicates that the weapon is reliable in an important sense. But what if the cluster is near the edge of the target rather than at the centre? In this case the gun is reliable as its bullets consistently give the same 'score' (a low one) but the weapon is *not* valid for the purpose of directing shots to the centre of the target. It is not meeting the user's requirements. Again, by analogy, it is possible to administer a reading test to a group of children and obtain consistent results, but the results may *not* be pertinent to the purpose you have in mind. For example, a test of reading comprehension can give very reliable results, but if the instructional objective in which you are interested is speed of reading, your test is most likely invalid for this purpose. Although your test is highly reliable, it is not valid for your specified purpose. High reliability does not *guarantee* the validity of a reading test, but is an essential pre-requisite of reading test validity. However, if a reading test can be shown to be valid, it *must* have good reliability. Both considerations are pertinent to the selection of *any* reading test for a specified purpose. Both terms can be expressed with considerable precision in relation to the vast majority of published standardised reading tests, although it should be pointed out that the detailed application of these two concepts to the uses of criterion-referenced reading tests is still in its infancy.

The following section considers validity and reliability in rather more detail, as the informed selection of a standardised reading test is to a large measure dependent upon an understanding of these terms.

The validity of a reading test

The usefulness of a reading test as a basis for making judgments about children's reading skills depends on its validity. Validity has two aspects: *relevance* and *reliability*. The former refers to the exactness with which the test measures what it is intended to measure. The latter refers to the accuracy and consistency of the instrument. If a reading test is used for different purposes, it will have different validities. For example, children's scores on a word-recognition test such as the *Schonell Graded Word Reading Test R*[1] are highly related to their ability to recognise a wide range of untimed flash-card-presented words. In this instance the Schonell test would be a valid one for the purpose of testing untimed word-recognition skill. However, children's scores on the untimed *Schonell Graded Word Reading Test R*[1] have a lower relationship with, say, children's speed of reading aloud continuous prose. In this case, the Schonell test would *not* be a highly valid test of children's rate of reading continuous prose.

The validity of a reading test can be defined as the degree to which a test measures what it purports to measure. The importance of the teacher using tests of reading that are valid in terms of her instructional objectives in reading should be quite clear.

In using a test of reading there are four major types of question that teachers frequently wish to answer. These are:

1. Will the test help in determining the child's current attainments in a given reading skill?
2. Will the test assist in the estimation of the child's attainment on some reading skill related to that being tested?
3. Will the test be effective in predicting the child's future attainment in the reading skill being tested or in some related reading skill?
4. Will the reading test score enable the teacher to infer the extent to which the child possesses some hypothesised psychological quality or 'construct' related to the reading process?

Questions of the type listed above are related to the following four types of validity:

1. Content validity
2. Concurrent validity
3. Predictive validity
4. Construct validity.

The *content* validity of a reading test is the extent to which the items comprising the test form a representative, sufficiently complete and uncontaminated sample of items of the ability to be measured at a suitable level of difficulty for the children. Thus, for example, the words chosen for use in a test of *general* word recognition must be carefully selected. They should be proportionately representative of different types of words such as phonically regular and irregular words, and *not* exclusively one or the other. The number of words included in the test must be sufficiently large so

that the children have a number of opportunities of being successful at a given level. The items must be uncontaminated. The
presence of a large copy of the reading test as a wall display/teaching
aid in the classroom will invalidate the test. Care must also be taken
to ensure that the difficulty level of the words in the test is appropriate to the children's abilities: 'chiaroscuro' would be unsuitable
for infants.

Those who construct tests should give potential users evidence of
its content validity. The onus is then *on the teacher* who is considering
using the test to decide whether or not it has a content validity
appropriate to her reading instruction objectives, the children she
teaches and the type of instruction provided.

The *concurrent* validity of a reading test relates the test scores to
other *present* performances. It is concerned with the relationship
between children's scores on a specific reading test and their scores
on a test of some related skill. Usually this latter skill is one which
is difficult and time-consuming to measure. A less time-consuming
testing procedure is therefore an efficient approach. Thus the test
score which can be obtained in a few minutes is used as a substitute
for some other criterion of performance which might require a
month's observation of a child. To say that a child has a reading age
of twelve years on a specified reading test assumes that the test
score has a high relationship with the typical twelve-year-old
child's attainment in the skill tested. When a test constructor gives
evidence of the concurrent validity of a reading test, he must also
show that the criterion measure is valid. Because information on
children's performances on both reading tests and the criterion can
be obtained at about the same time, i.e. concurrently, concurrent
validities of tests are fairly readily obtainable. Teachers' estimates
of children's reading ability and children's scores on other established reading tests are two commonly used criteria of concurrent
validity.

The *predictive* validity of a reading test is concerned with how well
the test will predict children's future achievements in the skill
tested. For example, if one tests children's reading comprehension
ability at the age of eight years, how well will the test predict the
same children's reading comprehension ability at the age of ten
years? If a reading test has a high predictive validity it can help to
identify the children most likely to succeed in acquiring, say,
competence in reading comprehension at a later date. Additionally,
it can be used to identify those children most likely *not* to succeed.
Thus the reading test with high predictive validity can help to focus

the teacher's attention on the instructional needs of these children. Test constructors should be expected to provide information concerning the predictive validity of their tests for defined groups of children and specific purposes. The teacher of reading tends to build up an intuitive knowledge of the predictive validity of a range of children's characteristic behaviours: for example, 'the fluent speakers have no difficulty in learning to read'. However, such relatively unsystematised knowledge can be dangerous *because* it contains an indeterminate element of predictive validity on which the teacher may over-generalise. She might thus tend to neglect those children who are fluent speakers but who in fact have difficulty in acquiring certain reading skills. Such children may well have problems of perception that the teacher might fail to detect.

Many variables influence children's performance on a reading test. Not all of these will be adequately accounted for in the previously described three types of validity. For example, a reading test with high content validity, concurrent validity and moderate predictive validity might not take into account the importance of motivational variables such as interests in and attitudes to the particular reading skill being tested. With *construct* validity, the test constructor is concerned to show that the items in the reading test are adequate samples of the behaviours included in the psychological construct under consideration, in this instance reading ability. The test constructor goes further than simply showing the relationship between a reading test score and some outside criterion. By using the scores of children on a number of different types of items and by looking at the inter-relationships between these, he uses techniques such as factor analysis in an attempt to specify the psychological quality that the particular reading test measures.

The validity of a test is usually expressed as an index ranging from 0 to 1. The former would indicate that for a group of children there existed no relationship between their scores on a test of reading and their scores on the reading ability that the test was intended to tap, i.e. the reading test was useless. The latter would show that there was perfect agreement between the two measures. The magnitude of validity coefficients vary, depending upon the type of validity or validities which the test constructor has examined. They are also affected by the specific conditions under which the validation data were obtained. It is up to the teacher selecting a test of reading to decide whether, on the evidence presented in the test manual, the test is valid for the particular purpose she wishes to use it.

It will be apparent that an understanding of the concept of the validity of tests in general and of reading tests in particular is crucial to the informed selection of reading tests. On such an understanding depends the extent to which the test is likely to help the teacher assess various aspects of her pupils' progress towards specified goals of reading instruction and to indicate areas in which children require additional help.

The reliability of a reading test

The reliability of a reading test is the extent to which an individual's scores on a test vary under different circumstances. There are a number of ways in which the reliability of reading tests can be measured. The results are usually expressed as indices known as *reliability coefficients*. A coefficient of 1 indicates perfect reliability whereas one of 0 would show that the test was completely unreliable. The four major reliability coefficients pertinent to the selection of a reading test are:

1. Coefficient of stability
2. Coefficient of equivalence
3. Coefficient of internal consistency
4. Coefficient of stability and equivalence.

Knowing how these coefficients are obtained will enable the teacher to make a more informed selection from the range of reading tests available to her.

Stability. We can administer a test of reading comprehension to a class of children on two occasions separated sufficiently in time to prevent practice effect from complicating the situation yet close enough to minimise the effects of intervening instruction and maturation. We would expect to obtain similar results for individual children on each occasion. John, aged eleven years, who obtained a reading age of fifteen years on the first administration would be expected to obtain a similarly high score on the second occasion. A child obtaining a low score on the first occasion would be expected to obtain a rather similar score on the second occasion. This is no more than saying that we expect the test to be reliable, to give consistent results.

In the above example we administer the *same* reading test on different occasions (a very common practice in the testing of reading) and then compare the results. The index of reliability obtained is called the coefficient of stability. This approach is known as the 'test-retest' method, for obvious reasons. The longer the time interval between the two testings, the lower the coefficient tends to be. If, from a class of children, one obtained an identical rank-order of scores on both occasions, the coefficient of stability could be expressed by a coefficient of 1. On the other hand, if the two obtained rank-orders showed no consistent relationship, the coefficient would be 0 and the teacher would almost certainly have grave doubts as to the value of such a test in helping her to make useful decisions concerning the attainment of her instructional objectives in reading.

Equivalence. In some tests of reading, for example the *Neale Analysis of Reading Ability* (Neale 1958) and the *Salford Sentence Reading Test* (Bookbinder 1976), there are parallel forms of the tests. Thus it is possible to test the same skill on *equivalent* but different items sampling the same reading skill. The relationship between children's scores on the administration of two such parallel forms of a reading test is called the coefficient of equivalence. It measures the consistency of the children's reading performance on two sets of *different* but parallel items covering the same skill.

Internal consistency. As most teachers will be well aware, equivalent or parallel forms of reading tests are not always available. A technique exists that enables an estimate of reliability to be obtained from *one* administration of a reading test having only *one* form. This is done by giving the test to a group of children and then dividing the test items into two halves. This could be done on the basis of odd and even item numbers respectively. This enables *two* scores to be obtained for each child, one on each of the two sub-sets of items. If the relationship between the two sets of scores obtained is high, this is an indication that each half of the test is measuring a similar attribute. Hence the result of comparing scores from two halves of a reading test is known as a coefficient of internal consistency. It is an approximation of the previously described coefficient of equivalence, provided that allowance is made for the shortening of the length of the tests inherent in splitting it into two halves. The method is inappropriate in highly speeded tests (for example, the *Ballard One Minute Reading Test*), where there is a wide range of items left unattempted by children taking the test due to shortage of time. Because of the ease with which the information can be obtained, coefficients of internal consistency are frequently given in reading test manuals.

Stability and equivalence. The final measure of reading test reliability to be described here is that obtained when a parallel form of the same test is administered after a period of time. Comparison of children's performances under these conditions yields a co-efficient of reliability more precisely known as the coefficient of stability and equivalence. In general, this coefficient will be rather lower than those obtained from the other methods of calculating reliability. This is because more possible sources of variation in children's scores occur between the two occasions and in the measures when the children complete the two equivalent reading tests.

Which coefficient of reliability matters most?

The answer to this question depends partly on the purpose for which the reading test is to be used. The *highest* coefficient of reliability is *not* necessarily the best recommendation for a test of reading. If the teacher is particularly concerned with measuring change in reading skill over time, she would be well advised to use a test with a high coefficient of stability and equivalence.

Frequently, reading test manuals do *not* contain the above index of reliability (or indeed any index of reliability). The manuals of American reading tests usually contain more information concerning reliability than many English reading test manuals. Fortunately this situation is changing quite markedly as professional organisations concerned with test construction have formulated policies specifying the requirements of a well constructed test and its accompanying manual.

From the above it will be noted that it is difficult to prescribe arbitrary standards concerning the reliability of tests of reading. However, it has been suggested that the minimum internal consistency reliability coefficients for attainment tests including tests of reading often exceeds 0·95, according to certain authorities (NFER 1977).

The reliability required of a test depends on the purpose for which it is to be used. Very high reliability is required where important decisions are to be made concerning individual children on the basis of a single administration of a reading test. It is also required in tests of reading ability that provide a profile of scores on a variety of measures if the importance of the differences between a child's scores on the sub-tests is to be interpreted in terms of a programme of remedial reading activities.

The reliability of reading tests used to determine the differences between the *average* scores of large groups of children need not be as high. The classroom teacher might be interested in the use of reading tests in all three of the situations described.

Work carried out by Kelley (1927) and making rather stringent assumptions* concerning the precision with which a test should discriminate for various purposes, has been extensively quoted in the literature relating to objective testing. The following table quotes the minimum reliability coefficients for tests used for various purposes calculated by Kelley. They have been related to the testing of reading, but have wider applicability.

Table 4.1

Purpose for which test scores are to be used	*Minimum reliability coefficient*
1 To evaluate the level of reading attainment of a group....	0·50
2 To evaluate differences in level of reading attainment of a group on two or more test administrations..............	0·90
3 To evaluate the level of individual reading attainment....	0·94
4 To evaluate differences in individual reading attainment on two or more test administrations.....................	0·98

Although many standardised reading tests measure up to the above requirements, a large number do not. Fortunately, there is evidence that tests with lower reliabilities than those quoted in the table can be useful in the assessment of reading. If the test has a reliability higher than that afforded by some subjective estimates of reading ability such as teachers' ratings, even if it does not measure up to the level of reliability suggested necessary for a given purpose by Kelley, it can usually be used to advantage. These considerations of reliability apply only to standardised tests of reading attainment and *not* to criterion-referenced tests.

Improving the reliability of a reading test

The reliability of a reading test can, in general, be raised by increasing the length of the test. It can also be improved by increasing the

* Kelley's figures are based on the assumption that a test should allow discrimination of differences in reading ability as small as one-fourth the standard deviation of scores for a year group, with the chances of being correct about the direction of the difference being five to one.

objectivity of the scoring procedure and by ensuring that the test administration is consistent. To test a child's reading comprehension ability on the basis of his reading one passage of prose and answering a maximum of five questions is likely to be a much less reliable test than the presentation of a number of paragraphs *each* having five associated questions to be answered. If the correctness of the answers is in any doubt, test reliability will decrease. If the teacher provides encouragement to one child and not to another whilst administering a reading test, the reliability of the test will be adversely affected.

Although the teacher selecting a test of reading for a given purpose can do relatively little about the first of the above variables influencing test reliability, she needs to be aware of the importance of the other two. They point up the often unrecognised conflict between the role of teacher and tester. 'Come on, Johnny, you *know* how to read this word. What sound does it begin with?' is a disastrous way to administer a standardised individual test of word-reading ability if one intends interpreting the results in a normative manner. It is a useful teaching approach, but the teaching of a standardised test should always be avoided.

The practicability of a reading test

The prime characteristic of a reading test is that it must be suited to the particular purpose that the teacher has in mind. Within this constraint, for tests of similar acceptable validity and reliability, other considerations are important in reading test selection. These include test availability, cost, ease of administration and scoring, together with the readiness with which the results may be interpreted and applied.

These very practical considerations are recognised by test constructors. The danger facing the teacher in selecting a reading test lies in the balance between such desirable practical characteristics as those listed above and the less well understood, but far more important ones, of validity and reliability. It is not unknown for a reading test to be used solely *because* it is available, economical, easy to administer and apparently easy to interpret. Teachers need to be sufficiently knowledgeable about the desirable characteristics of such reading tests to make an informed choice, rather than one governed solely by considerations based on convenience. If this appears to be asking too much of the teacher (*not* the writer's belief), she should at least be able to obtain the advice of someone who is aware of the importance of test validity (see Chapter 5).

The two most valuable sources of information concerning a reading test are the handbook or manual plus expert critical evaluations of the test. The test and its handbook should measure up to criteria that have been spelled out by both the British Psychological Society (1960) and by the American Psychological Association (1974). As yet, a number of British and American reading tests do not have manuals providing information on which teachers could make informed decisions. However, as teachers become increasingly aware of the information they require and critical of tests having inadequate manuals, the standard of manuals will tend to rise. The manual should provide answers to the questions concerning content, form and administration given in the following section.

Selecting a reading test: essential considerations

The choice of a reading test is a three-phase process of: (i) deciding the purpose the test is to fulfil, (ii) considering the range of tests available, and (iii) selecting the test or tests which best suit that purpose.

The most important consideration when selecting a test is the purpose that it is intended to fulfil. In other words, the tester must answer the question: 'Why do I consider the use of a reading test necessary?' This is a consideration that can only be made in the context of the instructional objectives and methods of the reading programme. The perspectives and interests of the class teacher, headteacher, administrator, parent and the researcher frequently differ in this respect. The teacher's prime interest is usually in helping children master increasingly complex reading skills. The administrator might be more concerned with general standards (although these depend upon the effectiveness with which the teacher can help individual children). Frequently, in the legitimate interests of economy of time, there are attempts at selecting one reading test that will satisfy a number of purposes. This can be achieved only in part, usually if the centre of interest of all parties lies in a child's relative attainments (Educational Testing Service 1969b; des 1975; Pumfrey 1976).

The question which follows specification of one's purpose in using a reading test is: 'Which *type* of test is most likely to give the information that will be of most value to me?' All too frequently, pressure of time, limitations in the availability of money or materials and a limited knowledge by teachers of the reading tests relevant to their purposes lead inevitably to the use of informal tests *where other types would be more appropriate.*

Should the teacher need advice or wish to discuss the selection of a suitable test, there are, within the majority of local education authorities, services employing educational psychologists and remedial reading teachers who frequently have an extensive knowledge of available reading tests. Nevertheless, the selection of a reading test is not something that the teacher should readily hand over lock, stock and barrel to some 'expert'. The person who uses a test should have a major say in its selection, provided she is able to make an informed choice.

Having decided one's purpose in testing reading, being aware of the range of tests available and of the theoretical and practical criteria that determine their suitability, the selection of a reading test is relatively straightforward. The choice involves the following five considerations, three instructional and two administrative:

1. *Content*
Is the content valid for my purpose? (For example, does it test the skill in which I am interested, such as 'ability to read regular three-letter words; to read accurately, or to understand instructions of a particular type'?)
Is the test reliable in the way important for my purpose?
Is the test intended for the group with which I am concerned?
Is the material appropriate to the children's background?

2. *Form*
What type of administration best suits my purpose? (For example, individual or group? oral or silent? timed or untimed? multiple-choice or constructed response? power or speed?)

3. *Marking and interpreting*
How are the results presented? (For example, will they be in terms of raw scores, reading ages, percentiles, or quotients?)
Will I be able to relate these results to my purpose?
How long does it take to administer, score and interpret?
How can the results best be recorded?
Has the test been given to the children before?
If so, when, and will this affect my interpretation?
Are the norms of the test up to date?
Is it important if they are not?

4. *Availability*
Am I qualified to use the test?
Is the test available already in the school or in the area?

Is it part of the reading assessment programme of the school or the
   local education authority?
Is the test 'open' or 'restricted'?
5. *Cost*
Is the test material expendable or reusable?
What is the cost per pupil of administering the test?
Is the expenditure incurred in both time and money justified?

The critical reviews of tests reported in the various Buros Yearbooks and Monographs (see Chapter 5) and other professional
periodicals help the teacher to make informed selections because
the reviewers often point to weaknesses that the unsuspecting reader
of a test manual might overlook.

Cumulative records of reading test results

Before we can understand and improve our control of a situation
we need to know what is happening in that situation. In the case of
the development of reading abilities, the use of *one* reading test on
one occasion is in some respects analogous to taking a photograph
of a changing scene from a given vantage point. In both cases one
obtains a static picture of a dynamic process. Such a picture can be
misleading. The changing nature of the skills comprising reading
and their inter-relationships can be understood most adequately in
the full knowledge of the changes in the process. In order to know
what is happening in the development of reading one would like
the equivalent of a cine recording of the moving scene from a variety
of vantage points. Such a record of the changes occurring would
enable one to analyse the processes involved, possibly to learn how
to modify the situation more effectively and, in this case, to be able
to help children achieve certain goals. An able teacher of reading
obtains an approximation of the individual child's 'reading scene'
because she is continuously involved with her pupils and views their
reading attainments from a variety of standpoints. However, when
another teacher accepts responsibility for the child, the important
understanding achieved by her predecessor cannot readily be con-
densed and summarised. The most practical approximation to a
record of the children's reading development that can be a guide to
the teacher is obtained through the use of an individual cumulative
record. In this the results of agreed tests related to the objectives and
methods of reading instruction used can be recorded *together* with
room for the observations that the teacher feels pertinent for a

colleague to know when a child transfers. If one teaches in a school where staff changes occur frequently, the value of such a record is soon apparent. Examples of simple cumulative records and their uses are given in Rance (1971), Dean (1972) and Foster (1972). The information concerning their pupils' reading attainments and attitudes collected by teachers should be recorded in relation to such other information concerning the individual as the school considers necessary. This point is emphasised as it is a direct consequence of the principles of diagnosis considered earlier in Chapter 2. The educational returns to the pupil and the teacher from the time spent in keeping records must justify this use of valuable resource. Waste of time and effort can occur when the school's policy on information concerning reading required by the LEA, the school and the individual teacher is not clearly specified.

Typically, the records of the infant school pupil's reading attainments are confined to a series of dated entries and page numbers on a child's book marker, indicating the pupil's current place in a series of graded readers. In a minority of cases reading test scores are available. At the junior stage, the monitoring of reading attainments using a normative test is likely to be carried out each year, whereas in the secondary school there is less likely to be as extensive a use of objective assessments of reading attainments except with those pupils experiencing difficulties.

Such information is sufficient for an LEA to obtain only an extremely unreliable estimate of the reading standards of its pupils. It is also insufficient for the development of individualised programmes of reading-related activities likely to optimise the pupil's progress. As a consequence of the first weakness, in consultation with their teachers some LEAs are introducing regular and comprehensive testing of reading in all their schools. In connection with the second, some schools are pioneering cumulative individual records based on the pupil's mastery of a specified series of skills of increasing complexity (e.g. Dean and Nichols 1974). An example of the type of record that can be developed by a class teacher is given in Chapter 8.

Despite reservations made earlier concerning our conceptualisation and understanding of the reading process, the use of checklists of skills which children must acquire during their progress towards becoming fluent readers has much to commend itself.

Many teachers of infants encourage their pupils to record aspects of their reading progress. For example, the number of words in a child's sight vocabulary can be recorded in a variety of ways (Harris

1970). Most teachers are well aware of the advantages of encouraging their pupils to keep such records in which the pupil's own progress is made clear to the child concerned.

By the time he is starting in the junior school, the child should be conscious of the progress he has already made in mastering the skills basic to reading. Thus an individual skills checklist is helpful to both child and teacher in that it specifies goals for both. One advantage of such lists—and there are many of them available—is that they encourage intra-individual assessment of progress which some teachers consider a more valuable form of motivation than a more inter-individual competitive system. Yet by virtue of all pupils needing to master certain skills, the checklists also provide the teacher with an overall view of the progress of her pupils towards the sub-goals. Thus testing and teaching draw together to the advantage of both pupil and teacher.

Some efficient ways of keeping records have been devised by Simpson (1962) and Zintz (1970). The latter, in particular, has developed individual progress records for use at various stages in the teaching of reading. Currently the NFER is carrying out a three-year project on record keeping. The team's strategy, in so far as reading is concerned, is to help teachers define specific objectives that can then be taught and the pupils' mastery or otherwise monitored. The researchers intend visiting some 200 schools that have made special efforts in developing record-keeping systems. The most promising ideas will be identified and work will be undertaken with groups of teachers to establish how these notions can be applied in various types of schools. The project's aims include the production of a set of explicit guidelines that will help other teachers systematise their record keeping, providing suggestions for summarising information without losing its essence, and consider the implications of problems associated with the confidentiality of records.

References

American Psychological Association (1974) *Standards for Educational and Psychological Tests and Manuals* (revised edition). Washington, D.C., American Psychological Association.

BLOOM, B. S. *et al.* (Eds.) (1956) *Taxonomy of Educational Objectives, Handbook 1 : Cognitive Domain*. New York, David McKay.

BOOKBINDER, G. E. (1970) Variations in reading test norms. *Educational Research, 12*, 2, 99–105.

BOOKBINDER, G. E. (1976) *Salford Sentence Reading Test*. London, Hodder and Stoughton.

British Psychological Society (1960) 'Technical recommendations for Psychological and Educational Tests' prepared by the Committee on Test Standards of the British Psychological Society. *British Psychological Society Bulletin, 41*, May, 1960.

CRONBACH, L. J. (1970) *Essentials of Psychological Testing* (third edition). New York, Harper and Row.

DEAN, J. (1972) *Recording Individual Progress.* London, Macmillan.

DEAN, J. and NICHOLS, R. (1974) *Framework for Reading.* London, Evans.

Department of Education and Science (1975) *A Language for Life.* London, HMSO.

Educational Testing Service (1964) *Short-cut Statistics for Teacher-made Tests.* Princeton, New Jersey, ETS.

Educational Testing Service (1969a) *Making the Classroom Test: a Guide for Teachers.* Princeton, New Jersey, ETS.

Educational Testing Service (1969b) *Selecting an Achievement Test: Principles and Procedures.* Princeton, New Jersey, ETS.

FOSTER, J. (1972) *Recording Individual Progress.* Basingstoke, Macmillan Education.

HARRIS, A. J. (1970) *How to Increase Reading Ability* (fifth edition). New York, McKay.

KELLEY, T. L. (1927) Interpretation of Educational Measurements. In ADAMS, G. S. (1965) *Measurement and Evaluation in Education, Psychology and Guidance.* New York, Holt, Rinehart and Winston.

KRATHWOHL, D. R. et al. (1964) *Taxonomy of Educational Objectives, Handbook 11: Affective Domain.* New York, McKay.

MACINTOSH, H. G. and MORRISON, R. B. (1969) *Objective Testing.* London, Hodder and Stoughton.

MARSHALL, J. C. and HALES, L. W. (1971) *Classroom Test Construction.* New York, Addison-Wesley.

MELNIK, A. and MERRITT, J. (Eds.) (1972) *Reading: Today and Tomorrow.* London, Hodder and Stoughton.

National Foundation for Educational Research (1977) *Catalogue of Tests for Educational Guidance and Assessment.* Windsor, NFER.

NEALE, M. D. (1958). *Neale Analysis of Reading Ability.* London, Macmillan.

PUMFREY, P. D. (1976) *Reading: Tests and Assessment Techniques.* London, Hodder and Stoughton.

RANCE, P. (1971) *Record Keeping in the Progressive Primary School.* London, Ward Lock.

SCHOFIELD, H. (1972) *Assessment and Testing: An Introduction.* London, Allen and Unwin.

SHEARER, E. (1974) Reading—2: New Words. *Times Educational Supplement*, No. 3078 (24th May), p. 34.

SIMPSON, G. O. (1962) *My Reading Design.* Ohio, Hubbard.

THYNE, J. M. (1974) *Principles of Examining.* London, Hodder and Stoughton.

ZINTZ, M. V. (1970) *The Reading Process: The Teacher and the Learner.* Iowa, W. C. Brown.

5. Sources of reading tests and information

Knowing why we wish to use tests of reading, being aware of the developmental nature of the reading process and of the principles governing the selection of a reading test, we can now turn to a consideration of the major sources of tests of reading and information concerning them.

There is a tremendous variety of tests of reading available to teachers. Elsewhere the writer has given detailed information about a selected range of reading tests that have been found of value by many teachers (Pumfrey 1976). In the following examination of sources of tests and test information, we will first consider national sources and then local sources in the UK.

National sources

National Foundation for Educational Research in England and Wales

Emerging as the major producer and distributor of objective tests in general and of reading tests in particular in the UK, is the National Foundation for Educational Research (NFER). Founded in 1946, the NFER is an independent organisation devoted to the improvement of education. It is supported mainly by local education authorities (LEAs) and by the Department of Education and Science, with teachers' organisations, universities and other institutions of higher education making smaller contributions.

Three of the NFER's activities are particularly pertinent to readers of this book. Firstly, its Test Department produces reading tests for specific purposes in the UK. This helps to meet the sometimes justified criticism of teachers that, for example, a reading test developed in the USA may not be entirely suitable for use with English children. An informative, free catalogue, *Tests for Educational Guidance and Assessment*, which includes technical details of

reading tests available to teachers, can be obtained from the
NFER.

Secondly, it produces a *Catalogue of Psychological Tests and
Clinical Procedures* covering a wide range of both English and overseas educational, psychological and other measuring instruments,
including tests of reading. These tests are *not* to be found in the
catalogue mentioned in the previous paragraph; neither are all of
the tests of reading and related skills listed in the *Catalogue of
Psychological Tests and Clinical Procedures* available to the teacher
who has not undertaken training and study in the use of psychological tests beyond that contained in the initial professional training
course.

Thirdly, the NFER has carried out a number of major investigations into the causes of failure and success in reading. It has also
completed a national survey of reading attainment on behalf of the
DES (see Chapter 1).

Classification of the NFER *tests.*   Recently the NFER test titles have
been amended to conform to a new system. This is intended to give
the potential user more indication of the age range for which the
test is intended than test titles formerly provided. The current
system is that the test titles will contain code letters specifying the
appropriate chronological age range as follows:

Code letter	A	B	C	D	E	F	G	H	I
Age range (years)	7–8	8–9	9–10	10–11	11–12	12–13	13–14	14–15	15–16

Thus NFER *Reading Test A* (formerly *Primary Reading Test 1*)
is intended for use with 7–8-year-old children. When a test is
designed for a wider age range than one year, the letters specifying
the limits of the age ranges are given. The NFER *Reading Tests EH
(1–3)* are intended for children at all ages between 11–12 years and
14–15 years.

Having explained the system for the benefit of potential users of
the excellent tests produced by the NFER, one wonders why it was
not considered better to enter the age ranges themselves in the test
titles rather than obscuring these by the above letter code.

Godfrey Thomson Unit for Academic Assessment (UK)

One of the earliest workers in the field of test construction was
Godfrey Thomson. At one time the Edinburgh University Depart-

ment of Education and Moray House College of Education were
housed in the same building, and the tests produced by Thomson
and his colleagues were known as 'Moray House' tests. These were
of extremely high standard and were extensively used in eleven-plus
selection in England and Wales. At present the work started by
Thomson is carried out in the Godfrey Thomson Unit, which is
part of the University of Edinburgh. Their tests are published by
Hodder and Stoughton. The decline in the demand for restricted
tests used in eleven-plus selection that has paralleled the secondary
school reorganisation on comprehensive lines in the UK means that
some tests that were restricted are now available to teachers.

The Godfrey Thomson Unit and a research team from Moray
House College of Education have been engaged in a project of considerable importance to all teachers concerned with children's
reading attainments. The aim of the project is to produce a series of
reading tests which will help class teachers to assess their pupils'
reading attainments and diagnose their reading difficulties. Four
sets of instruments suitable for all school ages from 7:0 to 16:0 years
have been produced. The name given to the complete series is the
Edinburgh Reading Tests.

The relationship between reading instruction objectives, assessment and teaching which has been stressed throughout this book is
emphasised in the statement by Dr W. Gatherer, HMI, who chaired
an important Scottish Primary School Research Group. The
Group's task was 'to determine goals and objectives for the development of competence in reading in the upper primary school and to
provide a number of evaluative instruments for use by teachers in
deciding the extent to which children were making progress towards
these goals'. As a result of this initiative, the Scottish Education
Department and the Educational Institute of Scotland jointly
sponsored the four-stage *Edinburgh Reading Tests* project.

Centre for the Teaching of Reading, Reading University (UK)

The Reading Centre provides both a local and a national service.
Here we are concerned with the national aspect. One of the Centre's
functions is to make available to the teacher information concerning
all aspects of reading, including its testing. Amongst other materials,
a brief manual called *Reading Tests* is currently available. This is
descriptive rather than evaluative, and at present the information
provided concerning particular tests is rather limited. The manual
is, however, of use to teachers wanting to see the content of some

reading tests as, for all but one of the reading tests described, a sample of the test material is included. At the Centre there are staff qualified to comment on the adequacy of reading tests for purposes specified by any teacher.

Dr E. J. Goodacre (1972) has produced for the Centre a pamphlet called *Hearing Children Read* which gives useful suggestions concerning ways of helping children who have particular difficulties.

Courses of training at univerisities, polytechnics and colleges of education (UK)

A small but increasing number of full-time and part-time courses having a large component concerned with the teaching of reading are run throughout the UK. The majority of these courses consider the need for the evaluation of children's progress in reading and the various tests that can be used to this end. Details of full-time courses can be obtained from the DES Teachers' Course Lists circulated to all state schools (DES 1977a, b). Where such courses are regularly organised, at either a university or a college of education, a polytechnic or elsewhere, its staff may be willing to offer guidance on the selection of reading tests for specific purposes. Mention should again be made of Centres such as the one at the University of Reading described earlier and of the Reading Centre at Craigie College of Education, Ayr.

Undoubtedly there will be an expansion of in-service training for teachers as a consequence of the James Report recommendations and the government white paper *Education: A Programme for Expansion* (DES 1972b). This will mean that opportunities for teachers to study the teaching and testing of reading will increase, particularly if teachers express interest in this area (DES 1972a). The Committee of Inquiry into Reading and the Use of English, under Sir Alan Bullock, has completed its work. The very concern which led to the Committee being set up has provided further impetus to the provision of in-service training opportunities for teachers to study the aims, methods and evaluation of work in the language arts at all levels (DES 1975).

The School of Education at the University of Bristol is offering a Master's degree course, which started in September 1976, intended to train specialists to advise on language and the teaching of reading. Those completing the course successfully will be qualified to undertake the specialist functions in this aspect of the curriculum as recommended in the Bullock Report (DES 1975). A further post-

Bullock Report development concerned with the diagnosis and treatment of reading difficulties is to be found at Bangor University. Professor Miles, of the Department of Psychology, is running in conjunction with the Department of Education a one-year M.Ed. degree course in the field of dyslexia. The first course was completed in 1976. It is worthy of note that the Psychology Department also provides assessment and tuition facilities for dyslexic children living in the Gwynedd Education Authority.

The Open University Post-experience Diploma in Reading Development

This is the first diploma course offered by the Open University; the structure and content of the Diploma has been developed from a need noted in the Bullock Report for a 'flexible interaction between practice and theory'. The full course consists of four modules of study. These have been constructed to provide specialist instruction for teachers, lecturers, advisers and educational psychologists who would like to undertake systematic study but who may be unable or unwilling to take time off work to do so. The course work is also claimed to be suitable for those teachers and volunteers engaged in alleviating adult illiteracy.

Module 1 is a course entitled 'Reading Development', which was started in January 1973 at the request of the Department of Education and Science (Johnson 1972). Professor John Merritt of the Faculty of Educational Studies at the Open University co-edited two texts specifically for the course. The first book of readings, *Reading : Today and Tomorrow*, was mentioned in Chapter 2 and is directed towards a discussion of the two central issues of 'What is reading?' and 'Present standards and future needs'. The second book, *The Reading Curriculum*, contains analyses of reading skills in various areas and at different levels, together with an excellent consideration of the development of reading competence. The theory and practice of the diagnostic teaching of reading is well covered and there is a section devoted to the assessment of reading (Melnik and Merritt 1972a, 1972b). These two books bring together conveniently and inexpensively the writings of many authorities on reading.

A revised version of the course began in January 1977. As would be expected, the Bullock Report (DES 1975) has now become a set book, replacing the two by Melnik and Merritt. Three new monographs have also been specially written to supplement the sixteen

correspondence texts and the sixteen television and radio programmes included in the course. The varied purposes for which
reading may be used are emphasised in these monographs. Thus
Reading, Writing and Relevance (Hoffman 1976) contains a collection of examples of language projects undertaken in British schools.
Print and Prejudice (Zimet 1976) examines the influence of the
printed media on attitudes and attainments in reading, as well as
examining psychological and political aspects. An analysis and
summary of the relationship between print and prejudice in Britain
comprises the fourth section of the book. The value of reading to
the consumer is discussed by the Consultant Education Adviser to
the Consumer Association in the third monograph *Reading and the
Consumer : A Practical Guide* (Williams 1976). The author emphasises the practical value of competent reading and shows how, in the
context of consumer education in schools, basic skills such as
reading and numeracy can be appreciated by pupils as being of
immediate relevance.

Module 2 is called 'Language and Learning'. It focuses on the
development of and interaction between language and learning in a
first language. The five major areas covered include: the nature of
language; ways in which language structures our world; language
acquisition, including individual differences and the effects of
language on learning; the teacher's use of language; and the per-
tinence of an analysis of language in areas such as morality, politics,
aesthetics and literary judgment.

Modules 3 and 4 are project-based courses. It has provisionally
been decided that the former will be concerned with 'Reading and
Individual Development' and the latter with 'The Reading Curriculum and the Advisory Role'. Both will require the student to carry
out action research projects.

Module 1, 'Reading Development', involves a consideration of
many aspects of measurement taken from the Bullock Report and
from the sixteen correspondence texts. Completion of Modules 3
and 4 is likely to involve the student in assessing some effects of his
action research. Thus the ability to utilise various aspects of measurement and assessment are likely to be required. The applications of
various observation and assessment techniques by students taking
the Diploma is likely to increase awareness of the contribution that
measurement can make to an effective language programme and
also enhance the professional competence of the individual to
utilise such techniques to the advantage of the pupils involved.

The Buros Mental Measurement Yearbooks and Monographs (USA)

A source of information about reading tests of which all teachers should be aware is the series of Buros *Mental Measurement Yearbooks* (Buros 1938, 1941, 1949, 1953, 1959, 1965, 1972) and their associated *Monographs*. These books contain references to, and critical reviews by specially selected reviewers of, tests of *all* types. The seventh Yearbook also contains a comprehensive list of the major test publishers and suppliers.

To the teacher concerned more specifically with the source of reading tests and reading test information, the most valuable books by Buros are *Tests in Print*, published in 1961, a second edition of which appeared in 1974, and *Reading Tests and Reviews* (Buros 1968). The former lists all paper-and-pencil tests then available. If one wished to find out about a particular reading test, *Tests in Print* would provide information as to whether it was available and to which of the Buros Yearbooks one should turn to read critical reviews.

The monograph *Reading Tests and Reviews* published in 1968 is of even greater importance and utility. It is the most comprehensive single source of information about, and informed comment on, reading tests. Its content is restricted to tests published in English-speaking countries. The monograph contains a comprehensive bibliography of reading tests in print as of 1 May 1968, together with reviews of those tests that had previously appeared in the *Mental Measurement Yearbooks*. A total of 209 reading tests in print and 83 out-of-print tests are listed. Tests are categorised as 'General, Diagnostic, Miscellaneous, Oral Reading, Readiness, Special Fields, Speed and Study Skills'.

Also included are 349 critical reviews of 158 reading tests, plus 608 references concerning the validity, reliability, construction and use of specific reading tests. The Publishers' Directory and Index contains the addresses of 86 publishers of 'in print' reading tests.

It should be pointed out that although the Buros series is the most extensive single source of information concerning reading tests, it is far from complete. Furthermore, not all of the reading tests listed have necessarily been reviewed. On the other hand, the most important ones will almost certainly have been dealt with. One further weakness is that such publications are inevitably not completely up to date and information on recently produced reading tests must be sought elsewhere. The UKRA monograph *Reading: Tests and Assessment Techniques* (Pumfrey 1976) in part meets the latter criticism of the Buros series in so far as British reading tests are concerned.

Professional journals (UK/USA)

Professional journals concerned with the teaching of reading are useful sources of information concerning the availability of reading tests. Such publications will also contain evidence and comment concerning the use of specific tests for given purposes. At present, most of these journals are American, but the United Kingdom Reading Association's journal *Reading* and their *Journal of Research in Reading* appear likely forums in which information concerning reading tests and their uses can be expected to develop.

In 1972 the United Kingdom Reading Association published a short descriptive list of mainly British reading tests grouped under six headings: (i) word reading tests, (ii) sentence completion tests, (iii) comprehension tests, (iv) diagnostic tests, (v) multi-purpose tests and (vi) reading-readiness tests (Turner 1972, second edition 1976).

Other journals associated with the International Reading Association (IRA) likely to contain information and comment on reading tests and their uses are *The Reading Teacher, Journal of Reading* and *Reading Research Quarterly*.

The IRA also publishes a wide variety of books on reading. One contains test reviews of reading readiness tests and is intended to enable teachers choose instruments suitable to their particular classroom requirements (Farr and Anastasiow 1969). Another focuses on reading tests for the secondary school population. As well as discussing some uses of standardised reading tests and informal reading inventories, the authors present reviews of some frequently used normative reading tests (Blanton, Farr and Tuinman 1972).

Additionally, the professional journals of teachers concerned with children experiencing learning difficulties sometimes contain articles on the diagnostic uses of reading tests. Two of the more widely known are *Remedial Education*, published by the National Association for Remedial Education, and *Special Education*, published by the Association for Special Education.

Frequently, journals concerned with problems of measurement will contain information of importance to the users of reading tests. Some of these publications are listed in Appendix 2 and, like the journals referred to above, are obtainable through the library services.

Commercial publishers and distributors (UK/USA)

A major national source of reading tests and reading test information is through various commercial publishers and distributors. These provide a wide range of reading tests, the major ones publishing annual catalogues of their tests. Selected lists of some of the major British and American test publishers and distributors are given in appendices 1 and 2 of the UKRA monograph referred to earlier.

Educational Resources Information Centres (USA)

The United States Office of Education has established a number of Educational Resources Information Centres (ERIC) concerned with particular aspects of education. These centres are situated in various academic institutions. Their function is to assemble, co-ordinate and disseminate information. Of particular interest to readers of this book will be the ERIC Clearinghouse on Reading and Communication Skills at Urbana, Illinois. There is also one concerned with Language and Linguistics in New York, and another on Tests, Measurement and Evaluation. Full addresses are given in Appendix 1 (pp. 191–2). Altogether there are sixteen Clearinghouses, each specialising in a particular area of education. Each is linked to a central computerised facility that enables anyone using ERIC to have access to information covering the full range encompassed by their network. Additionally, ERIC has associated with it a Document Reproduction Service and a Processing and Reference Facility. Details of the system are clearly set out in a readily available pamphlet (Brown *et al.* 1975). The British Library Lending Division has a collection of ERIC data on microfiche.

Center for the Study of Evaluation (USA)

This unit, based at the University of California, Los Angeles, was established in 1966. One of their projects has been the production of a series of books devoted to the evaluation of a wide range of psychological tests. For each test, information is provided concerning Measurement Validity, Examinee Appropriateness, Administrative Usability and Normed Technical Excellence. From the initial letters the acronym MEAN is derived to refer to these four aspects of test evaluation. The test reports produced have achieved a high degree of conciseness, comprehensive coverage, educational relevance, objectivity and consistency.

At present, the following publications are available from the Center:

The CSE Secondary Test Evaluations. This comes in three volumes containing evaluations of 5,400 tests for the 13–14, the 15–16 and the 17–18 year groups. It was published in 1974.

CSE–ECRC Preschool/Kindergarten Test Evaluations. This contains 550 test evaluations for children aged from $2\frac{1}{2}$ to 6 years of age.

CSE Elementary School Test Evaluations. Published in 1970, this book contains evaluations of about 750 scales for children aged from 6–7, 9–10, 11–12 and 12–13 years (grades 1, 3, 5 and 6). There are five sections devoted to reading tests as follows:

Oral-aural skills	(3 MEAN evaluations)
Word recognition	(45 MEAN evaluations)
Reading mechanics	(17 MEAN evaluations)
Reading comprehension	(97 MEAN evaluations)
Reading interpretation	(2 MEAN evaluations)

CSE/RBS Test Evaluations. The format of this book differs somewhat from the other three listed above. It contains evaluations of about 4,100 test scales for all ages. The majority of these are of 'higher-order cognitive, affective and interpersonal skills rather than academic course materials'.

While only a small proportion of the tests evaluated by CSE are reading tests, the unit's contribution towards the dissemination of test evaluations is considerable. In England we have no organisation that has carried out such an extensive evaluation of psychological tests.

The Educational Testing Service (USA)

The ETS is the largest organisation in the English-speaking world devoted to the theory and practice of educational measurement. Their address is given in Appendix 1, page 191. One of their most recent publications of interest to the teacher of reading is a series of Reading Test bibliographies. These contain brief descriptions of reading tests, plus reference to test reviews. The bibliographies cover the three age ranges 10 to 12 years, 12 to 21 years, and adult.

'Right to Read' Programme (USA)

This is the title of a colossal American programme aimed at eradicating illiteracy in the United States by 1980. It is estimated that between eighteen and twenty-five million functional illiterates will require help. Other than the 1 per cent of the population deemed ineducable, it is believed that people can learn the skills of literacy if programmes are designed to utilise their strengths and meet their needs.

In connection with the 'Right to Read' campaign inaugurated by the United States Commissioner of Education in 1969, a National Council of Reading was established. This led to the opening of the National Reading Centre intended to coordinate the efforts of both public and private organisations in training citizen volunteers, developing public support and assessing progress. A 'Right to Read' office was opened in the US Office of Education to stimulate activity in the development of educational programmes aimed at reducing the incidence of illiteracy. The scope of the 'Right to Read' programme can be gauged from the fact that in 1972 four hundred and sixty million dollars were allocated for spending on reading programmes, reading-related research and development and support activities.

The Officers responsible for the 'Right to Read' programme have expressed their wish to establish contacts with professionals in other countries concerned with the improvement of reading. Dr Ruth L. Holloway as Director of the 'Right to Read' programme has asked that information concerning projects related to reading in any country be sent to her office. Presumably the intention is to identify and make more widely known any practices that appear particularly promising. The area of assessment and diagnosis of reading difficulties is likely to be an important focus of attention. Dr Holloway's address is given in Appendix 1, p. 192.

In a report given at the UKRA Conference held at Totley-Thornbridge College of Education in 1973, Dr Holloway stated that 244 projects had been inaugurated. Every programme involves diagnosing the needs of the persons taking part and in prescribing techniques related to the individual's needs that will ensure the necessary motivation: 'As for evaluation, we have put a component into each of our kits that should reflect how all the children did on standardized tests but—even more significantly—how their interests have changed . . . The evaluation components should set guidelines for school personnel so that future programmes can be tailor made to the needs of students' (Holloway 1975). The office of the 'Right to Read' Programme, with its concern to overcome the problems of illiteracy, is likely to make a major contribution to the conceptualisation, modification and evaluation of literacy skills under a wide variety of conditions.

Local sources (UK)

Whilst the teacher needs to be aware of the major sources of reading tests and evaluative information concerning their usefulness, ready *access* to the source is perhaps of prime practical importance. Foresight and planning in obtaining the necessary information on which to make an informed choice is essential.

In the busy life of the teacher, activities other than the above type of planning may be given priority. There is then a chance that reading test selection will be done on an *ad hoc* basis against which there are cogent arguments. Fortunately, there are in most LEAs a number of important sources of reading test information that will probably already have established access to the sources mentioned earlier. If any of the following local sources of reading test information are available, they should be consulted if necessary.

Remedial Education Services

Many LEAs have Remedial Education Services. These employ staff to advise teachers concerning children's learning difficulties and to help individual children overcome their reading problems. Recognised as one of the most important parts of their work is the remedial teaching of reading. The senior staff of Remedial Education Centres have usually taken a course of training beyond basic teacher training and will also have had a number of years of successful teaching experience in school. In their advanced courses of training they will almost certainly have studied the uses and limitations of reading tests in the teaching of reading.

Contact with the staff of a Remedial Education Service, if not already established, can swiftly be achieved. This can be done either through a peripatetic remedial teacher who might visit a school regularly in order to help with children having reading difficulties, or by personally visiting a Remedial Education Centre. This is the base from which the Remedial Education Service usually operates. It may be in a building of its own, housed in a local school or situated in the local Child Guidance Clinic. Children with reading difficulties are frequently helped at the Remedial Education Centre. Centres are also used for running courses on the teaching and testing of reading.

A Remedial Education Centre will have available a wide range of tests and materials pertinent to the teaching of reading and some of the staff will be trained and experienced in the values and limitations of both. The staff's advice concerning the selection of a test suitable for a particular purpose is readily available. The majority of Remedial Education Services will also respond to requests for in-service courses on the uses and abuses of tests in the teaching of reading. The importance of remedial centres is recognised by the Bullock Committee. One of the principal recommendations in their report is that 'There should be a reading clinic or remedial centre in every LEA, giving access to a comprehensive diagnostic service . . . the centre should also offer an advisory service to schools in association with the LEA's specialist adviser' (DES 1975, p. 514).

Schools' Psychological Services and Child Guidance Clinics

In 1959, the Ministry of Education stated that '. . . there should be a comprehensive child guidance service available for the area of every local education authority, involving a school psychological service, the school health service and child guidance clinic(s), all of which should work in close cooperation' (Ministry of Education 1959). The organisation of these services is currently being reviewed.

Child Guidance Clinics provide a service oriented towards the emotional and learning problems of children who require intensive investigation. The work of the Schools' Psychological Service is slanted towards the more frequent learning and emotional problems that can be dealt with in the school. The precise relationship between Child Guidance Clinics and Schools' Psychological Services varies between LEAS.

The above two services are mentioned here because both employ educational psychologists who are highly trained in the selection, uses and interpretation of many tests including reading tests. At present there appear to be only four LEAs at the very most in England and Wales that do not have Psychological Services (DES 1968, para. 2:13). The number of educational psychologists employed by LEAS is about 850 and is increasing. The majority work for both the Child Guidance Clinics and the Schools' Psychological Services, although arrangements vary. The ratio of schoolchildren to educational psychologists is about 10,000 to 1. Hence it is not surprising that many teachers have never met an educational psychologist in their professional careers. Because they are concerned with children's attainments in the basic subjects and are trained at an advanced level in the theory and practice of testing, educational psychologists are probably the best qualified individuals within an LEA to advise on the selection of reading tests. One part of the educational psychologist's duties is to contribute to in-service courses for teachers. Those psychologists who have taken a particular interest in the development of the Remedial Education Service in general and of the remedial teaching of reading in particular should be looked upon by the teacher as a valuable source of reading test information and informed comment.

An example of what is available through Schools' Psychological Services will illustrate this point. The former Senior Educational Psychologist of the West Sussex County Education Committee has, with his colleagues, produced a series of helpful pamphlets. One entitled *Assessment of Reading Ability* contains some important comments on the use of reading test results in planning remedial work with children (Labon 1972). The pamphlet introduces a Reading Test Battery of five diagnostic tests intended to assess aspects of visual discrimination, auditory discrimination, knowledge of letter sounds and of phonic ability. It also shows how this battery can be used to help identify the area of a child's reading difficulties and to provide leads to reading activities likely to help the child acquire increased proficiency in the given skill.

In the writer's experience, there are many Schools' Psychological Services that provide similar materials.

Local inspectorate

The LEA local inspectorate of schools, particularly its members concerned with standards of literacy, is likely to be familiar with a variety of reading tests. The inspectorate will also have important views concerning the uses of reading tests. The extent to which the systematic use of reading tests can enable the inspectorate to obtain a more valid overview of reading standards in the schools in their area is well appreciated.

Currently the concept of accountability in education is receiving considerable political impetus. The Assessment of Performance Unit of the Department of Education and Science (see pp. 14–15) to some extent reflects this interest. The unit has already commissioned certain reading tests and 'In the next year or so it will be increasingly associated with the actual development of test materials for a national programme of monitoring standards in schools' (Kay 1976).

Remedial education departments in schools

The majority of secondary schools provide remedial teaching in reading as part of the activities of its Remedial Department. Thus some senior members of the Remedial Education Department are likely to be aware of the various available reading tests that are of use to them in their work. At present the majority of staff in Remedial Education Departments in secondary schools have not taken an advanced course of study and training in their specialism. Despite this, there will still be many who have and who will be knowledgeable about the uses of reading tests available to them.

Teachers' centres

The increasing provision of teachers' centres with one of their functions being that of a 'resources' centre is welcomed. At some, a variety of instructional materials are available for teachers to see, handle and discuss. Such centres are a potential source of information on reading tests, but too much should not be expected of them in this respect. Tests require that the teacher has some understanding of their limitations and the mere display of tests and testing material is, quite correctly, frowned upon by most authorities.

Local courses of training

The demand from teachers for local courses of in-service training in the field of reading is considerable. This reflects the importance with which the educational objective of literacy is seen by teachers. The view that teachers generally should acquire more specialist knowledge in the teaching and testing of reading is stressed in the James Report. This recommends, as top priority, that every teacher be given entitlement to regular in-service education and training. More specifically, teachers in schools faced with illiteracy or semi-literacy need to improve their competence in fostering children's language development and in the teaching of reading and writing (DES 1972a, 1975).

As has been indicated in the previous six sections, there are available in most LEAs the resources necessary to run courses on the uses and limitations of reading tests in the improvement of standards of reading. If there is sufficient demand from teachers for such courses in a given area, it is most likely that they will be arranged by the LEA. Other educational institutions also contribute.

The availability of courses on, and information concerning, the uses and limitations of reading tests

It has been suggested that within most LEAs the Schools' Psychological Services and the Remedial Education Services are important sources of expertise related to the above.

All the then 164 LEAs in England and Wales were circularised in 1973 in order to obtain information on the following two points:

1. Had any of the in-service courses for teachers run by either the Schools' Psychological Service and/or the Remedial Education Services within an LEA during the past year provided instruction and training in the uses and limitations of reading tests as a significant part of course content?
2. Do these LEA services produce pamphlets concerning reading tests and their uses for teachers within the LEA?

The response to the questionnaire was satisfactory; 96·95 per cent of the 164 LEAs approached replied. In the following table the Schools' Psychological Service and Remedial Education Service taken together within each LEA that replied have been categorised as *either* having run *or* not having run a course with the defined content. Additionally they have been classified as *either* having available *or* not having available appropriate pamphlets.

Table 5.1   Schools' Psychological Services/Remedial Education Services and the provision of courses and pamphlets related to the testing of reading

	At least one course during past year		No course during past year		Total pamphlets	
	N	%	N	%	N	%
Pamphlets available	48	30·2	5	3·1	53	33·3
Pamphlets not available	48	30·2	58	36·4	106	66·6
Total courses	96	60·4	63	39·5	*No. of replies =* 159/164 = 96·95 %	

The table shows that there are considerable variations in the extent to which the LEA services mentioned are involved in activities

Table 5.2 Number of courses organised in England and Wales during one year by Schools' Psychological Services and Remedial Education Services within 159 LEAs in which consideration of the uses and limitations of reading tests formed a significant part

Number of courses run in year	0	1	2	3	4	5	6	7	8	9	10	11	12	13	14	Over 30
i. SPS/RES providing number of courses	63	28	25	9	8	6	8	3	2	0	2	0	1	0	1	3
ii. Percentage of SPS/RES providing number of courses in i above	39·6	17·6	15·7	5·6	5·0	3·8	5·0	1·9	1·3	0	1·3	0	0·6	0	0·6	1·9
iii. Cumulative frequency of iii above	63	91	116	125	133	139	147	150	152	152	154	154	155	155	156	159
iv. Cumulative percentage of ii above	39·6	57·2	72·9	78·5	83·5	87·3	92·3	94·2	95·5	95·5	96·8	96·8	97·4	97·4	98·0	99·9

related to disseminating knowledge to teachers concerning the uses and limitations of reading tests.

In Table 5.2 the number of courses organised by these two services in a given year on the topic specified is presented. The provision is hardly extensive. However, it should be stressed that many other institutions such as university departments of education, polytechnics and colleges of education provide courses on the uses and limitations of reading tests. What can be provided by Schools' Psychological Services and Remedial Education Services depends on their resources, their priorities and the demands exerted on the services.

A fuller analysis of the survey has been reported elsewhere (Pumfrey 1974). The overall tendency for services running courses also to produce pamphlets was confirmed within different types of authority. The above analysis of the number of courses run during a given year shows this to be, on average, minimal with some honourable exceptions. The findings suggest that more could be done to meet teachers' needs in this field.

In April 1974 the local authorities of England and Wales were reorganised. This reorganisation has not materially increased the ratio of Educational Psychologists to pupils and teachers, and Schools' Psychological Services and Remedial Education Services in the newly formed local authorities are still staffed largely by the same personnel as prior to reorganisation. Courses on, and information concerning, the uses and limitations of reading tests still fall short of what is needed. However, there are some signs that in response to the survey mentioned above and to requests from teachers, more attention is being paid to meeting these needs (Marder 1976).

Qualifications required to purchase and use reading tests

Earlier it was stated that teaching and testing are complementary processes in education. However, it does not follow that any teacher can purchase and use any published test of reading solely because she is interested in the teaching of reading. The importance of training in the selection, administration and interpretation of test results is being increasingly recognised (BPS 1965, 1966).

In order to prevent the misuse of tests, in accordance with the recommendations of the British Psychological Society (BPS 1969), the NFER has categorised its tests as falling into three major groups. These are attainment tests, psychological tests and clinical instruments. They are defined as follows:

i. *Attainment tests* are concerned with acquired knowledge and/or skills such as reading.
ii. *Psychological tests* are concerned with more complex aspects of abilities, aptitudes, interests or attitudes.
iii. *Clinical instruments* are quasi-test devices not giving an objective score, but allowing a clinical diagnostic assessment of the subject's performance.

Within this framework, the NFER subdivides the second category into various levels which specify to whom the tests are available.

Attainment tests

Level A tests are objectively-scored attainment tests and inventories requiring minimum technical knowledge for their use. These include all the tests of reading contained in their catalogue *Tests for Educational Guidance and Assessment*. Teachers can order these tests on production of the written authority of their headteacher. Students hoping to use these tests in their research must obtain the written support of their supervisor.

Psychological tests

Psychological tests, which include many reading tests, are divided into three categories:

Level P tests require that the user has satisfactorily completed a course of training in test administration and interpretation. Alternatively, she must be able to show experience in the use of tests, under the guidance of a trained and qualified psychologist. The experience should be such that the British Psychological Society and the NFER consider it equivalent to attendance at a suitable course of training.
Level Q tests are available to individuals who have a thorough knowledge of the principles underlying testing, considerable practical experience in testing plus training in the particular test.
Level R tests are available only to individuals having a very substantial background in the theory and practice of mental measurement at a postgraduate level. Users of these tests must either be Associate Members of the British Psychological Society or have undergone training and had experience with tests to an equivalent standard.
The addition of the letter (T) after a test-level letter, e.g. P(T),

shows that the test is suitable for use in schools by teachers and is available to them.

The system of grading described is found in the NFER *Catalogue of Psychological Tests and Clinical Procedures*, but not in their other annual publication, *Tests for Educational Guidance and Assessment.*

Lest it be thought that the NFER is the only source of reading tests, it should be stressed that many useful tests of reading are available from the other sources previously outlined, including commercial publishers and distributors. There are considerable differences in the systems used by commercial publishers for grading reading tests in terms of their availability to teachers. These are best considered by consulting the appropriate catalogues.

A Test Commission?

In July 1971 the International Association of Applied Psychology drew up recommendations concerning the construction, distribution and use of psychological tests. It was proposed that each country should establish a Test Commission. This body would deal with matters such as test standards, evaluation of existing tests and the development of new tests.

The British Psychological Society has a Standing Committee on Test Standards. Its terms of reference were revised in 1974 in line with the IAAP proposals. The British Psychological Society considers that the implementation of these will form a long-term programme (British Psychological Society 1974).

References

BLANTON, W., FARR, R. and TUINMAN, J. (1972) *Reading Tests for the Secondary Grades.* Newark, Delaware, International Reading Association.

British Psychological Society (1965) Principles governing the employment of psychological tests and clinical instruments. *Bulletin of the British Psychological Society, 18,* 16.

British Psychological Society (1966) *Psychological Tests : a Statement by the British Psychological Society.* London, British Psychological Society.

British Psychological Society (1969) Classification of tests and test users. *Bulletin of the British Psychological Society, 22,* 109–11.

British Psychological Society (1974) A Test Commission. *Bulletin of the British Psychological Society, 27,* 206–7.

BROWN, J. W., SITTS, M. K. and YARBOROUGH, J. (1975) *ERIC : What it can do for you/How to use it.* Stanford Centre for Research and Development in Teaching, Stanford, California.

BUROS, O. K. (Ed.) (1938) *The Nineteen Thirty-Eight Mental Measurement*

Yearbook. New Jersey, Rutgers University Press. (This was the first of the mental measurement yearbooks. It is now out of print. A reprint is available from the Johnson Reprint Corporation, 111 Fifth Avenue, New York, N.Y. 10003, USA. The same firm also supplies reprints of the 1940, or second mental measurement yearbook.)

BUROS, O. K. (Ed.) (1941) *The Nineteen-Forty Mental Measurement Yearbook.* New Jersey, Gryphon Press.

BUROS, O. K. (Ed.) (1949) *The Third Mental Measurement Yearbook.* Highland Park, N.J., Gryphon Press.

BUROS, O. K. (Ed.) (1953) *The Fourth Mental Measurement Yearbook.* Highland Park, N.J., Gryphon Press.

BUROS, O. K. (Ed.) (1959) *The Fifth Mental Measurement Yearbook.* Highland Park, N.J., Gryphon Press.

BUROS, O. K. (Ed.) (1961) *Tests in Print: A Comprehensive Bibliography of Tests for Use in Education, Psychology and Industry.* Highland Park, N.J., Gryphon Press (second edition 1974).

BUROS, O. K. (Ed.) (1965) *The Sixth Mental Measurement Yearbook.* Highland Park, N.J., Gryphon Press.

BUROS, O. K. (Ed.) (1968) *Reading Tests and Reviews.* Highland Park, N.J., Gryphon Press.

BUROS, O. K. (Ed.) (1972) *The Seventh Mental Measurement Yearbook.* Highland Park, N.J., Gryphon Press.

Department of Education and Science (1968) *Psychologists in Education Services.* London, HMSO.

Department of Education and Science (1972a) *Teacher Education and Training* (The James Report). London, HMSO.

Department of Education and Science (1972b) *Education: a Programme for Expansion.* London, HMSO.

Department of Education and Science (1975) *A Language for Life.* London, HMSO.

Department of Education and Science (1977a) *Programme of Short Courses. Teachers' Course List No. 2.* London, HMSO.

Department of Education and Science (1977b) *Programme of Long Courses. Teachers' Course List No. 1.* London, HMSO.

FARR, R. and ANASTASIOW, N. (1969) *Tests of Reading-readiness and Achievement.* Newark, Delaware, International Reading Association.

GOODACRE, E. J. (1972) *Hearing Children Read: including a list of reading schemes and other materials.* Reading, Berks, Centre for the Teaching of Reading.

HOFFMAN, M. (1976) *Reading, Writing and Relevance.* London, Hodder and Stoughton.

HOLLOWAY, R. L. (1975) The Right to Read. In LATHAM, W. (Ed.) *The Road to Effective Reading.* London, Ward Lock Educational.

JOHNSON, R. (1972) The Open University Reading Development Course. *Reading, 6,* 2, 31–4.

KAY, B. (1976) Justified Impatience: Brian Kay describes the progress made by the Assessment of Performance Unit in its first two years. *Times Educational Supplement, 3200,* 1 October.

LABON, D. (1972) *Assessment of Reading Ability.* West Sussex County Education Committee Psychological Service.

MARDER, J. V. (1976) A register of activities related to the recommendations of the Bullock Report and reported from teacher-training institutions in England and Wales; with a contribution from the New University of Ulster. University of Southampton Education Library.

MELNIK, A. and MERRITT, J. (Eds.) (1972a) *Reading: Today and Tomorrow.* London, Hodder and Stoughton.

MELNIK, A. and MERRITT, J. (Eds.) (1972b) *The Reading Curriculum.* London, Hodder and Stoughton.

Ministry of Education (1959) *Report of the Committee on Maladjusted Children.* London, HMSO.

PUMFREY, P. D. (1974) Promoting more sophisticated use of reading tests: a national survey. *Reading, 8,* 1, 5–13.

PUMFREY, P. D. (1976) *Reading: Tests and Assessment Techniques.* London, Hodder and Stoughton.

TURNER, J. (1972) *The Assessment of Reading Skills.* UKRA Bibliography No. 2. (Second edition 1976.)

WILLIAMS, A. (1976) *Reading and the Consumer: A Practical Guide.* London, Hodder and Stoughton.

ZIMET, S. G. (1976) *Print and Prejudice.* London, Hodder and Stoughton.

6. Principles of test administration

While attention has been drawn to some of the similarities and differences between norm-referenced and criterion-referenced tests of reading respectively, the importance of the conditions under which test information is collected cannot be over-emphasised (Cronbach 1970).

The following consideration of principles and practices of test administration is particularly geared to norm-referenced or standardised tests of reading and relates to both group and individual tests. The first two areas are concerned with the importance of ensuring that the subjects to be tested do justice to themselves. The third is to ensure that the reading test is carried out under the conditions stipulated in the test manual and under which the test was standardised (Vernon 1964).

Principles and practice

1. To enable the subjects to do justice to themselves, it is essential that a suitable testing situation be arranged. The following practical considerations are important: (i) see that all materials, including spare pencils, are available for all subjects; (ii) ensure that the room in which the reading test is to be administered is not subject to intermittent and/or extraneous noise; (iii) check that the lighting, heating and ventilation are suitable before starting the test; (iv) if group testing, ensure that desks or tables are appropriately spaced; and (v) if possible, ensure that there will be no disturbance during the administration of the test, either from children leaving the room or from other individuals entering it.
2. It is also important that the pupils be suitably motivated. To this end it is helpful if the tester does the following: (i) explains to the subjects the reason for giving the particular test; (ii) briefly indicates how the results can be used to help each of the children

as individuals, and (iii) presents the task as an enjoyable activity and not one to be feared.

3. If the subjects' results are to be related to the population on which the reading test was standardised, it is necessary that the test be administered strictly in accordance with the conditions prescribed in the test manual. Thus the tester should ensure that she: (i) can clearly differentiate between her role as a tester and that as a teacher; (ii) has studied the test manual carefully; (iii) has both completed and scored the test herself *before* administering it to the subjects, and is thoroughly familiar with the mechanics of administration; (iv) reads the test instructions from the manual word for word; (v) keeps strictly to the timing specified in the test manual; (vi) keeps a record of the timing of the test administration; (vii) knows the extent to which she is permitted by the manual to help subjects asking questions (the principle which is usually applied is that questions relating to the test administration such as 'Is this the place for the answer?' or 'Do I have to underline the word or put a ring around it?' can be answered. Questions concerning test content cannot. For example, if a subject asks what a word means, the tester should reply along the lines 'If you are sure that you cannot do that one by yourself, try the next one'. With very young children this can be a difficult situation for a teacher/tester who wants to be 'helpful' in a teaching sense); (viii) goes carefully with the subjects over any prescribed examples; (ix) enquires whether there are any questions *before* the test administration starts; (x) ensures that her supervisory function does not distract the subjects; and (xi) remembers never to test more children than can be adequately supervised. In general, the younger the children, the smaller the group that can be tested.

The teacher's dilemma

Teachers by definition wish to teach and to help children to learn. This is the centre of their work. Only in so far as the testing of reading contributes to making decisions that improve the child's skill acquisition or attitude enhancement will reading tests and testing be seen as valuable by the teacher.

In informal tests that are an integral part of teaching, and in comprehensive criterion-referenced tests of reading content, teaching need not necessarily invalidate the test results. In standardised tests, however, the very helpfulness which is the hallmark of the competent teacher can reduce the validity of the results obtained.

In the administration of some reading tests, the repetition of certain key words is prohibited in the instructions in the test manual. Yet it is all too easy for the teacher/tester to respond to a plaintive 'Please could you say that again?' by so doing—and thereby administering the test under very different conditions from those prescribed. Similarly, in the individual testing situation where the child is asked to read a series of sentences of increasing complexity and length starting with: 'I saw a dog chasing a cat on my way home', care must be taken that the teaching function does not influence the child's response.

Child's oral response	Response appropriate to a tester	Response appropriate to a teacher*
I was	(NONE)	Are you sure? Look at the last word again. What does it begin with?
a dog (falters)	Yes	Well done! You wrote that word under your picture yesterday.
chase	(NONE)	You've got most of it right, but what about the ending? What sound do these three letters say? (points to 'ing').
a cat	(NONE)	Yes, you built that one up correctly.
no '	(NONE)	Look again. Does what you've said make sense?
way to	(NONE)	Slow down a little. Look again. Can you see the word 'to' anywhere? What is there before 'way'?
home	Thank you. Let's look at the next sentence now.	There! I knew you could read it. Now read it again from the start and see if you can get it all right.

* It is *not* suggested that these cues are ideal. It is suggested that they are fairly typical at a certain stage of reading instruction.

The tester has to establish and maintain rapport with the child being tested in an individual testing situation. At the same time she must beware of mixing the roles of teacher and tester if she wishes to obtain reliable and valid results that can be interpreted normatively.

Administrative procedures

The consideration of the principles and practice of reading test administration given earlier has indicated the many ways in which the inexperienced or naïve tester may quite unintentionally and unknowingly affect children's test scores. At this point attention is drawn to the apparently straightforward task of marking tests, totalling, converting raw scores to standard scores and transcribing marks to a record form. There is ample evidence that these activities are a frequent source of error. Even if the test has been administered correctly, a child's results can be seriously affected by errors at this later stage. Checking of the above procedures, preferably by a different teacher, is advisable, especially if an important decision is to be made on the basis of the results.

References

CRONBACH, L. J. (1970) *Essentials of Psychological Testing* (third edition, chapter 3). New York, Harper and Row.
VERNON, P. E. (1964) *Intelligence and Attainment Tests* (chapter 3). London, Hodder and Stoughton.

Further reading

ANASTASI, A. (1975) *Psychological Testing* (fourth edition, chapter 3). London, Cassell and Collier Macmillan.
GOSLIN, D. A. (1967) *Teachers and Testing*. New York, Russell Sage Foundation.
JACKSON, S. (1974) *A Teacher's Guide to Tests and Testing* (third edition). London, Longman.

7. What do reading test scores mean?

Individual differences and measurement

Comparison is the basis of measurement. A measure of a child's reading skills only has meaning to the degree that the measure permits comparison with someone or something else. For example, 'Did John read more fluently than Peter?', 'Is Helen as able at reading irregular words as regular ones?' or 'How many words from the book's vocabulary can Mary recognise out of context?'. The first question is focused on inter-individual differences, the second on intra-individual differences and the third towards content criterion-referenced measurement. The above types of question are related. Teachers of reading can use tests to help answer them. Equally important, the information obtained can be used to provide guidance in deciding the type of educational experiences required by the child if his reading attainments are to be advanced.

Considering inter-individual differences, it is well known that individuals differ in height and that a child can be described as either 'tall', 'short' or 'of average height' for his age group. Individuals differ on a multitude of dimensions, physiological, sociological and psychological. The uniqueness of the individual is a function of the vast range of attributes on which we differ from one another. Similarly, the uniqueness of the particular pattern of the individual's reading-related attainments has to be recognised and accepted if we are to help his acquisition of various reading skills. Individual differences in intelligence and school attainments are a central focus in education, including the teaching of reading. Any given individual can be placed on a continuum indicating his position in relation to other individuals on the same continuum. The teacher requires knowledge of the ways in which individual differences in a given ability are *distributed* if she is to be able to interpret a child's score on a standardised reading test. In so far as a reading test

Table 7.1 Scores of children on two reading tests

Reading Comprehension Test A : Distribution of marks for thirteen children, mean score equals 20, score range 14 to 26, in rank order.

											*			
14	15	16	17	18	19	20	21	22	23	24	25	26		Total = 260; Mean = $\dfrac{260}{13}$ = 20

Reading Comprehension Test B : Distribution of marks for thirteen children, mean score equals 20, score range 0 to 40, in rank order.

							*							
0	1	2	7	10	15	20	25	30	33	38	39	40		Total = 260; Mean = $\dfrac{260}{13}$ = 20

adequately samples a particular skill (say, reading comprehension) the distribution of children's scores on the test will reflect the distribution within the group of children of the ability it tests. The importance of a teacher knowing the distribution of individual differences in children's scores from a given reading test cannot be over-emphasised if she is to interpret a particular child's result *in a normative sense*. If *all* that is known about a child's score on a reading test is that he has scored 25 marks, the figure is meaningless. If the average mark of the group taking the test was 20, we know that the child's score is above average, but we do *not* know by how much with any precision. We need to know the range of scores obtained by children on the test, together with the extent to which these scores cluster together. The scores of the *same* thirteen children on two tests of reading comprehension are shown in Table 7.1. The mean score for each test is 20. However, the children's scores on Reading Comprehension Test A range from 14 to 26, whereas on Test B the range is from 0 to 40. Clearly, a score of 25 on Test A, i.e. five marks above average, and a score of 25 on Test B, also five marks above average, say very different things about the relative merits of a score of 25 marks.

The relative importance of a given score depends on two related considerations. The first is the extent to which the score is above or below average. The second is the magnitude of this difference from the average (mean) in relation to the differences between the other scores on the test and the mean score. The difference in the 'spread', range and variability on each of the above tests is shown graphically in Figure 7.1 (p. 94). We will return to a further consideration of measures of variability later.

If the two reading tests had the same mean scores and dispersion of scores, then marks would be comparable. This does not apply here. In the example given, 5 points above average on Test A represents a superior performance to 5 points above average on Test B.

For the teacher wanting to understand the results of normative reading tests, some knowledge of the most important characteristics of the distribution of children's reading test scores is essential. The two most fundamental of these are (i) measures of central tendency, and (ii) measures of the dispersion or spread of test scores.

Understanding these two aspects of mental measurement will help the teacher interpret normative scores, but by themselves are clearly insufficient. The psychological aspects of the test information

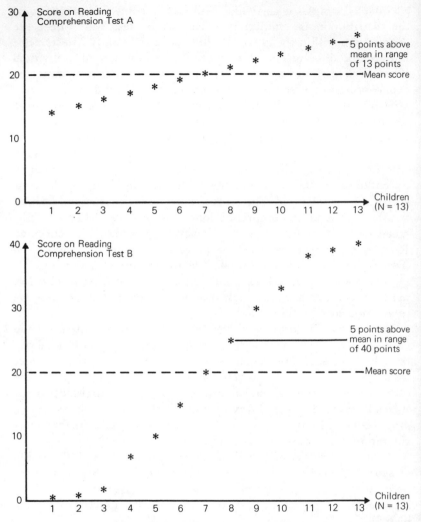

Figure 7.1   Scores of the same children on two reading tests

are equally important. Thus the *content* of the tests must also be considered.

Measures of central tendency

Any of the following three measures of central tendency may be found in reading test manuals. The first is the *mean*, or average,

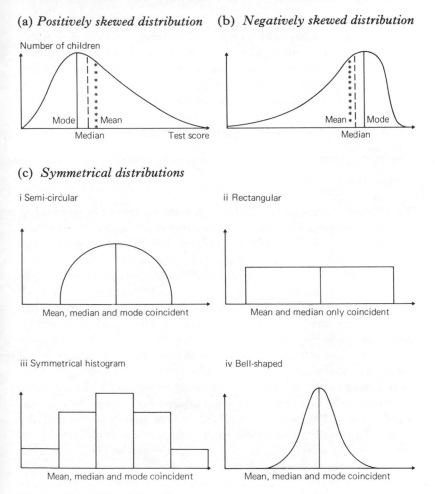

(a) *Positively skewed distribution*   (b) *Negatively skewed distribution*

(c) *Symmetrical distributions*

i Semi-circular

ii Rectangular

iii Symmetrical histogram

iv Bell-shaped

Figure 7.2   Measures of central tendency

which is obtained by adding up the scores of all children on the test and dividing by the number of children tested. The mean is the measure of central tendency which is most reliable. The second measure is called the *median*. This is a point on the scale of test marks which divides the scores of the group into two, with half of the children's scores coming above and half below the median score. The median is useful as a quickly calculated measure of central tendency. The third (rarely used) measure is called the *mode*. This is the most frequently obtained score on the test and provides a rapid, albeit extremely crude, indication of score concentration.

In the case of test score distributions (including the normal distribution) that are symmetrical, the mean, median and mode are usually coincident. Where the distribution of scores is markedly skewed, i.e. not symmetrical, these measures fall at different positions. This is shown in Figure 7.2 (p. 95).

The major value of these three measures is that they provide single descriptive indices of the whole group's performance. Thus they can be used in comparing the typical performance of a number of groups.

Measures of dispersion

There are many measures of the dispersion or spread of test scores. The two most important ones are the *range* of scores and the *standard deviation* of scores. The *range* of scores merely indicates the extremes of the scores obtained by a group on a particular test. For example, the range of children's scores on the *Schonell Graded Word Recognition Test* might be from 20 to 100. This information does not tell us whether the scores were evenly spread out over the entire range of the test or whether the scores clustered at one end or the other. Similarly, knowing that the range of reading ages obtained by a group on a test is from 10 years to 17 years gives no indication of the numbers of pupils scoring high or low. A refinement called the *interquartile range* indicates the range of scores on a test obtained by the middle 50 per cent of the children on whom the test was standardised. The semi-interquartile range specifies one half the range of scores obtained by the middle 50 per cent of children. Both the interquartile range and the semi-interquartile range are used in the manuals of some reading tests.

From the point of view of understanding the meaning of standardised reading test scores, the most important measure of test score spread is called the *standard deviation* (Amos *et al.* 1965; Gregory *et al.* 1969; Griffiths and Downes 1969; Crocker 1974; Lewis 1974; Vincent and Cresswell 1976).* The term is widely used in test manuals to describe the characteristics of the spread of test scores. The standard deviation of a particular reading test indicates the extent to which the children's scores spread themselves out around the group's mean score. Where the standard deviation is small, test scores tend to cluster closely around the mean score.

*The standard deviation of the scores of a defined population on a given test is typically indicated by the Greek letter σ (sigma). The standard deviation of a sample is usually indicated by the letters S.D. or *s*.

Where the standard deviation is large, the dispersion of children's scores is wider. In the example given in Table 7.1, page 92, Reading Comprehension Test A has a smaller range of scores and a smaller standard deviation of scores than Reading Comprehension Test B. As can be seen in Figure 7.1, page 94, in the former test the children's scores are more closely clustered around the mean than in the latter.

The standard deviation, or S.D., of a set of test scores can be calculated by finding the amount by which each individual score deviates from the mean. These deviations, both positive and negative, are then squared, summed and averaged. The square root of the figure so obtained is the S.D. of the set of scores. Thus:

$$\text{S.D.} = \sqrt{\frac{\Sigma x^2}{N}}$$

where $x =$ the deviation of a score from the mean of the set, $N =$ the number of scores, and $\Sigma x^2 =$ the sum of the squares of the x scores.

If the S.D. is considered as a unit of distance, its value in interpreting a child's score in relation to the scores of the rest of a class can readily be appreciated. The S.D. tells one *how much* the scores in a distribution are spread out around the mean. If the value of the S.D. is small, the majority of the scores are closely grouped around the mean. In contrast, a large S.D. indicates that the scores are more widely spread about the mean. In Figure 7.1, p. 94, we have two distributions with the same mean but markedly differing dispersions of scores about the mean. The S.D. for Reading Comprehension Test A is *less* than that for Reading Comprehension Test B. While a score of 25 on each is 5 above the mean, for Test A this deviation score of $+5$ will be more S.D. units above the mean than a score of 25 (also 5 points above the mean) on Test B.

Where the distribution of reading test scores forms a normal frequency distribution curve there is a known relationship between any score and the percentage of children who will achieve that score. For example, the mean score on a test in which the distribution of scores is normal will be obtained by *more* children than any other score. We will now look a little more closely at some of the characteristics of the normal frequency distribution curve.

The normal frequency distribution curve

There is strong evidence that individual differences in many human characteristics are approximately normally distributed in populations

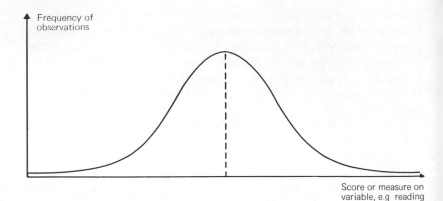

Figure 7.3   The normal frequency distribution curve

or very large groups (Linden and Linden 1968). In other words, when a distribution of scores (e.g. on a reading test) or of measures (e.g. height) is graphically presented as in Figure 7.3, it has a distinctive shape. This is frequently described as 'bell-shaped' or 'cocked-hat'. This type of frequency distribution has certain important characteristics from the point of view of understanding test scores.

As can be seen, the 'bell-shaped', 'cocked-hat' or normal frequency distribution curve is symmetrical about its mean. The two halves are mirror images. The tails of the curve never meet the baseline (in theory) as its limits stretch to infinity. Most scores or measures are concentrated near the average and decrease in frequency the further one moves away from the average, according to a known mathematical function. The belief that many of the abilities involved in reading are approximately normally distributed has led to the construction of reading tests that produce a normal distribution of scores when administered to a large representative group of children. Thus an understanding of standardised reading test scores demands an understanding of the characteristics of the normal frequency distribution curve.

In the normal curve shown in Figure 7.4, the distance from the mean to x is one standard deviation. It specifies the 'point of inflection' of the curve. This is the point at which the curve changes direction from concave downwards in the central section to concave upwards in the tails of the distribution. Because of the symmetrical nature of the curve, the distance from the mean to y is also one standard deviation (Akhurst 1970).

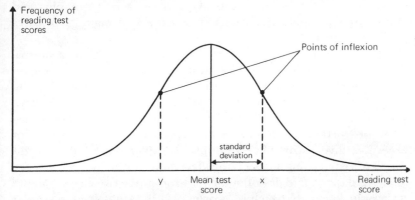

Figure 7.4 The normal frequency distribution showing the points of inflexion and the standard deviation of the distribution

If the distribution of scores on a reading test is normal and the standard deviation of the scores is known, it is possible to estimate the numbers of children who will obtain certain scores. The area under the normal curve can be divided up into the percentages of cases falling between certain limits. In Figure 7.5, the proportions falling between four standard deviations below and four above the

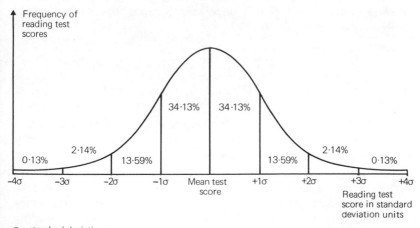

Figure 7.5 Percentage of subjects between certain limits under the normal curve

mean are shown. For all practical purposes a range of plus and minus three standard deviations covers the vast majority of cases (99·72 per cent).

Thus it can be seen that 34·13 per cent of scores in a normal distribution will fall between the mean and a score of plus 1 standard deviation; 68·26 per cent of scores will fall in the range of plus and minus 1 standard deviation from the mean. If we know the mean and standard deviation of a reading test we are in a position to say what proportion of children can be expected to fall below, or exceed, a given score. For example, consider one of the NFER's standardised reading tests giving deviation quotients with a mean of 100 and a standard deviation of 15. From these two characteristics we would know that a child scoring 115 had obtained a score 1 standard deviation above the mean. Furthermore, that $50\% + 34·13\% = 84·13\%$ of children for whom the test was designed would score 115* and *less*. Approximately $13·59\% + 2·14\% + 0·13\% = 15·86\%$ would score *more*.

The language of test scores

The scores obtained by children on reading tests can be expressed in various ways. This sometimes causes difficulties for a teacher in interpreting the meaning of the results from two tests that are not given in the same terms. The following are ways in which reading test scores are commonly expressed. An understanding of them and of their inter-relationships is necessary in order to make full use of scores expressed in different ways.

Raw scores

These refer to a direct, quantified report of a child's performance on a test of a reading skill. For example, the number of words correctly read from a list, the time in seconds taken to read a paragraph, the number of multiple-choice sentences completed correctly or the number of words read correctly in a given time.

Raw scores can easily be misinterpreted. If all we know is that a child has scored 70 on an unknown reading test, the raw score tells us nothing about the child's reading ability. Again, if a child scores 30 words correct on a teacher's *own* word recognition test of reading

---

*There is a convention of giving test scores correct to the nearest whole number. Thus in a continuous distribution a score of 115 theoretically includes scores from *above* 114·5 to *below* 115·5.

and 60 items correct on a test of comprehension, does this mean that the child has scored at a higher level on the one test than the other? The answer is 'We cannot say'. It is possible that the maximum marks obtainable on each of the two tests *might* have been 30 and 60 respectively—we just do not know. Additionally, we know nothing about the relative difficulty of the two tests. A low score on a 'hard' reading test might be considered superior to a high score on an easier test. An important question the teacher needs to ask when considering scores on reading (or any) tests is 'What is the content of the test?'.

Despite the above comments, raw scores on reading tests are not to be despised. Once their limitations for valid comparisons of the relative achievements of children on different reading tests are recognised, they can be used to measure change in children's mastery of a reading skill. If a child scores 12 on the first administration of a test and 30 on the second after a period of instruction, provided that improvement due to maturation and some practice effect is allowed for, it is likely that the change in the child's attainment is a real one attributable in part to the instruction. (From the discussion in Chapter 3, it will be appreciated that considerations of the validity and reliability of the test must also be made.)

Another valuable use of raw scores is in connection with a criterion-referenced test based on a content analysis of, for example, the total vocabulary used in a reader. A change in the raw score of the number of words recognised or understood could be a useful index of a child's progress. Indeed, this is common practice in most primary schools. Such information is not primarily normative, but is very valuable to the teacher.

Rank order

It is possible to make a quick comparison between children's reading attainments on, say, two different tests if the raw scores are put in rank orders of the group taking both tests. Table 7.2 (p. 102) gives the raw scores of a group of children who have each taken two tests of reading, one a word recognition test and the other a test of reading comprehension. These have then been converted into the rank orders for each test and the differences in ranks noted.

Whether or not it is psychologically sound to *expect* similar rank orders of performance on each of the two tests depends largely on their content and characteristics. Reference must be made to these

Table 7.2   Raw scores and ranks of fifteen children on two tests of reading

| | Tests | | | | |
	(1) Schonell Word Recognition Test Raw Score	(2) Schonell Silent Reading Test R2 Raw Score	Rank order for Test (1)	Rank order for Test (2)	Differences in rank order
Child					
A	50	20	1	2	1
B	45	22	2	1	1
C	41	14	3	5	2
D	39	16	4	4	0
E	38	18	5	3	2
F	36	9	6	9	3
G	35	10	7	8	1
H	34	13	8	6	2
I	33	11	9	7	2
J	32	8	10	10	0
K	30	6	11	11	0
L	28	0	12	14	2
M	24	1	13	13	0
N	20	3	14	12	2
O	15	0	15	15	0

Note : By looking at the test norms and converting the above raw scores it will be seen that the differences in children's *reading ages* on the above two tests are not great. However, if one set of results had been *severely* depressed for *all* children, looking at the rank orders of performance alone would not have revealed this.

before the implications of the differences in rank order for a given child can be interpreted.

A comparison of children's rankings serves to draw the teacher's attention to discrepancies between rankings for a child on different tests or on the same test given on two occasions. This then raises the question of whether the teacher should take any action. Differences in children's rank orders can only be of interest if the children in the group remain the same.

In some respects, the use of ranks is similar to a still common method of reporting children's schoolwork to their parents. It has many serious weaknesses (Vernon 1955). However, if the teacher interested in the use of reading tests for both description and diagnosis is aware of these weaknesses, rankings can be of value *to the teacher*.

Percentiles

These are a development of simple ranking in which children's scores on a reading test are manipulated so that they range from 0 to 100. A child's rank on a given test expressed as a percentile is only his rank expressed in percentage terms. Under this system, a child whose raw score was equivalent to a percentile of 15 would score better than 15 per cent of the group. Thus a very accurate reader would obtain a high percentile on a valid test of reading accuracy. The raw score equivalent to the fiftieth percentile indicates the score which divides the group into two numerically equal halves. Percentiles can be used with any group of children. They are of value in comparing results from different reading tests, provided that the tests are designed for the same population of children. The percentiles for given raw scores contained in many test manuals allow valid comparisons to be made between children's performances. If the percentiles are derived from different populations, e.g. junior and secondary school children, such direct comparison is not possible. However, on the basis of *one* group of children's raw scores on both tests, it would be possible to calculate and compare a pupil's percentile for each test.

Whilst percentiles are of some value in comparing results from different reading tests, they suffer from one major disadvantage. They cannot readily be combined and averaged in the usual way. This is because the marks in each of the distributions to be compared are rarely distributed evenly over the percentile range. The normal distribution of many reading skills results in a cluster of scores near to the test means. Thus the differences between consecutive percentiles in terms of their raw score equivalents is affected. A change in raw score of a few points near to the mean of distribution affects a child's percentile much *more* than a similar change in raw score would produce near the extremes of the raw score distribution (Lewis 1967, 1974).

In official reports and reading test manuals, percentile norms are sometimes presented in graphical form such as that shown in Figure 7.6. This type of graph shows the cumulative percentage of cases falling below each raw score on a reading test. Such curves have a characteristic shape and are called ogives. The Department of Education and Science and the NFER have used these curves to show standards of reading comprehension in various national samples of children on particular tests of reading comprehension both at the primary and secondary school levels (e.g. DES 1966;

Start and Wells 1972). The great advantages of presenting test results in percentiles is that they are very easy to calculate and relatively easy to understand.

In Figure 7.6, a child obtaining a raw score of 30 marks on the test would have a percentile of 50. Thus his attainment places him at the mid-point of the range of the group of children from whose scores the ogive was compiled. A child with a score of 44 would be at the 98th percentile. Only about two children in a hundred from the appropriate population of children would score at a higher level.

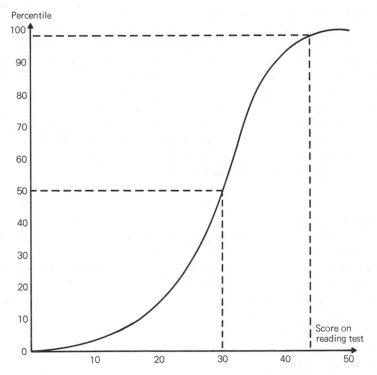

Figure 7.6   Cumulative frequency graph or ogive used to find children's percentile rank on a test from their raw scores

Where the group of children is representative of the entire range of ability, percentiles have an important relationship with the standard scores usually associated with standardised tests of reading attainment. After considering the nature of standard scores, we will return to this point (p. 107).

Standard scores

In comparing scores obtained by children on different tests that
have been standardised on the same population, it is useful to be
able to relate each child's score to the extent that it is above or below
the mean score for the test. In this way different test scores can be
expressed in comparable terms.

The basic way of expressing such scores is called a z-score and
from it all other standard scores can be calculated. A z-score ex-
presses the difference between a child's score on a test and the mean
score of the test, divided by the standard deviation of the test.

The z-score of a particular mark in a distribution of scores can
be calculated from the formula:

$$z = \frac{X - \bar{X}}{\text{S.D.}}$$

where z = the standard score, $\bar{X}$ = the mean raw score of the group
on the test, X = the child's score on the reading test, and S.D. =
the standard deviation of the distribution of X scores.

If a child obtained a score of 20 on a test with a mean of 16 and
a standard deviation of 4, his z-score would be:

$$\frac{20 - 16}{4} = +1$$

Although z-scores are useful, they seem not to appeal to teachers
perhaps because z-scores have a mean of 0 and a standard deviation
of 1. Thus a range of marks from -3 to $+3$ would cover most
children's relative attainments on any test. The z-scores would
have to be calculated to one or two decimal places if children's scores
were to be compared (see Table 7.3, p. 109). Fortunately, z-scores
can be readily converted to give *any* range of scores. The deviation
quotient with a mean of 100 and a standard deviation of 15 is
popular with reading test constructors. T-scores with a mean of 50
and a S.D. of 10 are also frequently used. The relationship of these
scales to the normal frequency distribution and to each other is
shown in Figure 7.7, p. 108.

By expressing test scores in terms of standard scores, one makes
possible the comparison of the relative strengths and weaknesses of
children from the same population on tests having very different
means and ranges of raw scores. For example, assume that we have
given a test of knowledge of letter sounds to a child and also a test of
reading accuracy, with a view to establishing whether lack of
knowledge of letter sounds might be adversely affecting the child's

reading accuracy. The information concerning these tests is as follows:

	Raw score	Mean for group	Standard deviation
Knowledge of letter sounds	18	24	6
Reading accuracy	28	40	12

Is there a marked discrepancy between the child's scores on these two tests? If we only look at the extent to which his scores are below the group mean on each test, we see that in the letter sounds test he is 6 points below and in the accuracy test he is 12 points below. Does this suggest that his accuracy score is markedly below his letter sounds test score? Until we take into account the means of each test *and* their standard deviations, we cannot say with any certainty. In the above example, after conversion to z-scores, it will be seen that *both* raw scores are in fact equivalent:

Conversion to z-scores:

Letter sounds test score

$$z = \frac{18-24}{6} = -1$$

Reading accuracy test score

$$z = \frac{28-40}{12} = -1$$

Thus the apparent difference in raw scores disappears when both tests are converted to a common scale. In every case, one would be vitally concerned with the content of the tests if the statistics are to be used effectively. The possibility of further diagnostic testing and teaching would be considered, particularly if a large discrepancy had been found.*

In converting raw scores to any type of standard score (z-score; deviation quotient; T-score, etc.), the relationships between the raw scores is preserved in the standard score distribution. If the distribution of raw scores is markedly skewed, this skew in distribution is retained in the distribution of standard scores. However, where the raw score distribution approximates to a normal distribution, the interpretation of standard scores from different tests presents little difficulty. For the majority of reading skills it is reasonable to assume that a normal distribution of individual differences exists, given that the test has been 'centred' for difficulty at about the average for the class.

Perhaps an example might help to show the equivalence of different ways of reporting a child's score on a test. Let us assume that Pat has obtained a raw score of 25 on a reading test and that we

* The reliabilities of, and intercorrelation between, the tests must also be borne in mind (see pp. 169ff).

know the mean raw score for the test is 25 and the standard deviation of raw scores is 5. It then follows that all of the scores given below are saying the same thing about her relative performance: Pat's raw score of 25 is equivalent to a standard deviation score of 0; a percentile rank of 50; a z-score of 0; a deviation quotient of 100; and a T-score of 50.

Thus in a very real sense, *provided one is aware of the different scales*,

25	=	50	=	0	=	100	=	50
(Raw score)		(Percentile rank)		(z-score)		(Deviation quotient)		(T-score)

If we take another example of a child obtaining a raw score of 60 on a test with a raw score mean of 80 and a standard deviation of 20, then: a raw score of 60 is equivalent to a standard deviation score of -1; a percentile rank of about 16; a z-score of -1; a deviation quotient of 85; and a T-score of 40. Thus:

60	=	16	=	-1	=	85	=	40
(Raw score)		(Percentile rank)		(z-score)		(Deviation quotient)		(T-score)

The relationship between percentiles and standard scores

When we considered the normal frequency distribution curve earlier, it was noted that certain proportions of scores on a reading test having such a distribution would fall between specified limits. These limits can be described in terms of the standard deviation of the test. We have also seen that a child's raw score on a test can be expressed as a percentile and as any of a variety of standard scores.

Where the distribution of scores on a reading test is normal, percentiles can readily be converted into deviation (z) scores, and vice-versa. The relationship between standard deviation scores and percentiles for a normal frequency distribution is shown in Figure 7.7 (p. 108) and Table 7.3 (p. 109).

Reading ages

Teachers often find it helpful if a child's raw score on a reading test is converted to a reading age. For example, instead of saying 'John has a raw score of 21 on the National Reading Scale', one says 'John obtained a reading age of 14 years on the given test'. Changing raw scores to reading ages means that the test constructor has to relate the raw scores to the *average scores* made by children of given ages.

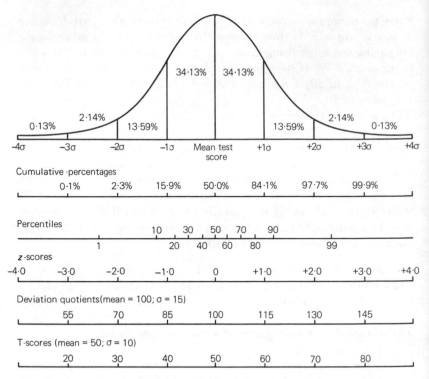

Figure 7.7   Standard scores and percentiles

If the average score on a test of reading comprehension for a nationally representative group of thirteen-year-old secondary school
children was 35, then the raw score of 35 would be considered
equivalent to a reading age of 13 years on that particular test, for
that particular age-group, at that point in time. Lest the provisos
appear pedantic, consider the national surveys of reading standards
in England and Wales carried out between 1948 and 1972. There
was a tendency for the average raw scores of eleven-year-old and
fifteen-year-old children to increase during most of this period.

In 1948 the average raw score for eleven-year-old children on the
test used was 11·6 items correct. By definition, this was equivalent
to a reading age of 11 years. The mean scores for eleven-year-old
children on the same test in other years are given below:

Year of survey	1948	1952	1956	1964	1970
Eleven-year-old mean raw score	11·6	12·4	13·3	15·0	14·2

Table 7.3 The relationship between percentiles and test scores
expressed in terms of standard deviations from the mean

Per-centile	Deviate* (or z-score)	Per-centile	Deviate (or z-score)	Per-centile	Deviate (or z-score)	Per-centile	Deviate (or z-score)	Per-centile	Deviate (or z-score)
1	−2·326	21	−0·806	41	−0·228	61	0·279	81	0·878
2	−2·054	22	−0·772	42	−0·202	62	0·306	82	0·915
3	−1·881	23	−0·739	43	−0·176	63	0·332	83	0·954
4	−1·751	24	−0·706	44	−0·151	64	0·359	84	0·995
5	−1·645	25	−0·675	45	−0·126	65	0·385	85	1·036
6	−1·555	26	−0·643	46	−0·100	66	0·413	86	1·080
7	−1·476	27	−0·613	47	−0·075	67	0·440	87	1·126
8	−1·405	28	−0·583	48	−0·050	68	0·468	88	1·175
9	−1·341	29	−0·553	49	−0·025	69	0·496	89	1·227
10	−1·282	30	−0·524	50	0·000	70	0·524	90	1·282
11	−1·227	31	−0·496	51	0·025	71	0·553	91	1·341
12	−1·175	32	−0·468	52	0·050	72	0·583	92	1·405
13	−1·126	33	−0·440	53	0·075	73	0·613	93	1·476
14	−1·080	34	−0·413	54	0·100	74	0·643	94	1·555
15	−1·036	35	−0·385	55	0·126	75	0·675	95	1·645
16	−0·995	36	−0·359	56	0·151	76	0·706	96	1·751
17	−0·954	37	−0·332	57	0·176	77	0·739	97	1·881
18	−0·915	38	−0·306	58	0·202	78	0·772	98	2·054
19	−0·878	39	−0·279	59	0·228	79	0·806	99	2·326
20	−0·842	40	−0·253	60	0·253	80	0·842		

*If a child has a score of 130 on a reading test with a mean of 100 and a
standard deviation of 15, his score as a *deviation* from the mean is +30. In
terms of standard deviation units or z-scores, this becomes +30/15 = +2.
Hence, from the above table, it is approximately equivalent to the 98th
percentile. The same result can be found from Figure 7.7.

Thus there are five raw scores equivalent to reading ages of 11
years, the validity of each dependent upon the time when the norms
were collected. The important point to remember is that such
reading ages are *not* absolute.

A further weakness stems from the teacher wanting one reading
test which will give valid reading ages for a very wide age range of
pupils. The fact that there is usually a greater range of attainments
amongst a group of older children than amongst younger ones bears
on this. For example, the average four-year-old may have little word
recognition vocabulary and the spread of scores on a test of such a
skill would be very small. By the age of seven years, the average
child will have quite a considerable word recognition vocabulary

and the spread of this skill among seven-year-olds will be much greater than in the four-year-old group. Similarly, the average eleven-year-old will have a sight vocabulary of many thousands of words, and the spread of words known in this way will be greater than at the age of seven years.

It follows that the standard deviations of children's scores on the ability 'word recognition' will differ from age group to age group with the older children showing the larger standard deviation. The situation shown below in Table 7.4 could easily exist:

Table 7.4 Variations in means, ranges and standard deviations of scores on a word reading test at different ages

Age group	Mean score on test	Range of scores	Standard deviation
7-year-old	20 equivalent to a Reading Age of 7 yrs	0 to 48	6 (Hence about 68% of the age group scores could be expected to fall between 14 and 26)
11-year-old	60 equivalent to a Reading Age of 11 yrs	0 to 108	16 (Hence about 68% of the age group scores could be expected to fall between 44 and 78)
15-year-old	100 equivalent to a Reading Age of 15 yrs	10 to 190	30 (Hence about 68% of the age group scores could be expected to fall between 70 and 130)

Yet in looking for an easy way of assessing reading attainment, teachers are possibly too ready to accept deceptively simple formulae. For example, ten words on a reading test are taken to be equivalent to one year of reading age. If such a yardstick is applied to the reading attainments of children, it is clear that proportionately *more* eleven-year-old children will be 'one year behind their chronological age in reading' than in the seven-year-old age group. Similarly, more fifteen-year-old children will be one year behind their chronological age than eleven-year-old children. No account has been taken of the differences between age groups in the spread of their scores. The difference in reading age of one year between a reading age of 4 years and one of 5 years for a five-year-old child is *not* the same as that between one of 10 years and 11 years for an eleven-year-old child. The first difference is relatively greater than the second because of the increasing spread of scores on the test of children at the older age level.

As a result of the above consideration, there is sometimes an unjustified concern with an apparent increase in the percentage of pupils who are considered backward in reading in relation to their chronological age as they grow older. In order to avoid such problems, many test agencies now construct reading tests only for restricted age ranges. The raw scores are converted into deviation quotients with a mean of 100 and a standard deviation of 15. Even if a reading test is constructed for, say, the fourteen-year-old age group it is important that the younger children in the group are not unjustifiably compared with their older peers if the teacher wishes to consider the pupils' relative attainments. Most recently constructed normative reading tests contain conversion tables. These include appropriate monthly age allowances even within the restricted range for which they are constructed (see p. 114).

A common question from teachers interested in the measurement of reading abilities is as follows: 'I can see from your conversion tables that by using a child's raw score on a reading test and knowing his chronological age it is possible to arrive at a standardised score for the child. However, I prefer to think in terms of reading age. Can these be worked out from the raw scores of the reading test?'

This type of question arises because many teachers are unfamiliar with the concepts underlying the use of standard scores. They are familiar with reading as a developmental process in which competence generally increases with age. Hence they are sympathetic towards the concept of reading ages. The question is also related to a failure to distinguish between normative and content criterion-referenced measurement. Teachers would like all their pupils to make observable and measurable progress in their reading attainments. Thus, for much of their work in the classroom, inter-individual differences in reading attainments are of less concern than the individual child's mastery of given material. Hence teachers find a simple age-related scale against which their pupils' progress can be assessed helpful in the evaluation of the reading programme. To some extent this accounts for the popularity of the two reading tests most widely used in UK schools, namely the *Schonell Graded Word Reading Test* and the *Burt (Rearranged) Word Reading Test*.

In both tests, raw scores of words correctly read are converted into reading ages based on the average scores of age groups. No account is taken of the increase in variability of scores as children mature. This does not, however, prevent teachers making valuable use of such tests.

If a teacher is concerned with inter-individual comparison of reading abilities, she would be well advised to abandon the use of reading ages. She should use some form of standard score as described earlier in this chapter, except when comparing children of the same age. This point has been discussed by a member of the NFER Guidance and Assessment Service (Vincent 1974).

If the focus of her interest is on assessing the individual child's mastery of particular skills and material, she should concentrate on content criterion-referenced measurement.

Currently, reading tests that provide conversion from raw scores to *both* normative and criterion-referenced scales are being developed. This is a recognition of the importance of both aspects of measurement to the reading teacher.

Age allowances and conversion tables

When we compare the reading abilities of a child aged 8 years 6 months with one aged 7 years 7 months we would normally expect the older child to have the more developed reading skills and to obtain a higher score on a reading test. A child aged 8 years 6 months who obtained a raw score on a reading test that was equal to the *average* score of all children aged 8 years 6 months would have a higher raw score than a child aged 7 years 7 months who obtained a reading test raw score equalling the *average* score for all children aged 7 years 7 months. Yet to say that the older child's reading test score indicated a *relatively* superior performance to that of the younger child would be unjustified.

The problem that children of different ages in the same year group will, on the same reading test, obtain different mean raw scores and standard deviations of scores, is recognised by test constructors. To facilitate comparison, most recently developed tests contain tables which convert raw reading test scores into standard scores for particular age groups. These standard scores are frequently adjusted to have a mean of 100 and a standard deviation of 15.

Table 7.5 (p. 114) presents an extract from the NFER *Reading Test AD* conversion table. Readers may well know the test better as the

Watts' Sentence Reading Test 1, a 35-item multiple-choice sentence-completion test. In the table, raw scores for any one-month age group between the ages of 7 years 6 months and 9 years 3 months are converted to standard scores. Such a conversion helps to mini-mise the chances that younger readers will be deemed relatively less competent than older readers in a year group. This is *not* to deny the existence of very real differences if the items in a test are considered as *absolute* criteria by which all children irrespective of their ages can be compared.

In the example given earlier, the average raw score for children aged 8 years 6 months on the test is 18; for children aged 7 years 7 months it is 11. Comparing a child aged 8 years 6 months with his own age group, and a child aged 7 years 7 months with his own age group, a score of 18 by the older child does not represent a superior performance than one of 11 by the younger child. In their daily work in the classroom teachers are apt not to take such considerations into account when appraising the relative reading attainments of children. Standardised tests with conversion tables such as that shown in Table 7.5 help to correct for this type of oversight. Where children are taught in year groups, the teacher's expectations of children's reading competence is frequently geared to the attain-ments of the child of average age for the class. Thus the reading attainments of older children are more favourably assessed than those of younger children in the same class. There is considerable evidence that teachers' expectations have a marked influence on subsequent pupil attainment. If this is so, it is vital that the teacher's expectations be based on valid inter-individual comparisons. The monthly age allowances built into certain standardised reading tests make possible such comparisons.

Lest it be thought that there can be only one possible age allow-ance calculated for children within a particular age range, the following qualification needs to be borne in mind. Change in raw score on a reading test might also be partly a function of the actual time during the school year when the standardisation data are ob-tained. It has been shown, for example, that a distinction can be drawn between differences in mean scores obtained at the same time by groups differing in six months of age (referred to as a 'cross-sectional difference') and the average change in score over a given period (called a 'longitudinal difference'). Goldstein and Fogelman (1974) point out that these two average differences need not be equal. Additionally, they question the assumption in the calculation of most age allowances that the change in mean raw score across

Table 7.5 Extract from NFER Reading Test AD conversion table (standardised scores)
Mean = 100; Standard Deviation = 15

Raw Scores 1-35 — Ages 7:6 to 9:3

AGE IN YEARS AND COMPLETED MONTHS AT DATE OF TEST

Raw Score	7:6	7:7	7:8	7:9	7:10	7:11	8:0	8:1	8:2	8:3	8:4	8:5	8:6	8:7	8:8	8:9	8:10	8:11	9:0	9:1	9:2	9:3	Raw Score
1	79	78	77	76	75	75	74	73	73	72	71	71	70										1
2	84	83	83	82	81	80	79	79	78	77	76	75	75	74	73	73	72	71	71	70			2
3	88	87	86	85	85	84	83	82	81	80	79	78	78	77	76	75	75	74	74	73	72	72	3
4	90	89	89	88	87	87	85	84	84	82	82	81	80	79	78	78	77	76	75	75	74	74	4
5	92	91	90	90	89	88	87	86	85	84	83	82	81	80	80	79	78	78	77	77	76	75	5
6	94	93	92	91	90	89	88	87	87	86	85	84	83	82	81	81	80	79	79	78	78	77	6
7	95	94	94	93	92	91	90	89	88	87	86	85	84	83	82	82	81	81	80	79	79	78	7
8	97	96	95	94	93	92	91	90	89	88	87	86	85	84	84	83	83	82	81	81	80	80	8
9	98	97	96	96	95	94	93	92	91	90	89	88	87	86	85	85	84	83	83	82	81	81	9
10	99	99	98	97	96	95	94	93	92	91	90	89	88	87	86	86	85	85	84	83	83	82	10
11	101	100	99	98	98	97	96	95	94	93	92	91	90	89	88	87	87	86	85	85	84	83	11
12	102	101	101	100	99	98	97	96	95	94	93	92	91	90	90	89	89	88	87	87	86	85	12
13	104	103	102	101	100	99	98	97	96	95	94	93	92	91	91	90	90	89	88	88	87	86	13
14	105	104	104	103	102	101	100	99	98	97	96	95	94	93	92	92	91	90	90	89	88	88	14
15	107	106	105	104	104	103	102	101	99	98	97	96	95	94	94	93	92	92	91	90	90	89	15
16	108	108	107	106	105	104	103	102	101	100	99	98	97	96	95	94	94	93	93	92	91	91	16
17	110	109	109	108	107	105	105	104	103	102	100	99	98	97	97	96	95	95	94	93	93	92	17
18	112	111	110	109	108	107	106	105	104	103	102	101	100	98	98	97	97	96	95	94	94	93	18
19	114	113	112	111	110	109	108	107	106	105	104	102	101	100	99	99	98	97	97	96	95	95	19
20	115	115	114	113	112	111	110	109	107	106	105	104	103	102	101	100	99	99	98	97	97	96	20
21	117	116	116	115	114	113	112	110	109	108	107	106	104	103	102	102	101	100	100	99	98	97	21
22	119	118	117	117	116	115	113	112	111	110	108	107	106	105	104	103	102	102	101	100	99	99	22
23	121	120	119	119	118	117	115	114	113	111	110	109	108	106	106	105	104	103	103	102	101	100	23
24	123	122	121	121	120	118	117	116	115	113	112	111	109	108	107	107	106	105	105	104	103	102	24
25	125	124	124	123	122	121	119	118	117	115	114	113	112	110	109	109	108	107	106	106	105	104	25
26	127	127	126	125	124	123	122	120	119	118	116	115	114	112	112	111	110	109	108	108	107	106	26
27	129	129	129	128	127	126	124	123	122	120	119	118	116	115	114	114	113	112	111	110	109	109	27
28	133	132	131	131	130	128	127	126	124	122	122	120	119	118	117	116	115	114	114	113	112	111	28
29	136	135	134	134	133	132	130	129	128	126	125	124	123	121	120	120	119	118	117	116	115	115	29
30	139	138	138	137	136	136	134	132	131	130	129	127	126	124	124	123	122	122	121	120	119	118	30
31					140	139	137	136	135	134	133	131	130	129	128	127	127	126	125	124	123	122	31
32											138	137	135	134	133	132	132	130	129	128	127	126	32
33															140	139	138	137	136	135	134	133	33
34																							34
35																							35
	7:6	7:7	7:8	7:9	7:10	7:11	8:0	8:1	8:2	8:3	8:4	8:5	8:6	8:7	8:8	8:9	8:10	8:11	9:0	9:1	9:2	9:3	

time is the same throughout the school year. In a study on samples drawn from the National Child Development Study, the two investigators looked at children's scores on a general ability test administered between April and September 1969. They found no increasing trend in score with age over this period. They conjecture that this may be a result of lower academic demands being made of pupils as the school year approaches its end. Alternatively, the skills the tests are designed to measure may develop, but the pupils' motivation to externalise this development in test performance may diminish. A further possibility is that test scores can be artificially increased during that part of a school year when various standardised tests are being used extensively in schools. As they say: 'It follows that a single age adjustment is inadequate and that standardisation procedures should, where possible, take account of the time of year of testing as well as the age of the child at that time. The age-time relationship for any given test would need to be determined by selecting standardising samples over the whole age range at different times of the year.'

It is extremely unlikely that their solution will be rapidly adopted by reading test constructors, and thus the imperfections of the current system of age allowances may continue for some time. The benefits of these imperfect age allowances to the making of valid inter-individual assessment of reading skills are still well worthwhile.

Normalised scores

In the measurement of individual differences in reading skills and other mental abilities, the normal frequency distribution curve is of use as a model. The distribution of scores on tests can be fitted to it, provided that the statistical model is congruent with the psychological phenomenon under consideration. The normal curve is assumed to be a valid approximation to the frequency distribution curve for certain mental abilities. A close approximation to the ideal curve shown earlier in Figure 7.7, page 108, is frequently obtained when large representative samples of subjects are studied, though within a small class of children the distribution of marks from a reading test may differ markedly.

Reading tests which produce frequency distributions rather different from the normal distribution, but of which there are sound reasons to expect the ability being tested to be normally distributed, can be scaled to the normal distribution. In this situation, the distribution of raw scores obtained during the construction of a reading test is *forced* to fit a normal distribution. A more usual approach is for the items comprising the test of reading to be changed so that the distribution of scores approximates normality. The normalising of distributions that are far from normal merely by the technique of area transformation is *not* to be commended in general and is rarely employed in the construction of reading tests.

However, the teacher should be aware of the distinction between standard scores and normalised standard scores obtained from tests. Where scores have been normalised, the test constructor should give a satisfactory explanation in terms of the nature of the ability being tested.

Sources of error

Irrespective of the type of reading test being used, teachers are well aware of the manner in which children's performances can fluctuate from day to day. The teacher is also aware that there are likely variations and unlikely ones. In other words, a host of influences over which the teacher may have no control can affect children's scores on reading tests to a greater or lesser extent. For example, if a child is not well, is emotionally upset, has had a late night watching TV, or is on drugs (legally or otherwise), his scores on successive reading tests might show great variations. In general, reading test results are expected to be reliable from occasion to occasion. We will now take a closer look at the way in which children's scores on reading tests can legitimately be expected to vary.

Standard error of a reading test score

Given a valid objective test of reading comprehension with a mean of 100 and a standard deviation of 15, a child might score 100 on it one day and 103 the next week on a parallel form of the test or on the same test taken again. A class of children might obtain a mean score of 100 on the first occasion of testing and 99 on the second. This type of variation in test scores would not cause the teacher undue concern as the changes in scores are not marked. However, if the changes for the individual's scores were from 100 to 125, and from a mean of 100 to one of 90 for the class, the teacher would probably wonder what had occurred to cause such a variation. One, if not both, of the scores would be suspect.

There are errors in any form of measurement, but their extent can be estimated and taken into account in the interpretation of reading test scores. According to conventional test theory, the score which a child obtains on a reading test can be considered as the combined result of his 'true' score plus an 'error' score. The former is the score that he would obtain if no influences other than his ability in reading affected his test score. The latter represents the effects of certain fortuitously occurring circumstances such as illness, anxiety, or poor motivation introducing 'error' into the child's test score. All three examples given specify circumstances likely to lower a child's obtained score on a test. Other circumstances would be likely to raise a pupil's score, for example, if his preparation had fortuitously been on identical material to that in the test. Thus 'error' may either increase or decrease an obtained score. Such errors are assumed to occur randomly.

If we had a number of parallel tests (say, about fifteen) and gave them to a pupil on a given day, the child would obtain a distribution of observed scores. The standard deviation of the distribution would be the standard error of the particular type of test for the individual. This standard error might be large for some children and smaller for others. A rather unstable extraverted child might well not apply the same effort consistently in all the tests, thus his standard error would be large. Another pupil, possibly a stable introvert, who applied consistent effort in all the tests would be likely to have a smaller standard error. In theory it is possible to calculate the standard error on a given type of reading test for every individual. In practice this is rarely done because the information is only of value in the particular instance. Typically the test constructor calculates an average standard error for persons with whom the test is to be used.

In terms of score variability, it is assumed that:

Obtained score on a test = 'True' score + 'Error'

Although one cannot directly measure a child's 'true' score on a reading test, its limits can be estimated on the basis of certain assumptions (Magnusson 1967). It is possible to calculate the standard deviation of *obtained scores* on a test for a group of children. One can also calculate the reliability of the particular test. From these two pieces of information it is possible to estimate the standard deviation of the error distribution. This in turn can be used to calculate the limits within which the obtained scores for individuals with a given 'true' score will lie. The standard deviation of the error

118   MEASURING READING ABILITIES

distribution is called the standard error of measurement. It can be calculated using the following formula:

Standard error
of measurement
of obtained score $= \delta_t\sqrt{1 - \text{Reliability coefficient of test}}$

Where δ_t = the standard deviation of the test.

In general, the more reliable the test, the lower is the standard error of children's scores on that test. In the case of the NFER *Reading Test AD* for children aged 7:6 to 11:1 years, the following standard errors are reported:

Age group	Reliability of test	Standard error
7:6– 8:1	0·94	3·6
8:2– 9:1	0·97	2·7
9:2–10:1	0·94	3·6
10:2–11:1	0·91	4·5

Assuming the standard deviation of test scores for the youngest age group to be 15 points, then the standard error $= 15\sqrt{1 - 0·94} = 3·6$. The test manual gives standardised scores that have been calculated for every month of age so as to give a mean of 100 and a standard deviation of 15. A child aged 7:7 years obtaining a raw score of 11 marks will obtain a standardised reading quotient of 100. A child aged 8:3 years would require a raw score of 16 marks to obtain the same quotient. An even older child aged 10:7 years would have to score 28 marks to obtain a similar quotient. But how much trust can we put in such quotients?

The standard error of measurement of standardised scores is used as an indication of the extent to which the *obtained* standard score on a reading test is likely to differ from the 'true' score. To do this it is assumed that errors of measurement are normally distributed. In this case by looking at Figure 7.7, p. 108, it can be argued that the chances of a child's obtained score deviating from the 'true' score by more than about plus or minus twice* the standard error of measurement of the test can be expected only once in twenty times by chance. For example, the child aged 7:7 years with a 'true' standardised score of 100 on NFER *Reading Test AD* is most unlikely to obtain scores fluctuating more than plus or minus 2 × 3·6 points in successive administrations of the reading test. Only five times in a hundred

---

*The precise range of scores covering 95% of obtained scores would be plus and minus 1·96 × the standard error of measurement.

would a swing of greater than plus or minus 7.2 points from the 'true' score occur by chance.

The reader will probably be asking 'But how do we know what the child's "true" score should have been?' The answer is that we do not know this. What is usually done is for the tester to assume that the obtained score is *an approximation of the child's 'true' score.* If, in a given instance, a child has had all the influences that affect a test score acting so as to *inflate* the child's obtained score, such an assumption can lead to misinterpretation. As some eminent workers indicate, this is a point frequently misrepresented to teachers (Guilford 1936; Cronbach 1970). It highlights the importance of a knowledge of the sources of error affecting children's reading test performances. While test theory takes account of randomly occurring errors of measurement, the definition of errors *excludes* the so-called 'constant error' analogous to using a ruler that has either been incorrectly calibrated or has been mutilated so that it always gives a result, say, one centimetre too short. Such systematic error is clearly important in considering a reading test score. In the knowledge of how these influenced a particular child's performance the teacher can decide whether the obtained result had been systematically affected and can interpret the results accordingly. The interpretation of an obtained score is still a long way from being purely mechanical! (Cronbach 1970, p. 163).

Test manuals often report only one standard error, but this is to oversimplify the situation as the above table shows. Also, to assume that the test has the same reliability and hence the same standard error for all children irrespective of score level, is highly suspect. In the case of the NFER test named above, the manual points out that errors in children's scores at the extremes of the range are 'not inconsiderable' and such extreme scores should be interpreted with caution.

The influence of test reliability on 'difference' scores between children's attainments on two tests such as a reading test and a non-verbal test of intelligence is discussed in Chapter 8, on the interpretation of reading test scores.

A wide-ranging and trenchant criticism of some of the assumptions on which conventional test theory is based has recently been published (Lumsden 1976). The author attributes what he sees as the failures of conventional test theory as '. . . partly because the problems are difficult and partly because of the obsession of test theorists with reliability theory'. Doubtless his article will stimulate the thinking of reading test constructors, among others, as well as generating considerable heat in academic circles. Many of his criticisms are justified.

We will now briefly consider some of the sources of fluctuations in children's reading test scores. These have important implications for the interpretation of test results.

A summary of factors that might affect any reading test score is given in the diagram opposite. Some of the more important ones are discussed in the text following.

Coaching and practice effects on test scores

If a child is given a reading test and then a series of tests with very similar content, the earlier tests in the series would be providing the child with practice for the later ones. If the answers are *discussed* with the child with the intention of helping him to avoid certain mistakes on future tests, the child is being *coached*. Both procedures can increase the child's score on subsequent tests.

Practice is sometimes legitimately prescribed by test authors and by LEAs arranging a large-scale testing programme. This is done in order to equalise children in terms of familiarity with the format of the standardised test and the accompanying procedures. Coaching on standardised test material is indefensible, except where specified in relation to introductory items in a test.

It must be realised that the items in a standardised test are only important because they represent many other items of similar difficulty. For example, the words used in the *Burt (Rearranged) Word Reading Test* are significant only because they have been selected from many other words of equal difficulty. The validity of a child's score on such a reading test assumes that his reading development has occurred under essentially similar conditions to the group on which the reading test was standardised. Hence, to teach a child to read the words on such a reading test *via the test* is to short-circuit the extensive learning the test aims to sample. If the only words the child can read are those on the particular test because only they have been taught, his score on the test gives absolutely no indication of his relative reading ability. This is because his experience is entirely different to that of the group from which the test's norms were derived. Standardised tests do *not* provide guides to the *content* of the school's reading programme.

To let the content and sequence of materials contained in a standardised test of reading affect the reading programme of the school would be considered by the majority of teachers to be a most

Figure 7.8 Some factors likely to affect a reading test score (adapted from Goslin 1963 with permission)

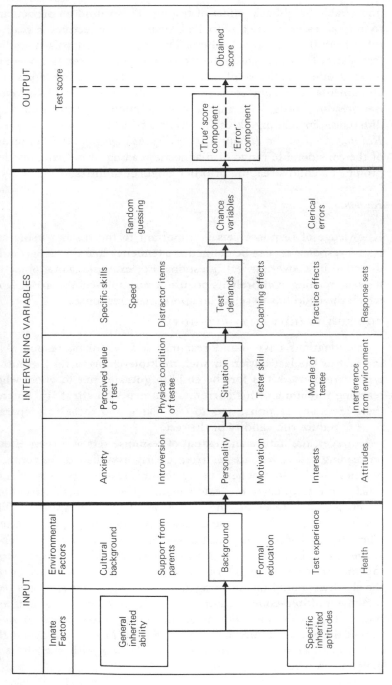

undesirable 'washback' effect of testing. This would be particularly so in those cases where a school's instructional objectives in reading differ from the majority of others. The use of a standardised reading test allows for comparison between children, classes, schools and other groups in terms of generally accepted reading goals and attainments. The same consideration applies to the use of standardised reading tests allowing a consideration of intra-individual differences in reading skills in tests such as the *Neale Analysis of Reading Ability*, the *Illinois Test of Psycholinguistic Abilities* or any of the considerable range of diagnostic reading tests that provide a profile of a child's reading or other language abilities.

Response sets

Knowledge of response sets is important to the teacher using any test. A response set can be defined as a tendency to follow a particular direction in answering test questions. For example, some objective tests of reading comprehension use a multiple-choice array from which the child has to select an appropriate response:

THE SUN IS (HUT/HIT/HAT/HOT).

Investigations have found response sets favouring responses to the first or the last option in such multiple-choice arrays. Another type of response set is for the child to guess or not to guess when reaching the limits of his current attainments on a test. In general, there are many response sets to test-taking and these *may* operate so as to reduce the validity of the test.

However, the nature and extent of response sets and their effects on reading test scores are far from clearly established. In terms of practical advice to teachers using reading tests, such sets operate much more frequently on tests containing ambiguous instructions which are also reaching the limits of the child's abilities. The 'readiness to guess' response sets will function to a greater extent when the child approaches the limits of his ability on a test. Evidence suggests that instructions concerning guessing can affect the extent to which it occurs. The instructions should indicate whether or not the children should be encouraged to guess when completing a test.

Some multiple-choice reading tests include such instructions and may also provide ways of correcting the obtained score so as to reduce the effects of guessing. The NFER *Reading Tests AD* and *BD* contain two contrasting approaches to dealing with the effect of guessing on reading test scores.

Anxiety

At a commonsense level, teachers are aware that children who are excessively anxious at taking a test of reading might not do justice to themselves. The interfering effect of their anxiety could depress test performance. At the other end of the scale a completely anxiety-free, perhaps disinterested in the situation, child might not apply himself to the task. He could consequently record a test result not representing his typical attainment level.

In general, the test user is best advised to encourage only a moderate amount of tension, sufficient to ensure that the children will be alert and ready to apply themselves to the task in hand. Children who appear highly anxious may need help in relaxing before they are ready to perform in any test situation, including reading tests.

One point is clear, and all who use reading tests should be aware of it. Standardised conditions of test administration do *not* ensure a common emotional response from the children being tested. Fortunately, in most circumstances the teacher/tester can minimise feelings of threat experienced by the children being tested (Gaudrey and Speilberger 1972).

Motivation

In contrast to measures of personality where one is concerned with the child's typical behaviour, it is sometimes argued that in attainment tests such as reading the child should be encouraged to try his hardest so that his *best* performance is obtained. As was noted earlier, it can be argued that an optimal performance might merely mean one in which the random error component fortuitously inflated a score to an unusual extent.

In practice, little is known about the differences between a typical and an optimal performance on reading tests and the implications for reading instruction. In one approach to measuring this type of difference, children have been tested under different test-instruction conditions. Clearly, instructions can be made more or less anxiety-arousing and this will differentially affect children's attainments. But for given levels of anxiety, motivation is still an important variable. Although there are ways of measuring children's motivation and attitudes at the time of taking tests, these techniques are still insufficiently developed to be of much value to the teacher concerned with the effects of motivation on reading test performance.

Perhaps the best advice that can be given to the teacher in terms of the children's motivation is that their interest in the test should be aroused, but not because of fear. Where children appear either under- or over-motivated, this should be noted at the time of administering the test, as the interpretation of the child's reading test result might require modification. Children are usually keener at working in a medium in which they feel competent (e.g. oral comprehension) rather than one in which they have experienced difficulties and failure (e.g. reading). There are some promising approaches to measuring differences in children's performance in different modes of presentation likely to have important motivational elements. The *Durrell Listening-Reading Series* and the Reading Comprehension and Listening Comprehension Tests of the *Progressive Achievement Tests* series are two examples. Children are presented with a test of reading attainment and a parallel test of equivalent difficulty and content that is presented orally and requires no reading by the child. Thus a child's reading comprehension can be compared with his listening comprehension. If the discrepancy between the two scores is considerable, the child scoring higher on the test requiring no reading, it is assumed that the child is not reading at a level commensurate with his potential reading ability. Whether or not the test requiring no reading ability is a test of reading potential is not as well established as Durrell suggests. The authors of the *Progressive Achievement Tests* take a less dogmatic line. Nevertheless, the approach is an interesting one which could usefully be developed. In the use of Informal Reading Inventories (see Chapter 8, p. 152), listening comprehension is sometimes used to assess a child's potential reading ability. Readers should be cautious of the deceptive simplicity of this formulation.

References

AMOS, J. R., BROWN, F. L. and MINK, O. G. (1965) *Statistical Concepts: A Basic Programme*. New York, Harper and Row.

CROCKER, A. C. (1974) *Statistics for the Teacher: or How to Put Figures in Their Place*. Slough, NFER.

CRONBACH, L. J. (1970) *Essentials of Psychological Testing* (third edition). New York, Harper and Row.

Department of Education and Science (1966) *Progress in Reading*. London, HMSO.

GAUDREY, E. and SPEILBERGER, C. D. (1972) *Anxiety and Educational Achievement*. New York, Wiley.

GOLDSTEIN, H. and FOGELMAN, K. (1974) Age standardisation and seasonal effects in mental testing. *British Journal of Educational Psychology*, *44*, 2, 109–15.

GOSLIN, D. A. (1963) *The Search for Ability*. New York, Russell Sage Foundation.

GREGORY, A. H., HARTLEY, J. R. and LEWIS, D. G. (1969) *Basic Statistics*. London, Methuen's Clearway Programmed Books.

GRIFFITHS, S. R. and DOWNES, L. W. (1969) *Educational Statistics for Beginners*. London, Methuen.

GUILFORD, J. P. (1936) *Psychometric Methods*. New York, McGraw-Hill.

LEWIS, D. G. (1967) *Statistical Methods in Education*. London, Hodder and Stoughton.

LEWIS, D. G. (1974) *Assessment in Education*. London, Hodder and Stoughton.

LINDEN, K. W. and LINDEN, J. D. (1968) *Modern Mental Measurement : A Historical Perspective*. Guidance Monograph Series, Boston, Houghton Mifflin.

LUMSDEN, J. (1976) Test Theory. In ROSENZWEIG, M. R. and PORTER, L. W. (Eds.) *Annual Review of Psychology*, vol. 27. Palo Alto, Annual Reviews Inc.

MAGNUSSON, D. (1967) *Test Theory*. London, Addison-Wesley.

START, K. B. and WELLS, B. K. (1972) *The Trend of Reading Standards*. Slough, NFER.

VERNON, P. E. (1955) *The Measurement of Abilities*. London, Hodder and Stoughton.

VINCENT, D. (1974) Reading ages and NFER reading tests. *Educational Research*, *16*, 3, 176–80.

VINCENT, D. and CRESSWELL, M. (1976) *Reading Tests in the Classroom*. Slough, NFER.

Further reading

AHMAN, J. S. and GLOCK, M. D. (1975) *Measuring and Evaluating Educational Achievement* (second edition). Boston, Allyn and Bacon.

AKHURST, B. A. (1970) *Assessing Intellectual Ability*. London, Hodder and Stoughton (Teach Yourself Books).

BROWN, F. G. (1970) Study Guide to Accompany *Principles of Educational and Psychological Testing*. New York, Holt, Rinehart and Winston.

BROWN, F. G. (1976) *Principles of Educational and Psychological Testing* (second edition). New York, Holt, Rinehart and Winston.

BROWN, F. G. (1971) *Measurement and Evaluation*. New York, Peacock.

GELLMAN, E. K. (1973) *Descriptive Statistics for Teachers*. London, Harper and Row.

GREEN, J. A. (1970) *Introduction to Measurement and Evaluation*. New York, Dodd, Mead.

HORROCKS, J. E. and SCHOONOVER, T. I. (1968) *Measurement for Teachers*. Columbus, Merrill.

LIEN, A. J. (1971) *Measurement and Evaluation of Learning* (second edition). Dubuque, Brown.

LYMAN, H. B. (1963) *Test Scores and What They Mean*. Englewood Cliffs, N.J., Prentice-Hall.

MCLAUGHLIN, K. F. (1965) *Interpretation of Test Results.* Washington, US Government Printing Office.

MILLER, D. M. (1972) *Interpreting Test Scores.* New York, Wiley.

SAVAGE, R. D. (1968) *Psychometric Assessment of the Individual Child.* Harmondsworth, Penguin.

SAX, G. (1975) *Principles of Educational Measurement and Evaluation.* Belmont, California, Wadsworth.

SCHOFIELD, H. (1972) *Assessment and Testing: An Introduction.* London, Allen and Unwin.

8. Interpreting reading test scores

Some important dimensions

It was stated in Chapter 4 that there are at least three important aspects of any reading test that concern the teacher. Firstly, which of the *goals* of the reading instruction programme does it purport to assess? Secondly, from which *source* does the information come? And finally, what is the emphasis of the *interpretation* to be? This third aspect is concerned with the purpose for which the test information has been collected. Each of the preceding three dimensions can be subdivided as follows:

(A) The goals of the reading instruction programme can be conceived in terms of reading skills (attainments) and attitudes towards the activity. Thus information concerning both the cognitive and affective aspects of Bloom's Taxonomy of Educational Objectives is included in the model.

(B) The three major sources of information can be described as: (i) informal tests of reading, (ii) standardised tests of reading, and (iii) criterion-referenced tests of reading.

(C) The emphasis given to the interpretation of the data obtained from these sources will depend on the purpose for which a given source of information concerning a particular goal of reading instruction is to be used. Adapting and modifying Goldman's (1971) model, there are three important levels of reading test interpretation: (i) descriptive; (ii) diagnostic, (*a*) historic and (*b*) predictive; and (iii) evaluative.

These three major aspects of reading tests can be represented visually as the three axes of a box, although it must be borne in mind that the spatial relationships between the axes do not show adequately the psychological relationships between the variables.

A moment's consideration of Figure 8.1 brings out some of the limitations of the classification. The teacher of reading is frequently involved in situations where both attainments in and attitudes towards reading are being considered simultaneously in relation to information from different sources. At the same time, interpretation of the information is also being carried out. However, at any given point in time, consideration of a specific goal of the reading programme in terms of information from one particular source looked at from a particular interpretative standpoint will frequently occur.

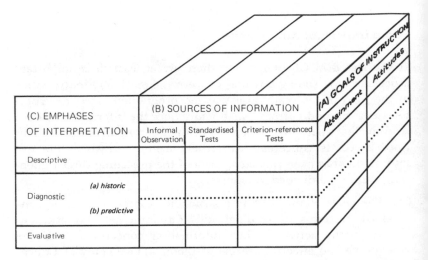

Figure 8.1 Model for the classification of reading tests in relation to goals of reading instruction, sources of information and emphases of interpretation

For example, a teacher might ask herself the question 'How do the reading standards of my class compare with national norms?' This concerns the goal of *attainment*. The source of information is probably a *standardised test* and the initial emphasis of interpretation *descriptive*.

The model provides a relatively simple and yet practical conceptualisation of the classification of reading tests in relation to the interpretation of reading test data.

Each of the major dimensions is considered in some detail below, followed by examples of the testing procedures involved in cross-classification of the three dimensions. The model has been used in the classification of reading tests by the writer (Pumfrey 1976).

(A) *Goals of reading instruction*

Bloom's classification of educational goals is described in two volumes entitled *Taxonomy of Educational Objectives* (Bloom *et al.* 1956; Krathwohl *et al.* 1964). The first of these deals with the cognitive domain, which includes such skills as reading. The second analyses the affective domain, which includes children's attitudes towards reading. Each domain is initially divided into categories. According to Bloom, these categories can be considered as successive stages in the development of a person's understanding and competence in an area of knowledge (in the cognitive domain) and in the growth of emotional involvement in a given area (affective domain). The categories are as follows:

Cognitive domain	*Affective domain*
1. Knowledge	1. Receiving
2. Comprehension	2. Responding
3. Application	3. Valuing
4. Analysis	4. Organisation
5. Synthesis	5. Characterisation by a value or a value
6. Evaluation	complex

The categories are roughly parallel in the two domains and are of increasing complexity. From the point of view of educational measurement, these categories have the considerable advantage that they can provide one basis for an absolute or criterion-referenced scale. This requires that the categories are translated into operationally defined objectives appropriate to a reading programme (Vargas 1972). Any adequate reading programme will contain objectives from both domains, but the *emphasis* allocated to each level will vary.

The objectives of *any* reading programme can usefully be considered at three levels: (i) Global, (ii) General, and (iii) Specific.

At the first level these might include the following examples from the cognitive and affective domains respectively:

'To enable every child to become a competent reader.'
'To enable every child to obtain pleasure from reading.'

At the second level the main thoughts included in the global objective are spelled out. For the first of the above, these could include the following:

(*a*) 'Knows the relationships between speech and printed language.'
(*b*) 'Develops the skill of translating text into speech.'
(*c*) 'Understands the meaning of what he reads', etc.

To move from global objectives about which there is agreement to general goals requires considerable thought on the part of those responsible for the reading programme. Even then the general goals have still to be translated into operationally defined, specific objectives. These must be such that they can be *observed*, *taught* and *measured*. The process is helped if the specific objectives of the reading programme satisfy the following six criteria:

1. The objective should be defined in terms of the pupil;
2. The objective should be observable and measurable;
3. The objective should be stated unambiguously so that it means the same to different teachers;
4. The objective should contain only one goal;
5. The objective should contain a specific action word such as 'names', 'tells', 'writes', 'explains', etc.; and
6. The objective should allow for individual differences in ability.

Thus, at the third level, each general objective is analysed into specific observable behaviours. Collectively, these could be expected to produce development towards the general and global objectives.

Hence, by analysing our *first* general objective of 'knows the relationships between speech and printed language' we could obtain for example the following (*knowledge* of specifics): (i) the child can *name* flash-cards correctly; (ii) the child can *match* pictures to printed words; and (iii) the child can *name* pictures of common objects, etc.

The operational definition of the objectives of a reading programme requires that a specific *content* be considered. In terms of the above three specific objectives, 'which words should be known?', 'which pictures and printed words matched?' and 'which pictures of common objects named?'. Such decisions are teaching ones made by the teacher.

If the instructional goals of a reading programme have been specified, the selection of appropriate reading tests is greatly simplified.

Reading is a complex developmental skill. It can be analysed in such terms and the component skills arranged in ascending order of complexity. It will be found that each skill can be categorised according to Bloom's taxonomy. Conversely, the taxonomy is a useful tool in the analysis of the components of competence in reading, in terms of both attainments and attitudes.

In order to help practising teachers solve the problems of evaluation facing them in their work, Bloom and his co-workers have produced a valuable handbook, which is in two sections. The first is concerned with educational objectives, various types of testing, teaching material and instructional processes. The second part is a translation of the points discussed earlier into examples from twelve subject fields, including sections by Cazden on the evaluation of early language development and by Moore and Kennedy on the evaluation of learning in the language arts (Bloom *et al.* 1971).

Of considerable interest to the teacher of reading interested in the specification of objectives as an integral part of the effective use of reading tests is the taxonomy of the cognitive and affective aspects of reading comprehension developed by T. C. Barrett. This particular taxonomy has received considerable attention in Britain as it is included in an article by Clymer in one of the books prepared for the Open University post-experience course 'Reading Development' (Melnik and Merritt 1972). It is presented here so that the reader can, if she so wishes, adapt the scheme to her own teaching situation.

THE BARRETT TAXONOMY
Cognitive and affective dimensions of reading comprehension

1.0 *Literal Comprehension.* Literal comprehension focuses on ideas and information which are *explicitly* stated in the selection. Purposes for reading and teacher's questions designed to elicit responses at this level may range from simple to complex. A simple task in literal comprehension may be the recognition or recall of a single fact or incident. A more complex task might be the recognition or recall of a series of facts or the sequencing of incidents in a reading selection. Purposes and questions at this level may have the following characteristics.

1.1 *Recognition* requires the student to locate or identify ideas or information *explicitly* stated in the reading selection itself or in exercises which use the explicit ideas and information presented in the reading selection. Recognition tasks are:
   a. *Recognition of details.* The student is required to locate or identify facts such as the names of characters, the time of the story, or the place of the story.
   b. *Recognition of main ideas.* The student is asked to locate or identify an explicit statement in or from a selection which is a main idea of a paragraph or a larger portion of the selection.
   c. *Recognition of a sequence.* The student is required to locate or identify the order of incidents or actions explicitly stated in the selection.
   d. *Recognition of comparison.* The student is requested to locate or identify likenesses and differences in characters, times, and places that are explicitly stated in the selection.

  e. Recognition of cause and effect relationships. The student in this instance
  may be required to locate or identify the explicitly stated reasons for
  certain happenings or actions in the selection.
  f. Recognition of character traits. The student is required to identify or
  locate explicit statements about a character which helps to point up the
  type of person he is.

1.2 *Recall* requires the student to produce from memory ideas and information *explicitly* stated in the reading selection. Recall tasks are:
  a. Recall of details. The student is asked to produce from memory facts
  such as the name of characters, the time of the story, or the place of the
  story.
  b. Recall of main ideas. The student is required to state a main idea of a
  paragraph or a larger portion of the selection from memory, when the
  main idea is explicitly stated in the selection.
  c. Recall of a sequence. The student is asked to provide from memory the
  order of incidents or actions explicitly stated in the selection.
  d. Recall of comparison. The student is required to call up from memory
  the likenesses and differences in characters, times and places that are
  explicitly stated in the selection.
  e. Recall of cause and effect relationships. The student is requested to
  produce from memory explicitly stated reasons for certain happenings
  or actions in the selection.
  f. Recall of character traits. The student is asked to call up from memory
  explicit statements about characters which illustrate the type of persons
  they are.

2.0 *Reorganisation.* Reorganisation requires the student to analyse, synthesise,
and/or organise ideas or information explicitly stated in the selection. To
produce the desired thought product, the reader may utilise the statements
of the author verbatim or he may paraphrase or translate the author's statements. Reorganisation tasks are:

2.1 *Classifying.* In this instance the student is required to place people, things,
places and/or events into categories.
2.2 *Outlining.* The student is requested to organise the selection into outline
  form using direct statements or paraphrased statements from the selection.
2.3 *Summarising.* The student is asked to condense the selection using direct
  or paraphrased statements from the selection.
2.4 *Synthesising.* In this instance, the student is requested to consolidate
  explicit ideas or information from more than one source.

3.0 *Inferential comprehension.* Inferential comprehension is demonstrated by
the student when he uses the ideas and information explicitly stated in the
selection, his intuition, and his personal experience as a basis for conjectures
and hypotheses. Inferences drawn by the student may be either convergent or
divergent in nature and the student may or may not be asked to verbalise
the rationale underlying his inferences. In general, then, inferential comprehension is stimulated by purposes for reading and teacher's questions which
demand thinking and imagination that go beyond the printed page.

3.1 *Inferring supporting details.* In this instance, the student is asked to conjecture about additional facts the author might have included in the selection which would have made it more informative, interesting, or appealing.

3.2 *Inferring main ideas.* The student is required to provide the main idea, general significance, theme, or moral which is not explicitly stated in the selection.

3.3 *Inferring sequence.* The student, in this case, may be requested to conjecture as to what action or incident might have taken place between two explicitly stated actions or incidents, or he may be asked to hypothesise about what would happen next if the selection had not ended as it did but had been extended.

3.4 *Inferring comparisons.* The student is required to infer likenesses and differences in characters, times, or places. Such inferential comparisons revolve around ideas such as: 'here and there', 'then and now', 'he and he', 'he and she', and 'she and she'.

3.5 *Inferring cause and effect relationships.* The student is required to hypothesise about the motivations of characters and their interactions with time and place. He may also be required to conjecture as to what caused the author to include certain ideas, words, characterisations, and actions in his writing.

3.6 *Inferring character traits.* In this case, the student is asked to hypothesise about the nature of characters on the basis of explicit clues presented in the selection.

3.7 *Predicting outcomes.* The student is requested to read an initial portion of the selections and on the basis of this reading he is required to conjecture about the outcome of the selection.

3.8 *Interpreting figurative language.* The student, in this instance, is asked to infer literal meanings from the author's figurative use of language.

4.0 *Evaluation.* Purposes for reading and teacher's questions, in this instance, require responses by the student which indicate that he has made an evaluative judgment by comparing ideas presented in the selection with external criteria provided by the teacher, other authorities, or other written sources, or with internal criteria provided by the reader's experience, knowledge or values. In essence evaluation deals with judgment and focuses on qualities of accuracy, acceptability, desirability, worth, or probability of occurrence. Evaluative thinking may be demonstrated by asking the student to make the following judgments:

4.1 *Judgments of reality or fantasy.* Could this really happen? Such a question calls for a judgment by the reader based on his experience.

4.2 *Judgments of fact or opinion.* Does the author provide adequate support for his conclusions. Is the author attempting to sway your thinking? Questions of this type require the student to analyse and evaluate the writing on the basis of the knowledge he has on the subject as well as to analyse and evaluate the intent of the author.

4.3 *Judgments of adequacy and validity.* Is the information presented here in keeping with what you have read on the subject in other sources? Questions of this nature call for the reader to compare written sources of information, with an eye toward agreement and disagreement or completeness and incompleteness.

4.4 *Judgments of appropriateness.* What part of the story best describes the main character? Such a question requires the reader to make a judgment about the relative adequacy of different parts of the selection to answer the question.

4.5 *Judgments of worth, desirability and acceptability.* Was the character right or wrong in what he did? Was his behaviour good or bad? Questions of this nature call for judgments based on the reader's moral code or his value system.

5.0 *Appreciation.* Appreciation involves all the previously cited cognitive dimensions of reading, for it deals with the psychological and aesthetic impact of the selection on the reader. Appreciation calls for the student to be emotionally and aesthetically sensitive to the work and to have a reaction to the worth of its psychological and artistic elements. Appreciation includes both the knowledge of and the emotional response to literary techniques, forms, styles and structures.

5.1 *Emotional response to the content.* The student is required to verbalise his feelings about the selection in terms of interest, excitement, boredom, fear, hate, amusement, etc. It is concerned with the emotional impact of the total work on the reader.

5.2 *Identification with characters or incidents.* Teachers' questions of this nature will elicit responses from the reader which demonstrate his sensitivity to, sympathy for, and empathy with characters and happenings portrayed by the author.

5.3 *Reactions to the author's use of language.* In this instance the student is required to respond to the author's craftsmanship in terms of the semantic dimensions of the selection, namely, connotations and denotations of words.

5.4 *Imagery.* In this instance, the reader is required to verbalise his feelings with regard to the author's artistic ability to paint word pictures which cause the reader to visualise, smell, taste, hear, or feel.

Under the aegis of the Australian Council for Educational Research, an extensive and detailed examination of the hierarchical structure of comprehension skills has been published in two volumes (Clark 1974). It can usefully be read in relation to the Barrett Taxonomy, which is an adaptation of the Bloom taxonomies outlined earlier in this chapter.

(B) *Sources of information*

Informal tests of reading. The importance of the informal test of reading given by the teacher as an integral part of the teaching of reading must never be overlooked. Its importance is, for example, one of the many reasons why the teacher of young children in the early stages of reading acquisition should hear her pupils read *individually* and *regularly* as *one* part of a reading programme. The information that the teacher receives instantaneously in such a situation helps her to identify both those children who are having reading difficulties and the type of difficulty. This knowledge makes it possible for the teacher to arrange experiences that are likely to reduce the child's reading difficulties; for example, by the use of appropriate material from the *Programmed Reading Kit* (Stott 1971). Such information can also help prevent the child developing an unnecessary aversion to the sight of material with which he cannot cope. With this informal approach to the testing of reading should go a systematic, albeit simple, method of recording what has been done with the child and what action, if any, has been taken by the teacher. Such a record allows the efficacy of intervention based on informal diagnosis and treatment to be evaluated and not merely forgotten in the host of activities the teacher undertakes daily (Rance 1971; Goodacre 1972).

Within this category of the 'informal' testing of reading, is included the use of teacher-made tests. Frequently these are devised to see whether a particular skill that has been taught has been mastered. Such tests are related to criterion-referenced tests (see below, p. 138). There is currently a move to help the class-teacher devise rather more adequate tests of particular skills than has hitherto been the case. The Educational Testing Service, Princeton, New Jersey, publish two small pamphlets called *Making the Classroom Test : a Guide for Teachers* and *Short-cut Statistics for Teacher-made Tests*. These can readily be related to the testing of reading, but they have a normative emphasis. Further details of these and other helpful publications are given at the end of this chapter.

The careful observation of children's reading behaviours can be an important source of information for the teacher. Systematic, planned, regular observation and recording of the observations can enable the teacher to assess children's reading standards, difficulties and progress. Indeed, one of the strengths of both standardised and criterion-referenced tests of reading is that they help the teacher to organise her observations in an efficient manner.

There have been a number of moves to improve the informal testing of reading. The development of Informal Reading Inventories is one of the most promising. The technique, which is briefly described later (p. 152), helps systematise the teacher's observation of children's reading behaviour with any material. This approach can help bridge the gap between the testing of reading and the type of teaching likely to help a child develop his reading competencies.

Standardised tests of reading.   From the summary given earlier of
the construction of a standardised test of reading, it will be recalled
that children are compared with one another on such a test. From
such instruments reliable measures of individual differences between
children in various aspects of reading attainment can be obtained.
This is a consideration of *inter-individual* or between-individual
differences in a skill. For example, the question 'Can Johnny read
faster than Peter?' could be answered with a known degree of
accuracy. Children can be compared both in relation to their immediate peers and also to other appropriate groups, for example, the
scores of a national sample of children. In a national survey of
reading attainment, it would be theoretically possible to compare
the scores of children of the same ages from different parts of the
country, from different socio-economic backgrounds or from any
of a variety of other sub-groups on whom normative information
had been obtained. If a teacher wishes to know whether her class of
children is reading as well as the generality of children of the same
age, a standardised reading test on a national sample of children
would enable her to make a valid judgment. Clearly, such a test
also informs the teacher how the children in her class perform on the
particular skill in relation to one another. Relative achievement is
central.

A refinement of this approach leads to the standardised diagnostic
reading test. This type of test can give a *number* of scores for *one*
child on the basis of a number of sub-tests. These different scores
can be presented in the form of a profile. For example, the *Neale
Analysis of Reading Ability* (Neale 1958) gives scores for speed of
reading, accuracy and comprehension as well as a record of the type
of reading error made by the child. Thus one begins to see a picture
of the relative strengths and weaknesses of the child in various
reading skills. Here we are looking at *intra-individual* differences.
Again, because the test is standardised, comparisons with other
children and groups can be made. There is a wide range of diagnostic
reading tests giving profiles of the child's abilities. Their central
tenet is that, having identified the child's strengths and weaknesses
in specified reading skills, it should be possible to devise an individual programme of remedial reading activities that will help the
child's reading development.

The profile on page 139 is taken from the *Illinois Test of Psycholinguistic Abilities* (ITPA) previously referred to in Chapter 3. It

shows one way in which an individual child's psycholinguistic abilities underlying reading may be analysed. At present, the effectiveness of specific remedial reading programmes based on profile analyses of this type is not clear cut. The use of such tests in conjunction with research into teaching methods and the more basic research into the nature of the reading process appears one potentially fruitful line of enquiry. Kirk has produced some useful guides to the remediation of psycholinguistic weaknesses identified using the ITPA (Kirk and Kirk 1971). An example of the pre- and post-remediation profile and scores from the record sheet of an eight-year-old boy is shown on pages 139–41. The following table briefly describes the twelve ITPA sub-tests. (See also Pumfrey 1974.)

Table 8.1 The sub-tests of the ITPA

Abilities tested at the representational level:

Name of Sub-Test

Auditory reception: This tests the child's ability to understand verbally presented material. The examiner asks a series of up to fifty short questions to which the answers are either 'Yes' or 'No'. This response can be shown either verbally or non-verbally by the child nodding or shaking his head.

Visual reception: The child's ability to understand visual symbols is tested. The examiner shows the child a picture for three seconds. The picture is replaced by one with four articles portrayed on it. The child has to select one of the four most like the picture previously seen alone. There are a maximum of forty pictures in the series.

Auditory-vocal association: This forty-two item sub-test examines the child's ability to relate concepts presented orally. For example, the child must complete an analogy such as 'A dog has hair, a fish has . . .' The channel through which the child receives information is auditory and that through which his response is expressed is vocal.

Visual-motor association: The channel through which the stimulus is received is vision and the child's response is expressed manually by pointing. The child is presented with a series of twenty cards each containing a stimulus picture with four optional pictures surrounding it. The child has to indicate which of the options goes with the central picture. There are also twenty-two visual analogies, comparable to the auditory ones, for older children.

Verbal expression: This tests the child's ability to use speech to transmit an idea. He is shown pictures of four common objects and asked to tell the tester about them.

Manual expression: Children are able to express their ideas in gestures. In this test fifteen pictures of common objects are shown to the child who has to *demonstrate* what is done with the objects.

Abilities tested at the automatic level:

Name of Sub-Test

Grammatic closure: This thirty-three item task examines the child's ability to respond automatically to commonly used standard speech. The items are presented orally accompanied by pictures. The examiner points to a picture as he makes a statement such as 'Here is a dog. Here are two . . .' which the child has to complete.

Auditory closure: The thirty item supplementary test Auditory closure is related to Grammatic closure. It tests the child's ability to fill in parts of a word that have been deliberately omitted by the tester, and to produce a complete word.

Sound blending: Sound blending is a thirty-two item supplementary test in which the child is given the sounds of a word by the tester and asked to say what the word is.

Visual closure: This tests the child's ability to identify a common object from a partial presentation of it. There are four pictures each with fourteen to fifteen examples of the object hidden within it. The child has to find as many of these as he can in a given time.

Auditory sequential memory: The focus of this sub-test is the child's ability to repeat from memory a series of between two and eight digits presented by the tester.

Visual sequential memory: This test is analogous to the previous one except that the child is presented with a series of between two and eight patterns. These he has to recall from memory by putting correspondingly patterned cards in the same order.

Criterion-referenced tests of reading. The previously mentioned normative approach has many uses, but there is another important type of reading test available. Some tests of reading are based on the premise that *all* children must master certain lower-order reading skills if they are to cope adequately with reading skills at the next level of complexity (Block 1971). Thus, the aspects of a child's reading attainment deemed significant for the teacher is not so much a normative consideration as an examination of the level of reading skill that the child has attained in relation to what it is deemed reasonable and necessary that he achieve (e.g. Jackson 1971).

Although norm-referenced tests constructed in the traditional manner can be used to measure the comparability of children's reading attainments, it is true to say that not all teaching decisions important to the child's reading progress can be based on normative information. What is required is some way of comparing the individual child's attainment with the criterion of mastery of the reading skills that the teacher has specified as her instructional objectives. This is a central characteristic of content criterion-referenced

pre- and post-remediation scores of an eight-year-old
poor reader (short-term effects)

Pre-remediation profile X————————X   Post-remediation profile O————————O (Each ITPA sub-test has a mean scaled score
of 36 and a standard deviation of 6 for the standardisation sample)

PROFILE OF ABILITIES ‡ John Smith

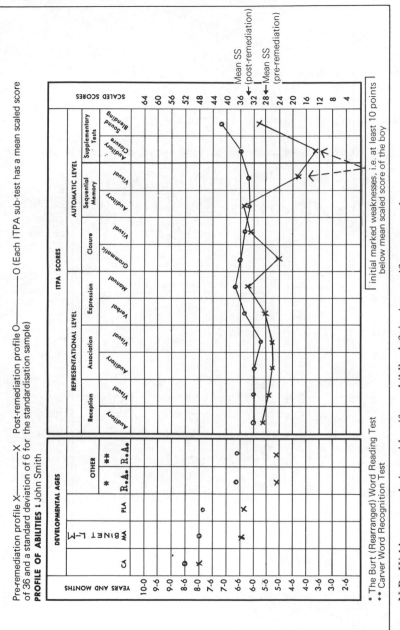

* The Burt (Rearranged) Word Reading Test
** Carver Word Recognition Test

N.B. Kirk's approach is to identify a child's deficits in specific areas and
attempt to rectify the weakness by remedial treatment.

Figure 8.2b *Illinois Test of Psycholinguistic Abilities*—Summary Sheet: pre-remediation scores

SUBTEST	REPRESENTATIONAL LEVEL						AUTOMATIC LEVEL					
	AUDITORY-VOCAL			VISUAL-MOTOR			AUDITORY-VOCAL			VISUAL-MOTOR		
	Raw Score	Age Score	Scaled Score	Raw Score	Age Score	Scaled Score	Raw Score	Age Score	Scaled Score	Raw Score	Age Score	Scaled Score
AUDITORY RECEPTION	26	6-3	29									
VISUAL RECEPTION				19	6-2	27						
VISUAL MEMORY										10	4-4	18
AUDITORY ASSOCIATION	22	7-3	26									
AUDITORY MEMORY							27	7-7	35			
VISUAL ASSOCIATION				19	5-9	26						
VISUAL CLOSURE										25	7-6	33
VERBAL EXPRESSION	20	5-10	28									
GRAMMATIC CLOSURE							17	6-0	24			
MANUAL EXPRESSION				25	7-6	34						
(Supplementary tests) AUDITORY CLOSURE							10	4-4	14			
SOUND BLENDING							14	6-8	30			

SUMMARY SCORES:	Sum of Raw Scores	Composite PLA	Sum of SS	Mean SS	Median SS
	210	6-5	280	28.0	27.5

(First ten tests)

Figure 8.2c Illinois Test of Psycholinguistic Abilities—Summary Sheet: post-remediation scores

SUBTEST	REPRESENTATIONAL LEVEL — AUDITORY-VOCAL			REPRESENTATIONAL LEVEL — VISUAL-MOTOR			AUTOMATIC LEVEL — AUDITORY-VOCAL			AUTOMATIC LEVEL — VISUAL-MOTOR		
	Raw Score	Age Score	Scaled Score	Raw Score	Age Score	Scaled Score	Raw Score	Age Score	Scaled Score	Raw Score	Age Score	Scaled Score
AUDITORY RECEPTION	32	7-6	32									
VISUAL RECEPTION				24	7-4	32						
VISUAL MEMORY										20	7-3	34
AUDITORY ASSOCIATION	27	7-8	32									
AUDITORY MEMORY							25	6-10	33			
VISUAL ASSOCIATION				22	6-6	30						
VISUAL CLOSURE										27	8-0	35
VERBAL EXPRESSION	32	8-1	35									
GRAMMATIC CLOSURE							26	8-6	36			
MANUAL EXPRESSION				29	9-2	38						
(Supplementary tests) AUDITORY CLOSURE							22	7-11	36			
SOUND BLENDING							26	8-7	42			

SUMMARY SCORES:	Sum of Raw Scores	Composite PLA	Sum of SS	Mean SS	Median SS
	264	7-9	337	33.7	33.5

measurement of reading attainment. Thus, for example, if it were considered that *all* children needed, and could be expected to be able, to recognise by sight the twelve irregular words in English that comprise about 25 per cent of typical prose, the criterion is the ability to recognise *all twelve* words (McNally and Murray 1962). This shows in an absolute sense how well the child is performing and whether or not he requires additional learning opportunities.

In discussing the similarities and differences between norm-referenced and criterion-referenced tests, Cronbach (1970) has drawn the following distinction: 'A test is said to be *criterion-referenced* when provision is made for translating the test score into a statement about the behaviour to be expected of a person with that score. A test is norm-referenced when the translated score tells where the person stands in some population of persons who have taken the test. The same test can be used in both ways. The former tells what the person is able to do, the latter tells how he compares with others. The former is useful in judging him as an isolated individual, the latter in judging his ability to compete.'

A content criterion-referenced reading test, as is implied in the name, is primarily concerned with the child's ability to cope with items representative of a specified criterion of reading attainment. What matters is whether the child has achieved the criterion and *not* whether he is better or worse than his peers. Criterion-referenced tests tell us what the child can do, usually in terms of a content analysis of reading instruction. The reading tests produced by Woodcock (1973) attempt to combine the advantages of criterion-referenced measurement of reading skills with normative scores.

The criterion-referenced approach to the testing of reading is built into some graded reading series; for example, in *Programmed Reading* (Buchanan 1963). A test on the material covered is an integral part of the programmed book and must be coped with before the child can proceed to a more complex level. The *Prescriptive Reading Inventory* uses criterion-referenced reading tests as a direct guide to a pupil's educational requirements (see Chapter 3, page 24).

In the writer's opinion, many of the diagnostic reading tests contained in the handbook by Daniels and Diack (1970) can be used as criterion tests of certain important components of reading attainment. The popularity of these tests with teachers suggests that *both* the norm-referenced tests and the criterion-type tests are appreciated by teachers of reading as helpful instruments.

The appeal to the teacher of the criterion-referenced test of reading is that it provides a very straightforward way of assessing the effectiveness of her reading instruction programme.

There is a marked movement towards objectives-based tests of reading. It could be claimed to be one of publishing's growth points. One firm which produces a wide range of objectives-based tests of reading skills also distributes a selection of extensively used 'objectives collections'. The latter are booklets containing sets of measurably defined instructional objectives together with examples of possible test items. The idea is that educators can select whatever objectives suit their particular reading curriculum (Instructional Objectives Exchange 1976). One of the dangers in such an approach is the obscurity of the inter-relationships between the various objectives and the implications of these relationships for the teaching of reading. A further danger is that one might end up teaching only the skills purported to underlie reading, if such an approach was taken to its extreme. Those teachers who accept the principle that the whole is more than the sum of its parts, and who advocate that children learn to read by reading in all its complexity, are likely to be particularly antipathetic to the more extreme advocates of the skills-based approach to the teaching of reading.

In the 'cloze' test procedure (see p. 161), children are presented with passages from reading material with words and/or groups of words deleted (Turner and Gilliland 1972; Gilliland 1972). As an objective of the pupils' reading instruction, they are expected to be able so to read that the context of the missing words enables the child to say what is missing. This is one way in which a content criterion-referenced test can readily be constructed by the teacher. The pupils' ability to perform this type of task would be *one* of the objectives of their reading instruction (Rankin 1970). The 'cloze' procedure can be used to study a child's progress through a hierarchy of reading skills and also to rank the difficulty of reading material (Spooncer 1974). Additionally, it can readily be used in constructing normative reading tests.

The criterion-referenced approach is clearly related to the informal approach used by the teacher in the immediacy of its link with the child's reading programme. It is a move away from the normative approach. This type of approach can, *if formalised*, lead to a convergence of reading measurement, the operational definition of reading objectives and the analysis of instructional procedures. It appears likely that developments in reading testing in the immediate future will be orientated increasingly towards criterion-referenced measurement. A most pertinent article on this topic by Ward was published in 1970. It deals with the implications of criterion-referenced measurement to diagnostic assessments and their joint relationship to programmes of remedial activities. The article's implications for the testing and teaching of reading are considerable. The *Prescriptive Reading Inventory* developed by CTB/McGraw-Hill is one of several ambitious ventures systematically linking criterion-referenced testing with the teaching of reading (see p. 24).

(C) *Emphases of interpretation*

It is clear that the three levels of interpretation which have been identified are increasingly removed from the reading behaviour under consideration. The first, description, merely specifies the situation as it is *now*. It is sometimes used in school reports and surveys. This is an aspect of interpretation only of interest to teachers as a starting point in the consideration of a child's reading ability. The second, diagnostic level is much more important to the teacher even if the result of her deliberations is that no special action need be initiated for the individual child concerned. The diagnostic emphasis of interpretation has two components. The *historic* is concerned with the possible causes of the current reading attainments and attitudes of the child. The *predictive* is forward-looking and considers the implications of a child's current pattern of cognitive and affective attributes for the future development of reading competencies. The third level, the evaluative, considers the goals of the school's reading instruction, its resources and the adequacy of these to the tasks that the school sets for itself and its pupils. Thus the values of the school and the legitimacy of its instructional goals in reading are brought into consideration. Testing alone cannot determine whether or not the bases on which evaluative judgments are made are sound. It can, however, provide pertinent, objective data.

In practice, the teacher rapidly moves between these three aspects of reading test interpretation, with the evaluative emphasis usually dominating. Developing Goldman's (1971) approach further, each of the levels of reading test interpretation can be characterised by the types of question concerning the child's reading that it arouses. For example:

Descriptive :
What is the pattern of the class's and/or the individual child's reading strengths and weaknesses?

What are the class's and/or the individual's attitudes towards reading and the language arts?

What interests or skills has the class and/or the individual at present which are related to reading?

Diagnostic :

(*a*) *Historic*—What has resulted in this class's or this child's current attainments in and attitudes towards reading?

How much has good or poor teaching contributed?

To what extent has the child received help and support from home in his school work in general and in reading in particular?

To what extent is dullness, brightness or specific disability implicated?

Have there been any marked changes over the years in his relative reading skills and attitudes?

Are any of his current difficulties attributable to previously unnoticed physical or sensory defects?

(*b*) *Predictive*—What are the chances of the child continuing to make poor, satisfactory or excellent progress respectively in the light of his current attainments and attitudes?

What will be his future progress if some modification to his reading instruction is arranged, such as remedial help or coaching?

Can we help the child to find use and enjoyment in reading?

Will the child always be a relative failure in reading?

Evaluative :

Considering the instructional objectives of the school reading programme, are the children's current attainments in and attitudes towards reading adequate?

Should more or less be expected?

Should additional resources such as the help of the Schools' Psychological Service be sought?

As has been said earlier, there is a tendency for teachers to want a *single* reading test which will provide them with all the information they require concerning a child's attainments and attitudes, both from the descriptive and diagnostic points of view. One is less likely to be disillusioned about the contribution that the testing of reading can make to the effectiveness of reading instruction if the limitations of various types of reading tests are appreciated. A fuller discussion of the types of tests available to teachers is provided in *Reading : Tests and Assessment Techniques* (Pumfrey 1976), which identifies twelve categories within which tests of reading might be classified. These categories are summarised in Figure 8.3 (p. 146).

Figure 8.3 Categories of comment in relation to sources of information, interpretive emphasis and goals of reading programmes

	(A) Goals of Reading Programme					
	Attainments			Attitudes		
(B) *Sources*	Informal observation	Standardised tests	Criterion-referenced tests	Informal observation	Standardised tests	Criterion-referenced tests
(C) *Emphases*						
Descriptive	(1)	(2)	(3)	(4)	(5)	(6)
Diagnostic	(7)	(8)	(9)	(10)	(11)	(12)

The following are examples of the type of teachers' comments pertinent to the assessment of reading, selected to illustrate categories 1 to 12 in Figure 8.3. It will be seen that these categories are the same as the first two 'layers' of the box in Figure 8.1, p. 128.

Mary appears better at mechanical aspects of reading than at

1. *Attainment, informal observation, descriptive data*
   Mary appears better at mechanical aspects of reading than at comprehension. She doesn't seem to understand a great deal of what she reads.

2. *Attainment, standardised, descriptive data*
   Mary's score on the *Schonell Graded Word Recognition Test* was average for her age. On the NFER *Reading Test AD*, a test of reading comprehension, she obtained a reading quotient of 84. Her mechanical reading appears to be markedly superior to her comprehension on these two tests.

3. *Attainment, criterion-referenced, descriptive data*
   Mary can recognise out of context all the words in her reader as listed at the back of the book. This is our criterion of mastery expected before a child moves to more complex material. She is unable to answer correctly the ten questions set as our criterion of understanding of the content of the book.

4. *Attitude, informal observation, descriptive data*
   Mary's attitude towards reading is ambivalent. I am uncertain whether or not she enjoys it.

5. *Attitude, standardised, descriptive data*
   On the *Williams' Attitude to Reading Scale* (Williams 1965), Mary obtained a scale score of 5·5 which indicates a neutral attitude towards reading.

6. *Attitude, criterion-referenced, descriptive data*
   Of the eight criterion behaviours listed on our check-list, Mary only exhibits five spontaneously. The others have to be elicited. Our criteria of an acceptable attitude towards reading require that all eight criterion behaviours be exhibited spontaneously.

7. *Attainment, informal observation, diagnostic data*
   Mary is having some difficulties with her reading. I'll try and find out what they are by hearing her read. I wonder what is causing them and whether I can help her to overcome them?

8. *Attainment, standardised tests, diagnostic data*
   On the *Neale Analysis of Reading Ability* Mary's Reading Comprehension Age is $6\frac{1}{2}$ years. Her Accuracy Age is $8\frac{1}{2}$ years, whilst her Speed of Reading is at the seven-year-old level. The pattern

of her errors shows no unusual features. Why should her level of comprehension be so far below her reading accuracy? It is quite likely that in the past undue emphasis has been given to accuracy rather than to understanding and enjoyment. Perhaps instead of pressing on further and further up the reading scheme some reading requiring a reading comprehension age of about seven years or so might be more satisfying to her and within her understanding. Work at such a level could provide the basis for a less uneven development of reading skills and improved understanding of its content.

9. *Attainment, criterion-referenced, diagnostic data*
Using the Daniels and Diack *Standard Reading Tests* 2 to 9, Mary showed that she has the necessary abilities, with no weaknesses in visual or oral discrimination, in visual-motor coordination or between other modalities. In terms of the requisite mechanical skills involved in reading, she has mastered the expected skills.

10. *Attitude, informal observation, diagnostic data*
Mary is not keen on reading yet she is quite a good reader in some ways. She used to be interested and enjoy it when she was in the infants' class. Perhaps the book she is on in the reading scheme isn't suitable. If I can find a book she will enjoy reading it will be a move in the right direction. I'll find out what her interests are and see if we can provide anything. Failing that, she could make up her own reader.

11. *Attitude, standardised test, diagnostic data*
On the *Georgiades' Attitude Test* Mary's total score is a little below average for the class. The pattern of her likings on the five items in the scale shows great variability. Consideration of the pattern suggests the need for helping Mary to realise through experience that reading can be pleasurable and not merely a chore engaged in *only at school*.

12. *Attitude, criterion-reference, diagnostic data*
Reading is the one aspect of the language programme that Mary does not appear to be showing the behaviour consonant with the attitudes we wish all our children to acquire. She does not change her class library book unless reminded; nor does she enter comments concerning it in the 'Comments Book' that we have. Her attitude towards spoken work is good. Perhaps we can use this to help her get more satisfaction and pleasure from her reading by concentrating more on her own language than on that contained in reading schemes.

Uses of reading test results: some examples

Reading test results and the teaching of reading

In the teaching of reading, teachers are frequently making decisions concerning how the facilities available within a school can best be used to improve a child's attainments and attitudes. This important decision-making process can be improved if the teacher has reliable information concerning the child's current reading skills and attitudes, the school's instructional goals and the resources available. Measurement and testing are components of evaluation, but they are far from all that matters.

A child's score on a reading test can be interpreted at three different levels as we have seen, namely, descriptive, diagnostic and evaluative (Figure 8.1, p. 128). When teachers begin to interpret reading test results in terms of action likely to help the child improve his reading competencies and/or his attitudes towards the activity, the interpretative emphasis is on diagnosis and evaluation. Testing and teaching are, at this point, united in the teacher's endeavour to facilitate children's acquisition of the reading skills and attitudes specified in the school's objectives. The testing of reading ceases to be an isolated aspect of the teacher's work. It is seen as an inevitable and indispensable aspect of competent instruction.

The teaching and testing of reading can be considered as integral parts of a hypothesis-testing situation. At the level of global objectives, the teacher may hypothesise that 'The children will all learn to read satisfactorily provided that I teach them adequately'. Assuming this objective to be operationally defined, reading tests are the *only* means by which the teacher can check reliably that her original hypothesis is being confirmed or otherwise. If because of the results of reading tests it appears that the hypothesis is not being confirmed, there are many paths open to the teacher. She may modify her hypothesis to 'These children are lazy/dull/get no home support/are cross-lateral/etc., and cannot be expected to achieve the goals I had anticipated their achieving'. She might question her methods and decide to modify these. It might be considered that her own expertise was insufficient and that she needed to learn more about the teaching and learning of reading to ensure that the specified goals were achieved.

Only if the information concerning the children's current attainments, attitudes and progress in reading is checked against hypotheses implicit in the goals of the reading programme can children be helped other than at an intuitive level. It is the writer's opinion that teachers owe it to their profession and their pupils to be increasingly aware of the complexity of the reading process. To become knowledgeable about the vast range of instructional aids available and to know *which* materials help *which* children in *which* situations is also essential. Reading tests are an integral part of this process.

The central requirements of the evaluation of reading are:

1. specifying instructional objectives;
2. defining these objectives in terms of observable behaviours;
3. choosing appropriate measures of the behaviours;
4. administering the reading test specified in 3 at a suitable time to establish a baseline from which progress can be assessed;
5. keeping a record of the reading test results;
6. interpreting the results;
7. specifying the experiences the class or the child needs in order to make further progress;
8. further testing to check the validity of the interpretation (6) and the effectiveness of 7;
9. retesting the skill specified in 1, 2 and 3; and
10. repeating the cycle, with modified objectives in the light of the results obtained.

Two examples of the above procedure are given in Tables 8.2 and 8.3.

Table 8.2 Relationships between one objective of a reading programme, methods and evaluation. Situation A: A class of first-year junior school children of mixed ability.

1. e.g. the group to achieve an average word recognition vocabulary at about the eight-year-old level by the middle of the school year, i.e. in February.
2. e.g. children to read aloud a number of words out of context from an individually administered word-recognition test of satisfactory reliability and validity.
3. e.g. the *Schonell Graded Word Reading Test R1* using up-to-date norms by Bookbinder (1970) or Shearer (1974), if appropriate to your area.
4. e.g. administer individually when the class has settled in if the school is organised on a year group basis.
5. e.g. enter each child's raw and converted scores on a cumulative record card. Summarise results for the class. Note the average attainment and the range.
6. e.g. taking into account the information in 5, plus other information concerning the children and the resources available decide how best to deploy your resources, so as to lead to the attainment of the reading objective.

7. e.g. (for the class) ensure that each child is given regular opportunities of reading books appropriate to his reading age and interest age. Set up a programme of reading activities based on a graded reading scheme with related materials and games, or a systematic language-experience approach.

(for an individual) if, say, signs of directional confusion appeared in the child's reading, prescribe activities likely to improve direction-ality and hence word recognition skills. Items from the Stott *Programmed Reading Kit* could help. Daniels and Diack's *Diagnostic Word Recognition Test 7G* 'Reversible words' could be used to establish a baseline assessment of the child's problem.

8. e.g. Daniels and Diack's *Word Recognition Test 7G*. Making such further prescription as seems appropriate.

9. e.g. at an appropriate time, say in February, re-administer the *Schonell Graded Word Reading Test* to children individually.

10. e.g. the results should be discussed with the staff who co-operated in the specification of the instructional objectives of the school's reading programme.

Table 8.3 Relationships between one objective of a reading programme, methods and evaluation. Situation B: A class of first-year secondary school children of mixed ability

1. e.g. the group to be able to understand explicit meaning of written material at a level commensurate with their age and ability.

2. e.g. individually, to read silently a passage of writing and to answer questions requiring comprehension of the explicit meaning of the passage.

3. e.g. the NFER *Reading Comprehension Test DE* intended for children aged from 10:0 to 12:6 years gives separate scores for both global under-standing and the ability to draw conclusions from what is read, as well as other indices. Here we are concerned with only the first two. Currently provisional norms only are available.

4. e.g. if the school is organised on a year group basis, administer after the children have settled into the school.

5. e.g. enter each child's raw and converted scores on a cumulative record which will accompany him during his school career.

6. e.g. if required, these should enable one to match the reading compre-hension level required by specific materials to the individual's level of reading comprehension skill.

7. e.g. reading material suited to the interests of first-year secondary school children are available in a wide range of reading difficulty. Matching of child to material can be arranged. The *SRA Language Laboratory* and the Ward Lock *Reading Workshops* might be considered suitable. These have the advantage of containing placement reading tests. These tests can be considered supplementary to 3 above.

8. e.g. use of individual records and tests built into the SRA and Ward Lock materials.

9. e.g. after an appropriate time, re-administer the NFER *Reading Comprehension Test DE*.
10. e.g. the results should be discussed with the staff who were concerned in the specification of the instructional objectives of the school's reading programme.

Improving the informal testing of reading

One approach to the testing of reading which appears promising is that of the Informal Reading Inventory (IRI) and the complementary analysis of individual children's error patterns. The IRI is not informal in the sense that it can be applied anyhow. There are well-defined procedures that must be followed. It does, however, have the virtue of tremendous flexibility. In a sense it brings together informal and criterion-referenced approaches to measuring reading abilities.

The technique merely requires that the teacher presents the pupil with a number of extracts from a book and assesses the level at which the child copes. Frequently the teacher will record the child's oral reading accuracy and will also set questions to test understanding of the content of the passages. Often a series of passages from a graded basal reading scheme is used to assess a child's reading standard in this way (Betts 1957).

The attraction of this approach to the measurement of the match between a child's reading skills and specified material is that it can be applied to any textual material, in or out of context, by any teacher of any subject at any pupil age level. Hence its great flexibility as a procedure.

Informal reading inventories are based on the idea that readers of any age have not *one* reading level, but several. It is important for the teacher to recognise these. Most already do so, but at an intuitive level. A greater awareness of these levels is likely to make the teacher conscious of her own previously unconscious assumptions concerning children's ability to cope with various reading materials. She will also see the situation from the child's viewpoint rather more clearly than before. Both of these possible consequences of using IRIs appear desirable.

Typically, four levels of reading ability are distinguished. Each is defined arbitrarily in terms of the percentage of the given material that a child can cope with successfully. Whilst accuracy of reading and comprehension are most usually assessed, rate of reading can

also be considered. The figures given below are based on the consensus of expert opinion in this field for *words in context*.

1. *Independent level* (accuracy, 99–100%; comprehension, 90–
   100%). At this level the child can cope readily with the material
   presented. Also, he is usually well aware of his competence with it.
   Provided that the content is appropriate in terms of its interest,
   the motivation provided by conscious mastery ensures that the
   learner obtains enjoyably that degree of practice essential to
   consolidation. It will also encourage the development of positive
   attitudes towards printed material. A considerable amount of
   reading at this level is desirable, particularly in the early stages of
   learning to read.
2. *Instructional level* (accuracy, 95–98%; comprehension, 70–89%).
   Children reading at this level are likely to benefit from systematic
   instruction. The child can recognise that he faces some difficulties
   in coping with the material, but these are not so frequent that his
   motivation drops to an undesirable level. He can both read and
   understand the vast majority of the material he encounters.
3. *Frustration level* (accuracy, below 95%; comprehension, below
   70%). Reading at this level is characterised by many and frequent
   errors, very slow reading and a failure to understand the content.
   Material at this level often has an aversive effect on children.
   There is some evidence supporting the view that too many
   children spend much of their school 'reading time' with material
   at this level.
4. *Capacity level* (comprehension of 75% of orally presented
   material). It is assumed that a useful index of a child's potential
   reading level can be gauged from the extent to which he is able
   to comprehend orally presented material and shows an oral
   language ability consonant with the material. If asked to *read* and
   show his understanding of the same material, a child's performance could well be at the Frustration Level. This approach is
   an alternative to the suspect method of using a child's non-
   verbal I.Q. or mental age as an index of his reading potential.

There are several reading tests which, in a more formal manner,
compare a child's listening comprehension with his ability to read
and understand equivalent material. The *Durrell Listening-Reading
Series* (Durrell 1970) and the *Progressive Achievement Tests* (Elley
and Reid 1969, 1971) are two good examples. In his *Reading Mastery
Tests*, Woodcock (1973) has linked normative and criterion-

referenced methods of scoring to the levels of competence characterised in I R Is.

The non-reading infant starting school usually has an extensive
ability to understand spoken language, although it is sometimes
underestimated. This ability is often taken as a rule-of-thumb guide
to the child's readiness for reading. Whilst oral comprehension
ability is almost certainly a useful index of potential reading proficiency, it must be remembered that reading involves skills specific
to the interpretation of print. There are some children who are
extremely able verbally yet who find great difficulty in learning to
read.

A major weakness of the I R I approach is the rather misleading
precision with which criteria of reading performances of the various
levels are given.

The tremendous flexibility of the informal reading inventory has
been emphasised. An I R I appraises the individual's level of mastery
of a given task without referring to the standards achieved by others.
In attaching no importance to individual differences in attainments
between children, it is in marked contrast to conventional test
theory on which normative reading tests have been developed. This
approach leads naturally to the use of checklists.

The following example of a checklist devised and tested by use
with pupils by a teacher* exemplifies the adaptability of the procedure. The particular list (see pp. 156–7) was designed to analyse and
record the development of reading skills (*other than comprehension
or word-attack skills*) for carrying out work on projects in school. It
was made to be used over a period of time, thereby providing a
record of the child's progress in the mastery of the skills tested. It is
also intended to be of use to colleagues and to be used by the
children themselves in certain circumstances. The inventory can be
used as a whole, or a section at a time, dependent on the teacher's
purposes and the time available.

This particular checklist was designed for individual use. The
skills needed for work on school projects using textual materials,
particularly books, are listed under the following five headings:

A. The structure of books
B. Goal setting
C. Locating and selecting resources
D. Abstracting information
E. Evaluation.

*With acknowledgments to K. R. Pumfrey.

The order of the reading skills to be tested was determined using two criteria. Firstly, as far as possible, the skills are categorised in a sequence approximating the order in which they might be needed by the reader for efficient project work. Secondly, each section is planned to facilitate ease of testing in that all items in a section could be checked at the appropriate stage in any project being carried out. To some extent the sequence of skills within sections is arbitrary, but the five sections form groups important from the points of view of instruction and assessment.

It might be argued that Part A (The structure of books) is not in the sequence claimed and that the skills listed could more appropriately be included in Part C (Locating and selecting resources). The teacher concerned decided to separate them because she considered that those contained in Part A can be quickly taught. In many cases, any teaching that might be required could be done during the first use of the checklist by the teacher.

Listed alongside each of the skills are questions for the teacher to ask. These questions should elicit an answer which enables the teacher to decide whether or not the pupil has mastered the particular skill. Sometimes the teacher's own rephrasing of the question may be necessary to give a little extra confidence to the child.

Assessment of some skills requires observation by the teacher rather than direct questioning. Where this is required, a note to the effect is made in upper-case letters in order to make the differentiation apparent on the checklist. It was decided that the convenience of having the questions immediately to hand was greater than the inconvenience of the resulting large form. If the inventory was to be used by subsequent teachers, the fact that all had used the same questions would be likely to improve the reliability of the assessments. Each teacher would have some understanding of how previous teachers had defined a positive score.

Scoring is done on a three-point scale:

$$+ \ = \text{mastery of a skill}$$
$$- \ = \text{non-mastery}$$
$$R \ = \text{review required.}$$

The form presented here has room for six separate testings, but can be readily extended as required. A class summary sheet is also included (p. 158). This simply contains the numbers of all the skills listed, with spaces for the pupil's names and for certain total scores. It is intended to help in the organisation of group and individual instruction revealed by the checklists to be necessary.

Name _____   Date of birth _____

CHECKLIST for assessing progress in the reading skills (other than comprehension and word attack skills) required for work on school projects

Inventory of skills	Questions and notes for assessment	Dates of testing					
PART A. The structure of books							
1 Title.	What is the title of this book?						
2 Author.	What is the name of the author?						
3 Qualifications of author.	What tells us that he ought to know his subject?						
4 Edition.	Is the book likely to be up-to-date?						
5 Contents.	How do you know what the book contains?						
6 Headings and sub-headings.	Show me a heading and a sub-heading.						
7 Index.	How many references to —— are there in this book?						
8 Glossary.	How would you use the glossary?						
9 Graphic materials.	Show me a picture, chart, map, graph, diagram.						
PART B. Goal setting							
10 Defines sub-purposes.	What part of this work are you going to do? What could the others do?						
11 Defines specific purposes.	What will you try to find out? What headings will you use?						
12 Constructs purpose hierarchy.	OBSERVATION AND ASSESSMENT REQUIRED.						
PART C. Locating and selecting resources							
13 Identifies those information needs to be met by reading.	What will you need to know that you can find out by reading?						
14 Identifies possible media.	Where will you find this information? Books, magazines, journals, leaflets, letters, etc.						
15 Writes letters requesting information.	OBSERVATION AND ASSESSMENT REQUIRED.						
16 Uses alphabetical order.	Request the finding of six words of different lengths (with same initial letter) in a dictionary.						
17 Uses subject index.	What is the reference number for this subject?						
18 Uses author index.	Has the author written anything else relevant? How do you know?						
19 Uses general bibliography.	Are there any other books likely to be useful that are not in the library?						
20 Uses encyclopaedias.	On which page does the information you want start?						
21 Locates all possible media.	COMPLETION OF PURPOSE-RESOURCE GRID ENABLES						
22 Constructs purpose-resource grid.	ASSESSMENT OF SUCCESS IN MEDIA LOCATION.						

PART D. *Abstracting information and producing outcomes*

23	Skims.							
24	Scans.							
25	Accepts or discards materials.							
26	Formulates questions.	Look briefly and tell me what this section is about. What are the important points in this section? ASSESSMENT AND ASSESSMENT REQUIRED. ASSESSMENT OF ACTUAL QUESTIONS REQUIRED. ARE THEY ADEQUATE?							
27	Selects sections for intensive reading.	Which parts will you read carefully?							
28	Reads and abstracts information by (a) making meaningful notes. (b) producing flow diagrams. (c) producing topic cards.	How will you remember what you have found out? OBSERVATION AND ASSESSMENT REQUIRED.							
29	Produces acceptable outcomes (a) verbal accounts. (b) written accounts. (c) pictures. (d) graphs. (e) diagrams. (f) maps. (g) charts. (h) creates stories relevant to topic. (i) creates poems relevant to topic. (j) creates plays relevant to topic.	OBSERVATION AND ASSESSMENT REQUIRED							
30	Communicates information to others by (a) giving talks. (b) setting up meaningful exhibitions. (c) producing books. (d) writing letters exchanging experiences.	OBSERVATION AND ASSESSMENT REQUIRED							
31	Effectively stores and indexes information obtained.	OBSERVATION AND ASSESSMENT REQUIRED							

PART E. *Evaluation*

32	Evaluates the work (a) affectively. (b) cognitively.	Did you enjoy this work? Did you find out all you needed to know? If not, could you now fill in the gaps? Do you wish to develop this work in other directions?							
33	Produces written evaluation of the project.	OBSERVATION AND ASSESSMENT REQUIRED.							

Scoring system: $+$ — mastery of a skill; $-$ — non-mastery; and R — review required.

Class summary sheet (abbreviated) for a checklist of school project reading skills

Names	A Structure of books		B Goal setting		C Locating and selecting resources		D Abstracting information		E Evaluation		TOTALS A+B+C+D+E	
Skills No.	*	R**	–	R	–	R	–	R	–	R	–	R
	1…9		10…12		13…22		23…31		32 33			
	TOTAL	TOTAL	TOTAL	TOTAL	TOTAL	TOTAL	TOTAL	TOTAL	TOTAL	TOTAL	TOTAL	TOTAL
John Adams												
etc.												
Children showing non-mastery of a skill { N %												
Children requiring review of a skill { N %												

* — = non-mastered skills ** R = skills require review

N.B. A full summary sheet would have columns for *each* of the thirty-three items in the checklist. The same scoring system would be employed.

Weaknesses
1. One big disadvantage of this checklist is its size. Reproduced in a handwritten form it is unwieldy to handle and difficult to store. If produced commercially on a smaller scale the problem can be overcome.
2. The length of the list of reading skills might prove daunting to a teacher who was asked to use it (a very different matter from designing and wanting to use such a list). It is suggested that the inventory could be used a section at a time to minimise this effect. Before starting a project with her pupils the teacher could specify, if she so wished, on which items she intended concentrating her teaching.
3. Scoring on a checklist such as this is necessarily crude. There is no scope for recording minor improvements. Thus the teacher may be aware that a pupil, due soon to leave her class, is working towards mastery of a particular skill but there is no way of recording this for the benefit of the next teacher other than the 'R' scoring which gives no details of near-mastery.
4. Scoring has to be subjective in some instances and a standard deemed adequate for a particular pupil by one teacher may not satisfy another.
5. Item 9 (Graphic materials) only scores for recognition of the different graphic aids and does not assess levels of interpretation. Some indication of the level achieved is given in the pupil's own graphic materials produced as outcomes, but the scope of such materials is vast. Niles (1969) considers them to be very important: 'Since they are found in the study materials of every subject field, developing student skill in handling graphics is an important responsibility of all teachers' (p. 37). However, to check the necessary skills adequately would require a separately designed list.

Strengths
1. The checklist was designed by the teacher for a specific purpose. Its content was determined by the teacher's analysis of the skills of reading (other than word-attack and comprehension) demanded of pupils working on projects.
2. The questions devised did elicit whether or not the child had mastered the particular skill.
3. Areas in which the individual child requires teaching are easily identified from the pattern of scores.
4. The list has useful diagnostic and assessment aspects. Negative and Review scores show what teaching is needed. Subsequent testing indicates whether or not the teaching was effective.

5. The children with whom the checklist was used all learned something at the actual time of testing. For example, one thirteen-year-old boy quickly learned how to check on the qualifications of an author, what a glossary is and how to use a general bibliography.
6. It follows from 5 above that the device is a useful teaching medium with none of the restrictions that apply to standardised tests, where to teach from the test would be to invalidate the score.
7. A pupil who is a fluent reader could be encouraged to study his own checklist and to take some responsibility for acquiring the remaining skills that he needs to master. Most children would gain great satisfaction from a completed list of mastered skills.

On the subject of locating information, Guszak (1972) states that 'Locating information includes the tasks of locating specifics within written materials, locating information with book parts, and locating information with reference aids' (p. 60). It is suggested that the checklist here presented goes some way towards testing all three of these tasks, in addition to the more complex ones of producing meaningful outcomes and evaluations for both pupil and teacher.

Many authors have produced checklists of reading skills. An interesting series of developmentally based checklists of reading and writing skills based on work in British schools has been devised (Dean and Nichols 1974). Such lists, whether devised by the class teacher herself or by someone else, are of value because they require that the objective of the reading instruction be operationally defined and systematically assessed (e.g. Spache and Taylor 1963).

As might be expected, the types of reading errors made by children depend in part on the difficulty level of the material with which they are faced. This leads us to a consideration of error analysis.

Error analysis

When reading, a child is engaged in what has been described as 'a psycholinguistic guessing game'. The reader uses various cues to help him both to decode print to sound (if reading aloud) and to understand the meaning of the material before him. The more proficient the reader, the fewer cues he requires. Thus the errors a child makes in his reading are indicative of an inappropriate use of certain cues. By considering the pattern of these, the teacher can gain insight into the ways in which the child is processing the incoming visual information. The teacher can then help the pupil to recognise and distinguish between the appropriate and the inappropriate use of various cues. This is the essence of error analysis (Goodman 1973).

Certain diagnostic reading tests allow the tester to record the types of errors made by children. For example, in the *Neale Analysis of Reading Ability* the following types can be recorded: mispronunciations, substitutions, refusals, additions, omissions and reversals. From the pattern of errors revealed on the child's individual record sheet, the teacher can decide where the child most needs help. Identification of this type is a useful first step in providing the necessary experiences likely to develop a child's mastery of specific skills (Neale 1958).

This approach can readily be adapted by the teacher to the reading material she uses. Goodacre (1972) has described one such system of error analysis. An example has also been given in some detail in a recent UKRA monograph (Pumfrey 1976).

The great strength of such systems of error analysis is that they focus the teacher's attention on the child's reading performance and encourage her to identify error patterns of diagnostic importance. Merely by listening to a child read, a teacher might correct errors made, but fail to notice the recurrence of certain types of errors; for example, reversals ('was' for saw; 'on' for no, etc.). When a pattern of errors is noticed, the teacher will tend to develop ideas and materials likely to reduce the occurrence of the pattern. Thus the vital link between error-pattern identification and remediation is established.

If the categories of errors to be recorded are idiosyncratic, the interpretation of the resultant patterns presents many problems. Indeed, interpretation can only be at an intuitive level unless the teacher knows a great deal about the inter-relationships between the error categories. This point is considered in some detail later in the chapter. Despite such limitations, the practice of error-pattern identification can readily and usefully be incorporated by any teacher into her reading programme. No complex material is required. All that is needed is a sheet of paper with a copy of the material to be read by the child written on the left-hand side, preferably with only a few words to each line. On the right-hand side of the paper are drawn columns for whichever error categories the teacher has decided to record.

A further application of error analysis that combines a linguistic analysis of the reading process with the use of 'cloze' procedure will be briefly described. The aim of this particular technique is to give the teacher a framework within which she can, for an individual child, establish which cues the child has difficulties in utilising when reading a passage of writing. If the nature of the cues needed can be specified and their effects on the child's reading understood, the teacher is then more likely to be able to provide the instruction that will enable a child to tackle a text more effectively (see p. 143).

Cues are signs provided by a text that enable the reader to decode unfamiliar words and meanings. It is helpful to group such cues initially under the following three headings: (i) grapho-phonic, (ii) syntactic, and (iii) semantic.

The first refers to cues contained in the written and spoken aspects of words and their inter-relationship. The second group of cues derives from the reader's knowledge of grammar, syntax and sentence structure. This enables the reader to deduce which words are likely to follow earlier ones in a sentence. The third group depends on the meaning of the passage and this effectively limits the variety of interpretations or meanings that can follow from a sequence of words.

Commonly, the decoding of print to sound involves the child using grapho-phonic cues. Their use enables the child to read aloud correctly words unknown to him, provided that their decoding involves principles of translation with which he is familiar (e.g. does the child know the sounds of the letters and can he synthesise these appropriately?). Using such cues, the child can read aloud, often with correct pronunciation, words unfamiliar to him that he may or may not understand. He can also read aloud nonsense words, provided that their decoding involves translation rules with which he is conversant. Thus the notion of the 'meaning' of what is being read is not dominant in relation to this group of cues. None the less, the word analysis skills which comprise a knowledge of phonics and of the structural analysis of words are important (Hunter and Merritt 1973). For example, the addition of the prefix 'un' to a wide variety of words results in a meaning which is the antithesis of the word without the prefix. Thus structural aspects of word analysis such as roots, suffixes, contractions and others can contribute towards the child's ability to read and understand unfamiliar words.

The other two groups of cues are frequently referred to as context cues. Their major contribution is towards determining the meanings that are conveyed by a passage of writing.

Having specified the three major types of cues in terms of their linguistic level, each in turn can be considered in relation to the following three dimensions: (a) direction of action, (b) modality of action, and (c) source of uncertainty reduction.

(*a*) *Direction of action.* Reading is characteristically a 'left to right' procedure and cues can be either forward-acting or backward-acting. While this is clearly so in phonically regular words (for example, forward-acting as when decoding to sound the word 'mat' or backward-acting as when applying the 'final e' rule when decoding the word 'mate'), it is also true for the other levels. At the semantic level the meaning of the word 'bat' may be almost completely determined by the words that *follow* it, as can be seen in the following example: 'A bat is used in the game of cricket'; 'A bat flew from the belfry'.

The meaning could as well be determined by words preceding 'bat' if the sentences were rearranged (e.g. 'Have you seen the cricket bat'; 'The word flittermouse vividly describes the bat'). Typically, 're-reading' parts of a word or of a passage may help a child having difficulty where the cue is forward-acting, whereas 'reading on' is usually helpful if the pronunciation of a word or its comprehension is dependent on a backward-acting cue.

(*b*) *Modality of action.* For both syntactic and semantic levels, cues can either act *within* a sentence or *between* sentences. With grapho-phonic cues the locus of attention is restricted to the particular word and the modality distinction is not pertinent.

(*c*) *Source of uncertainty reduction.* In the case of grapho-phonic cues, the child's ability to read aloud accurately may be determined by the information present in the script, coupled with whatever he has either learned inductively by himself or been specifically taught concerning decoding print to sound. In addition the child's general experiential background can contribute towards his ability to decode a word. Children who have been exposed to and have acquired extensive vocabularies are likely to bring to this situation previous knowledge that enables them to supplement the cues available from the script. Thus the ability to use cues depends on both the information contained within a text and the experiential background of the individual. There is more to reading than meets the eye!

The importance of the reader's previous knowledge is similarly important in relation to his ability to extract meaning from a text. While in some instances the text itself severely limits the variety of meanings possible, in others the reader's earlier experience can either curtail or enhance his ability to comprehend the writer's meaning.

Thus the cues important in considering a child's errors of reading accuracy and reading comprehension can be conceptualised as in Figure 8.4.

CUE LEVEL	DIRECTION		MODALITY		SOURCE	
	Forward-acting	Backward-acting	Inter-sentence	Intra-sentence	Textual	Reader's experience
Grapho-phonic			////	////		
Syntactic						
Semantic						

//// Not applicable at this cue level.

Figure 8.4   Error analysis. Cue levels and characteristics

The preceding analysis enables the teacher to establish which cues at which levels present the individual with difficulties. The analysis then leads to a consideration of ways in which the class teacher can help the pupil to make more effective use of cues. In the next section we turn to a consideration of the use of context cues (as distinct from grapho-phonic cues) from the point of view of the class teacher.

Texts for identifying and teaching the use of context cues

The reading matter chosen or devised by the teacher for the identification of context cues should be at the instructional level of the child. If the teacher is preparing materials to identify or teach the use of context cues, it is essential to remember that the more complex the sentence, the more difficult it is to use the cues available. Younger and less able pupils should initially work on material containing short sentences where each sentence occupies only one line. As the child's ability to use context cues develops, the materials used can progressively approximate conventionally presented prose.

Exercises employing 'cloze' procedure can be devised both to identify the types of contextual cues the child finds difficult and also to provide opportunities for the child to learn how to use particular types of cues. The gaps in a passage require the pupil to use contextual cues to determine the missing words (and ideas) indicated by them. The greater the ratio of text to gaps, the more helpful is the context in general.

In selecting or constructing texts for the above purposes, a knowledge of the pupil's interests and background experiences is helpful. One can then use a content that, because of its significance to the child, optimises the likelihood of his bringing to bear experiences that will help him to use the available cues.

Methods of helping pupils use context cues

Certain types of questions are helpful in encouraging a child to examine context in detail, in order to extract the information that will enable him to comprehend a passage. Questions beginning with the words who, which, what, why and how elicit definite information. In contrast, questions such as 'Can you think of a word for that space?' have relatively little value.

Dependent on whether the cue that a child is missing is forward- or backward-acting, the instruction to 'read on' or to 're-read' is often all that is needed to encourage re-examination of the context and the identification of a missing word or idea.

The child's answers to such questions as 'How did you know that it was that word?' or 'Which word/s helped you to decide?' have a dual purpose. They enable the reader to become aware of how he is using context. Additionally, the pupil's response helps the teacher assess the amount of help actually being derived from the context and what types of cues the reader is failing to use. The Bullock Report says: 'We are suggesting that the teacher should be aware when the child is reading of why he is making particular errors. She can then base her teaching on her understanding of the kind of context cues to which the child is not making adequate response' (DES 1975, p. 253).

When using 'cloze' procedure a child can only suggest words which are already within his vocabulary. This points to the importance of helping children to increase their vocabularies as far as possible. A 'speaking knowledge' of grammar is needed by the child in order that the constraints of the language can be imposed. For example, a child must appreciate that the words 'a apple' do not sound right, even if unable to explain why.

One of the valuable aspects of 'cloze' procedure exercises is that they can stimulate discussion. Indeed, Walker is of the opinion that such exercises should only be used in discussion situations. He states: 'Deletion exercises are intended as a group activity. . . . Closures are made as a result of oral discussion of all relevant possibilities. . . . Final choices are made by group consensus' (Walker 1974, p. 45). Few who have used this technique with groups of children would deny the value of such discussion. A group can draw on its combined vocabulary to the members' mutual benefit.

The oral and visual uses of context also have their places. Glennon has pointed out that skills learned in speech are applied also in aspects of learning to read. Context cues can be used in both listening to speech and in reading (Glennon 1975, p. 52). One type of oral context exercise is the group prediction type, in which a paragraph is read aloud by the teacher and a group of pupils is asked to predict the possible outcomes (i.e. what will happen next?), basing their predictions on the context. The next paragraph when read confirms, modifies or rejects some of the predictions, and so on.

Occasionally the context is not helpful in identifying unfamiliar words. In such instances the child needs to recognise the fact and refer to a dictionary or a helpful adult. Being aware when context is unhelpful will enhance the child's recognition of the many times when all the help required by the reader is contained in the text and in himself, thereby eliminating the need for recourse to other sources.

Helpful context increases the reader's vocabulary. It facilitates the understanding of multiple meanings and different pronunciations of words (e.g. minute, wind). The realisation that the meaning of such words is in fact determined by their context might be reached intuitively by the child. More probably, he will need to be taught this.

Conclusion. Instruction in the use of context cues can be given at any level throughout the entire educational system. This will improve children's learning to read by integrating it with reading to learn, thus bringing together skill learning and content learning.

One use for a content criterion-referenced reading test

In the IRI discussed previously, the criteria for the four levels were defined in terms of children's performances. It is also possible to define one's criterion in terms of a specified content analysis. A teacher might legitimately consider that one of the aims of her reading programme was to enable all the participants to be able to recognise on sight a particular selection of important words. She might, for example, consider the first hundred words in the McNally and Murray list *Key Words to Literacy* to form the criterion. As these hundred words account for approximately 50 per cent of those in common use, the goal can be seen as justifiable provided that the age and ability of her pupils have been taken into account (McNally and Murray 1962).

The actual words in the list can then be used as a test. There is no need to sample items, as is essential in a normative test, because the words selected form the complete specification of the criterion. The word-recognition attainment for each child can then be measured in terms of the number of words in the list recognised. There is no need for items to optimise individual differences in attainment between pupils as in a normative test. Progress can be measured by the increase in the number of words read correctly on subsequent testing. The teacher may have no norms for such a test, but by keeping records for a period these could be built up. Thus the teacher would develop a normative interpretation of what was initially a content criterion-referenced reading test. There are many lists of words that can be used in the above manner.

Thus it can be seen that word frequency counts provide one possible basis for specifying content suitable for content criterion-referenced tests of both word recognition and comprehension. For example, Dolch has presented a Basic Sight Vocabulary comprising the 220 words which make up 70 per cent of first readers and 65 per cent of second and third readers in graded reading series (Dolch 1942). Other word counts have been carried out for various age groups on a number of different criteria. The spontaneous writing of five- to seven-year-old school children in Leicestershire formed the basis of a frequency count analysis (Edwards and Gibbon 1964).

There have been attempts to adapt this content criterion-referenced approach to measure the individual's vocabulary on a scale having an upper limit of 36,000 words. According to Diack, this range is sufficient to 'include everybody except perhaps lexicographers and polymaths'. Thus Diack has produced a series of parallel forms of short tests from which an estimate of the individual's vocabulary can be made. Diack call these 'Literacy Tests'. There is a standard version using six levels of vocabulary for the series of parallel tests and a 'School Edition' which uses only the first three levels of the standard edition, plus a lower level not used in the standard edition (Diack 1975).

A selected list of word frequency counts in which teachers of various age groups might be interested is given on pages 189–90.

Readability formulae

Another important approach to assessing the suitability of reading material for children is to use one or more of a number of formulae that have been developed to measure the relative difficulty level of such matter. A wide variety of formulae have been developed. They are usually based on a selection of samples taken from a text followed by the counting of some objective characteristic of the samples. Thus, for example, the mean number of words in each sentence or the percentage of 'hard' or infrequently used words as defined by reference to a word frequency count might be calculated. These and other methods have been described in detail and their various limitations discussed in a UKRA monograph (Gilliland 1972). Gilliland describes the Idea Analysis Technique (Morriss and Halverson 1938), the Reading Ease and the Human Interest Formulae (Flesch 1948), the Dale-Chall formula (Dale and Chall 1948), the 'Fog Index' (Gunning 1952) and the 'SMOG Grading' devised by McLaughlin (1969). These are the formulae Gilliland considers the most valuable from the point of view of the teacher of reading. There are many others, as he points out, thirty-one being listed in a survey of this field carried out some time ago (Klare 1963). Others have been developed since. Among those not discussed by Gilliland, the Spache Readability Formula, which is designed for assessing reading materials in the 6 to 8 year age range, has much to commend it (Spache 1958). However, the older readability formulae have only a limited value to the reading teacher in, firstly, narrowing down the range of materials likely to be appropriate to a particular child and, secondly, in increasing the teacher's sensitivity to and knowledge of those characteristics of written material which contribute towards increasing or decreasing readability.

In this context it is worth drawing the reader's attention to a method developed in New Zealand by which the difficulty level of written prose is calculated on the basis of a *noun* frequency count. Nouns are grouped into nine levels, level 1 being for those used most frequently. Thus by taking three samples of twenty-five nouns and referring to a table giving the frequency level of nouns, it is possible to calculate a mean noun frequency rating for the passage from which the nouns were taken (Elley 1969). This work has been related to the construction of an impressive series of reading tests devised under the aegis of the New Zealand Council for Educational Research (Elley and Reid 1969).

Perhaps the most promising development in this area of readability is in the application of 'cloze' techniques. The essential characteristic of this is the deletion of randomly selected words in a text. The reader is then requested to fill in the missing words using context cues. There are many variations on this theme. Thus it has been noted that the use of 'cloze' tests which omit words of various types and functions systematically, are potentially of great diagnostic value (Schneyer 1965).

Comparing test scores, or 'take care when interpreting reading profiles'

Quite frequently teachers will compare the scores obtained by children on two tests, for example, a reading test and a so-called 'non-verbal' test of intelligence, the assumption being that the latter will be less influenced by educational experiences than the former. Thus a large discrepancy between scores, with a child's non-verbal test score being higher than the child's attainments in reading, is sometimes interpreted as indicating that these attainments are depressed due to environmental reasons (e.g. absence from school, poor teaching). It is also often assumed that such children's reading attainments can be raised so as to decrease the gap between the intelligence test score and the reading test score by appropriate help with reading.

The central point is that the one test is assumed to give an indication of children's reading potential, whereas the reading test indicates current performance only. Statistically, this situation can be considered as a particular case of the relationship between *any* two correlated measures. Psychologically, the matter is more complex, as we shall see.

If important decisions are to be made concerning, for example, the provision of remedial help in reading for such children, the teacher/tester needs to know *initially* whether the *differences* in scores between tests are attributable to errors of measurement or whether, if the testing were repeated, the same intra-individual differences would appear. In other words, are the discrepancy scores representing real or chance differences? Whilst the answer to this question cannot be given definitively, knowledge of the effects of the reliability of tests and their intercorrelation on such difference scores is vital if important decisions concerning the allocation of resources are to be based on them.

It is a fact that, where tests are correlated, the reliability of *differences* between pairs of test scores is *lower* than the separate reliabilities of each test. The two major factors causing this are, firstly, that the errors of measurement in *each* test *both* affect the amount of error in the difference scores; and secondly, that whatever the two tests measure in common is to a large extent removed in looking at the difference only. If a reading test and an intelligence test both measure, in part, common aspects of the thinking processes, much of the variability of true scores in each test is due to their tapping the same processes. The effects of looking at differences between test scores is shown below.

As noted earlier, the variability in scores on every test can be considered as being made up of a True componenent and an Error component. Hence:

Obtained reading test score = True reading score + Error;*
Obtained intelligence test score = True intelligence score + Error.

Now if the reading test and the intelligence test are correlated, they are in part sampling the same cognitive functions. Thus the True component of the reading test score consists of two parts: that which is specific to the reading test and that which it has in common with the intelligence test. Similarly, for the intelligence test, the True score component consists of a part specific to the intelligence test and that part which it shares with the reading test. Presented as an equation, in terms of their *variabilities*, we have:

	(1)	(2)	(3)
A. Obtained Reading Test Score	True score = specific to the reading test	True score in + common with intelligence test	Error + specific to the reading test

	(4)	(5)	(6)
B. Obtained Intelligence Test Score	True score = specific to the intelligence test	True score in + common with reading test	Error + specific to the intelligence test

When the *difference* score between two test results is obtained (A−B), elements (2) and (5) cancel each other out. The errors shown in elements (3) and (6) *do not* cancel each other out as they are uncorrelated.

In other words, when difference scores are considered, the *common* true variability is removed by the subtraction of one score from the other. Thus the remaining errors form a much higher *proportion* of the spread of difference scores. As was said earlier, the

*Errors can be either negative or positive, thereby either decreasing or increasing the obtained score.

Table 8.4 The reliability of differences between standard scores on two tests of known reliability

Correlation between any two tests	The reliability of coefficients for difference scores where the mean reliability coefficient of the two tests is given in the row below						
	·65	·70	·75	·80	·85	·90	·95
0·00	·65	·70	·75	·80	·85	·90	·95
0·10	·61	·67	·72	·78	·83	·89	·94
0·20	·56	·63	·69	·75	·81	·88	·94
0·30	·50	·57	·64	·71	·79	·86	·93
0·40	·42	·50	·58	·67	·75	·83	·91
0·50	·30	·40	·50	·60	·70	·80	·90
0·60	·01	·25	·38	·50	·62	·75	·88
0·65	·00	·14	·29	·43	·57	·71	·86
0·70		·00	·17	·33	·50	·67	·83
0·75			·00	·20	·40	·60	·80
0·80				·00	·25	·50	·75
0·85					·00	·33	·67
0·90						·00	·50
0·95							·00

(While this table is given to illustrate points made in the text concerning the interpretation of difference scores between a test of reading and a non-verbal test of intelligence, the table applies to all types of standardised tests.)

difference scores are thus *less* reliable than the separate reliabilities of scores on the two tests considered.

The phenomenon is illustrated in the table on page 171 in which the correlation between two tests, a reading test and a non-verbal test of intelligence, is compared with the reliability of the difference scores.

The following example will illustrate the point. Let us consider the case where we have a test of reading and a non-verbal test of intelligence with the following characteristics:

Word Recognition Test for 7–8-year-old children: reliability = 0·94 (Mean standardised score for group = 100; standard deviation of scores = 15).

Non-verbal Intelligence Test for 7–8-year-old children: reliability = 0·86 (Mean standardised score for group = 100; standard deviation of scores = 15).

Average reliability of two tests = 0·90

Correlation of the Word Recognition and the Intelligence Test = 0·50

Looking at Table 8.4, in the column headed ·90 we can see that the reliability of the difference scores will only be ·80, i.e. *less* than either of the individual tests.

If we consider the standard error of measurement of obtained scores of each test we see these are:

Word Recognition Test standard error = $15\sqrt{1-0·94} = 3·7$

Non-Verbal Intelligence Test standard error = $15\sqrt{1-0·86} = 5·6$

However, the standard error of the difference scores =

$$\sqrt{(3·7)^2 + (5·6)^2} = 6·7.*$$

* If the standard error of difference scores, which is the standard deviation of difference scores obtained on a series of administrations of parallel forms of the tests, is 6·7, then about 68% of obtained difference scores must lie between the 'true' difference score plus and minus 6·7. The 'true' difference score plus and minus 1·96 times the standard error of observed difference scores indicates that 95% of observations will fall within these limits. Thus the range of scores of 13·13 points centred on the 'true' score is known as the 95% confidence limit. If we extend the range to plus and minus 2·58 × the standard error of measurement of difference scores, such a range from a 'true' difference score will contain 99% of the obtained difference scores on the tests.

Here, as in Chapter 7 when we were concerned with the meaning of the standard error of measurement as an indicator of obtained score unreliability, we are faced with the difficulty of estimating a 'true' score. In the case of profile analysis the difficulties are compounded.

This indicates that the chances are two out of three that such students' difference scores are within 6·7 points of their true difference scores. The odds are about 20 to 1 that the difference scores are within 1·96 × 6·7 points of the true difference scores. Thus, *the errors inherent in difference scores are considerably greater than in scores for the two tests alone.*

In the normal population of children we might reasonably find a correlation between a reading and a non-verbal intelligence test of 0·5. However, if we look at only *those children failing to read*, the correlation between the two tests is much *lower*. Indeed, if the failing children's scores on the reading test were all zero or were all the same, the correlation between the two tests would be zero. Yet from Table 8.4 we see that the *lower* the correlation between the two tests being considered, for a given average reliability coefficient, the difference score becomes increasingly reliable.

Thus in poor readers one might well find very reliable differences between reading attainment and intelligence as measured by the test. But what does this tell the teacher? If, in the group under consideration, the correlation between the tests is *low*, knowledge of the children's intelligence test scores is largely unrelated to the reading ability being tested. What has been gained in this situation in measuring an almost unrelated variable such as non-verbal intelligence?

The argument concerning the use of such difference scores between reading and non-verbal intelligence test scores in identifying children likely to benefit from remedial teaching in reading is much more complex than is generally realised by teachers. Even here only some of the considerations have been touched upon. In practical terms, if one is interested in the improvement of reading skills, there is a strong case for *concentrating on these skills*. One should not adopt suspect identification procedures based on difference scores between reading tests and non-verbal intelligence tests.

Albeit rarely, very 'bright' children in terms of their scores on non-verbal (or verbal) tests can find reading excessively difficult. There are situations in which their progress is often less than that of so-called 'dull' poor readers (Yule 1973).

It can also be shown that the standard deviation of the distribution of *obtained differences* depends both on the standard deviations of each of the two tests and on their intercorrelation. The standard deviation of the obtained differences distribution increases as the standard deviations of the two tests increase, but decreases as the intercorrelation between the two tests rises (see p. 179). As the intercorrelation between the tests rises, the proportion of error variance to total variance in the difference scores rises; that is, the difference scores become progressively less reliable. Additionally, the standard deviation of *random* differences is the same for different values of the intercorrelation coefficient, but is dependent on the test reliabilities (Magnusson 1967).

The need to consider both the reliabilities of sub-tests and their intercorrelations cannot be overemphasised if one is to avoid giving undue weight to difference scores. Focusing the argument on the individual child, the position is admirably summed up in a technical paper on techniques for considering multiple measurements (Cooley 1971): 'One very serious shortcoming of such within-profile contrasts, especially in the achievement area, is the un-reliability of difference scores. This unreliability is partly the result of the high correlations among the traits measured by the battery. Some publishers "solve" this problem by not reporting these correlations! Where they are available, or the user computes them himself, it becomes clear that it is almost impossible to talk about the differences an individual exhibits from trait to trait because of the extremely low reliability of the differences between highly correlated traits.' And later on the same page: 'To provide a battery that measures a set of highly related traits and then to encourage educators to make interpretations regarding trait differences for students without even reporting the typical correlations among these traits is certainly an irresponsible practice' (p. 603).

Yet, as we have seen in our earlier consideration of the comparison of scores on a reading test and those on a non-verbal intelligence test, the extremely reliable difference scores obtainable when the variables under consideration are unrelated would be of little value to the teacher attempting remedial or corrective reading in the majority of cases.

None the less caution is still essential. Even though the non-verbal test scores may have no concurrent validity, they may under specified conditions have some predictive validity of which the teacher engaged in the diagnosis and remediation of reading difficulties needs to be aware. At the practical level, given a group of young non-readers having a range of scores on a non-verbal intelligence test, the teacher might reasonably expect the more rapid progress in learning to read to be made by the children with the higher scores on the intelligence test. If, however, another group of non-readers with a similar spread of non-verbal intelligence had been in receipt of formal education for some years, the predictive validity of the non-verbal test score could be minimal.

Some readers may feel that these points have been laboured. In defence it must be pointed out that *many* reading tests, especially diagnostic ones, give a number of test scores for a child. Often the results are displayed in a graph intended to show the student's weaknesses and strengths. For example, the use of a profile chart such as that of the *Illinois Test of Psycholinguistic Abilities* (p. 139) is becoming increasingly popular as a means of presenting test results. The simplicity of the visual presentation is, however, deceptive. In interpreting profiles the following points should be borne in mind:

1. If one is to plot individual profiles, the norms for the various sub-tests in the battery must be comparable. Thus, for example, all sub-tests in the ITPA can be scaled to a mean of 36 and a standard deviation of 6.

2. The scores of all sub-tests must be based on equivalent groups of subjects. This is best done by using a common population for all sub-tests when collecting the standardisation data.

3. By its very nature, the profile focuses attention on the differences between different sub-test scores within the individual. For example, in Figure 8.5 (p. 177) it appears evident that the pupil does better on sub-test 1, Reading Accuracy, than on sub-test 4, Visual Discrimination. How much confidence can we have in such a difference? How certain can we be that we would obtain a similar difference if we re-tested the child on a parallel form of the sub-tests? Once more we are brought back to the problems of reliability and intercorrelation touched on earlier (p. 169).

4. It must never be forgotten that a profile based on normative scores indicates the areas of relative strength and weakness of the individual in relation to a given population. It is likely that certain groups of children can, for sound psychological reasons, be expected to have reading ability profiles that differ markedly from the profile of the general population (e.g. Kirk and Kirk 1971).

In Figure 8.5 is plotted a graph of the results obtained from a child on a diagnostic reading test. The sub-tests are all scaled to a mean of 100 and a standard deviation of 15. The differences between the sub-test scores are given in Table 8.5 (p. 176).

In the previous section it was shown that the differences between two test scores are of lower reliability than the reliabilities of the two tests considered separately. The lower reliability of such difference scores is obviously pertinent to the interpretation of profiles. Both the reading test/non-verbal intelligence test discrepancy

Table 8.5 The scores of a child on the sub-tests of the diagnostic test presented in profile form in Figure 8.5, together with the *differences* between sub-test standardised scores

Sub-test number	Sub-test (arranged in rank order of sub-test performance)	Sub-test score	Differences between sub-test standardised scores					
			1	4	6	2	3	5
			120	112	108	105	97	77
1.	Reading accuracy	120	0					
4.	Visual discrimination	112	8	0				
6.	Phoneme blending	108	12	4	0			
2.	Reading comprehension	105	15	7	3	0		
3.	Auditory discrimination	97	23	15	11	8	0	
5.	Reading speed	77	43	35	31	28	20	0

considered earlier and the comparison of the differences obtained between any pair of sub-tests in the above profile are only particular examples of the relationship between any two or more correlated measures.

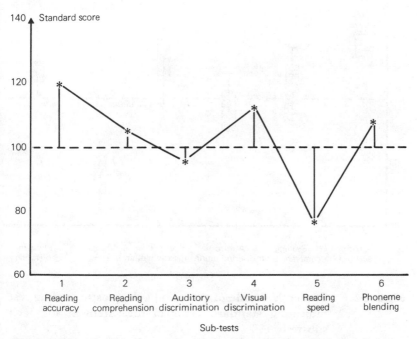

Figure 8.5 Student's profile of scores on a diagnostic reading test

Yet in profiles the visual presentation often tempts the user to over-interpret the significance of differences. Such an undesirable tendency can be largely offset if it is remembered that an individual's obtained score may fall anywhere within certain limits on either side of the true score. Thus, the possibility of over-interpretation in a profile is reduced if, instead of representing the pupil's score on a sub-test by a point, it is represented by a band of scores extending on either side of the obtained score as in Figure 8.6. There would be less chances of remedial teaching of reading being planned on the basis of differences in abilities that, by virtue of the profile, are more apparent than real.

A useful practice with profiles is to use a broad band to indicate one standard error of measurement on each side of the obtained score and a thin line extending to two standard errors of measurement.

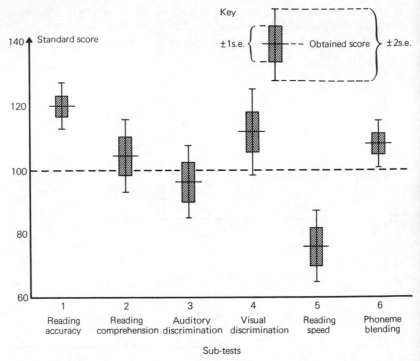

Figure 8.6 Student's profile of scores on a diagnostic reading test indicating standard error of measurement for each sub-test

ment. Doing this draws the teacher's attention to the overlap between sub-test scores rather than only to the differences. The technique is useful in comparing the scores of different groups on the same tests (inter-group comparisons) and can also be used informally in comparing differences between individual pupils on the same tests (inter-individual comparison). *Intra*-individual comparisons, as in Figures 8.5 and 8.6, are more complex. Despite certain reservations mentioned earlier (pp. 116–19), such a procedure helps the person interpreting the profile to think of the pupil as obtaining bands of scores, rather than in terms of the apparent precision inherent in, say, a score of 120 for sub-test 1, Reading Accuracy. While such an approach is possibly a help towards due caution in the interpretation of differences between scores obtained in a profile of reading abilities, it is not itself sufficient unless the sub-tests are independent, as is claimed for the ITPA.

To appreciate the limitations of differential diagnosis in terms of both sub-test reliabilities and their intercorrelation, it is necessary to consider together in more detail two related concepts touched on earlier. These are the *standard deviation of a distribution of differences* and the *standard error of measurement of the difference*. In Chapter 7, pp. 96–7, it was stated that the dispersion or variability of a set of scores could be expressed by a statistic called its standard deviation. Similarly, the dispersion of variability of a set of differences between two scores can be characterised by the standard deviation of the distribution of differences. The formula for this is:

$$S.D._{1-2} = \sqrt{S.D._1^2 + S.D._2^2 - 2r_{12}S.D._1S.D._2} \qquad \ldots (1A)$$

where $S.D._{1-2}$ = the standard deviation of the difference scores, $S.D._1$ = the standard deviation of Test 1 scores, $S.D._2$ = the standard deviation of Test 2 scores, and r_{12} = the intercorrelation of Tests 1 and 2.

In the case where both tests have equal standard deviations, the above formula becomes:

$$S.D._{1-2} = S.D._1\sqrt{2(1-r_{12})} \qquad \ldots (1B)$$

The standard error of measurement of the difference, that is the standard deviation of mean difference scores obtained on a series of administrations of parallel forms of the tests, is given by the following formula. It assumes that errors of measurement for the two tests are uncorrelated.

$$S.D._{meas.(1-2)} = \sqrt{S.D._{meas.1}^2 + S.D._{meas.2}^2} \qquad \ldots (2A)$$

If the standard deviations of the two test distributions are equal, this formula becomes:

$$S.D._{meas.(1-2)} = S.D._1\sqrt{2 - r_{11} - r_{22}} \qquad \ldots (2B)$$

where r_{11} = the reliability of Test 1 and r_{22} = the reliability of Test 2.

Any reader interested in the derivation of the above formulae is advised to consult Magnusson (1967).

As was noted earlier, a difference score is easier to evaluate when both tests are expressed in the same manner. The average expected difference is then zero. Using formula (1B) it is possible to estimate the unlikeliness of a difference score. Formula (2B) enables us to calculate the probability of differences not less than the obtained difference resulting solely from errors of measurement. To illustrate the uses of these formulae in interpreting difference scores we will apply them to sub-tests 1 and 4 in the profile of reading-related abilities presented in Figures 8.5 and 8.6. Each of the sub-tests is scaled to the same mean (100) and standard deviation (15). Thus:

Sub-test 1, Reading Accuracy: reliability $= 0.94$, Pupil's score $= 120$
Sub-test 4, Visual Discrimination: reliability $= 0.80$, Pupil's score
$= 112$
Intercorrelation between sub-tests 1 and 2 $= 0.6$, Difference $= 8$

By formula (1B)

$$\text{S.D.}_{1-4} = 15\sqrt{2 - 1.2}$$
$$\text{S.D.}_{1-4} = 13.4$$

By formula (2B)

$$\text{S.D.}_{\text{meas.}(-4)} = 15\sqrt{2 - 0.94 - 0.80}$$
$$\text{S.D.}_{\text{meas.}(1-4)} = 7.65$$

We will now consider how the figures 13.4 and 7.65 help in the interpretation of the pupil's Visual Discrimination sub-test score 8 points below his score on sub-test 1, Reading Accuracy.

By dividing the eight-point difference by the standard deviation of the differences (13.4), we obtain a deviate score of approximately 0.60. Referring to the normal curve or to Table 8.6, we find that in a survey a score on sub-test 4 of eight points or more below the sub-test 1 score can be expected in about 28 per cent of cases.

Dividing the difference score of 8 points by its standard error of measurement (7.65), we obtain a deviate score of approximately 1.05. If we turn to either a normal curve or to Table 8.6, we can see that errors of measurement can be expected to produce a Visual Discrimination sub-test score eight points or more below the Reading Accuracy sub-test score in about 15 per cent of cases.

The first of the above two percentages, 28 per cent, indicates the usualness of the difference. The second figure, 15 per cent, gives an indication of the lack of dependability of the difference. Both aspects must be considered in interpreting the difference.

The unusualness of a difference depends on the intercorrelation of the two tests involved. With a correlation of 0.6, a survey of pupils on sub-tests 1 and 4 could be expected to produce eight point or more deficits on sub-test 4 in relation to sub-test 1 in about 28 per cent of cases. The effect on the probability of such a difference occurring when the correlations between sub-tests 1 and 4 are either lower or higher than 0.6 can readily be examined by substituting other correlation coefficients in formula (1B). If the correlation drops to 0.1, the likelihood of such an eight-point difference arising increases to thirty-five in a hundred. On the other hand, if the correlation rises to, say, 0.80, the probability of a difference of eight points or more is only about twenty in a hundred. In the last instance, fifteen of the twenty differences would have to be considered as the consequences of chance errors of measurement. These figures vividly illustrate the marked reduction in the reliability of difference scores when the sub-tests are highly correlated. Where intercorrelation is high, large difference scores are unusual and those that do occur are generally attributable to chance effects of measurement.

Table 8.6 Deviates of the normal curve for each percentile of frequency

Percentile	Deviate (or z-score)	Percentile	Deviate (or z-score)	Percentile	Deviate (or z-score)	Percentile	Deviate (or z-score)	Percentile	Deviate (or z-score)
1	−2·3263	21	−0·8064	41	−0·2275	61	0·2793	81	0·8779
2	−2·0537	22	−0·7722	42	−0·2019	62	0·3055	82	0·9154
3	−1·8808	23	−0·7388	43	−0·1764	63	0·3319	83	0·9542
4	−1·7507	24	−0·7063	44	−0·1510	64	0·3585	84	0·9945
5	−1·6449	25	−0·6745	45	−0·1257	65	0·3853	85	1·0364
6	−1·5548	26	−0·6433	46	−0·1004	66	0·4125	86	1·0803
7	−1·4758	27	−0·6128	47	−0·0753	67	0·4399	87	1·1264
8	−1·4051	28	−0·5828	48	−0·0502	68	0·4677	88	1·1750
9	−1·3408	29	−0·5534	49	−0·0251	69	0·4959	89	1·2265
10	−1·2816	30	−0·5244	50	0·0000	70	0·5244	90	1·2816
11	−1·2265	31	−0·4959	51	0·0251	71	0·5534	91	1·3408
12	−1·1750	32	−0·4677	52	0·0502	72	0·5828	92	1·4051
13	−1·1264	33	−0·4399	53	0·0753	73	0·6128	93	1·4758
14	−1·0803	34	−0·4125	54	0·1004	74	0·6433	94	1·5548
15	−1·0364	35	−0·3853	55	0·1257	75	0·6745	95	1·6449
16	−0·9945	36	−0·3585	56	0·1510	76	0·7063	96	1·7507
17	−0·9542	37	−0·3319	57	0·1764	77	0·7388	97	1·8808
18	−0·9154	38	−0·3055	58	0·2019	78	0·7722	98	2·0537
19	−0·8779	39	−0·2793	59	0·2275	79	0·8064	99	2·3263
20	−0·8416	40	−0·2533	60	0·2533	80	0·8416		

With a correlation between sub-tests 1 and 4 of 0·6, twenty-eight cases out of a hundred show a difference as large as eight points in favour of sub-test 1. Of these, fifteen are attributable to errors of measurement. In other words, 15/28 or more, approximately 54 per cent of the cases having an eight-point discrepancy, would disappear if we retested on parallel forms of the sub-tests. Put another way, for any individual the odds are about one in two that the observed difference of eight points indicates a replicable difference in score between sub-tests 1 and 4 in the direction specified.

Such findings emphasise the caution needed in attempting differential diagnosis for an individual on the basis of the scores of a group. The following comment makes this point forcibly (Thorndike and Hagen 1955): 'When we have carried out a survey and have, on the basis of the survey, identified a number of atypical cases, we must expect a substantial proportion of those cases to evaporate upon retesting. We have capitalised upon peculiar combinations of errors of measurement. We have picked out the cases with plus errors on one test and minus errors on the other. Cases so identified will not hold up under closer scrutiny. Incidentally, some of these cases will provide miraculous "cures" if we apply any type of treatment and then retest them' (p. 537).

Rather different considerations obtain when an individual child is put forward for an assessment of his reading abilities because the teacher is puzzled by certain difficulties the child is experiencing. If the scores of such a child on the same two sub-tests are 120 and 112 respectively, how can this be interpreted? Here it is important to draw a distinction between an interpretation based on the psychometric characteristics of the instruments and a psychological interpretation intended to modify some aspect of the child's reading skills. The only pertinent consideration is the standard error of measurement of the difference (7·65), the major point being that a difference of this magnitude in the direction indicated could occur by error of measurement alone fifteen times in a hundred. On the assumption that the difference is a consequence of errors of measurement, differences not less than the obtained difference would occur about once in every seven such trials.

To summarise, in the case of formulae (1A) and (1B) based on population surveys, the interest is in trying to establish hypotheses concerning differences in the reading sub-skills of children. The approach capitalises on the differences produced by chance. In the second situation, a particular hypothesis concerning the child's relative weakness in Visual Discrimination is being tested. In such a situation the likelihood of a given difference being attributable to chance is much less.

This distinction between screening a year group and testing hypotheses concerning an individual child is vital in so far as the confidence with which differences in test scores can be interpreted. Any interpretation is always tentative. The chances of genuine differences being identified are higher when specific hypotheses are being tested. Additionally, in such circumstances, the test results of a particular child can be considered an unbiased estimate of the true scores because there is no systematic tendency for the observed difference to reduce as occurs when a survey is used to identify extreme cases. In the given circumstance, it is legitimate to accept the eight-point difference as a real difference at a known level of confidence and then move to the psychological interpretation. This requires the creative, innovative thinking of the teacher, coupled with an awareness of available resources for remediation, to come into play.

The *intuitive* interpretation of profiles of children's reading skills obtained from diagnostic reading tests giving a number of scores is a stage of professional competence that the teacher should soon leave behind her. Considerations of the validities, reliabilities and inter-correlations of tests in a battery should be given the importance that is their due if reading profiles are to be interpreted correctly.

When considering a child's reading profile in order to make either predictions about future progress or causes of current reading difficulties, the following points should be borne in mind:

1. Expertise in the interpretation of a reading profile requires considerable practice, application and study by the teacher. No reading test available contains a foolproof prescription for minimising the reading problems it identifies in the children with whom it is used. The teacher's experience of various methods and materials and an appreciation of their relative efficacy in helping develop certain skills is an essential corollary to the efficient use of reading tests.

2. If possible, the teacher should use or develop a test battery in which the sub-tests are based on the same group of children. This makes interpretation easier than if the sub-tests are based on different groups.

3. Knowledge of what is required of the child by a given skill is the best way to effective diagnosis of reading difficulties.

4. The teacher should use reading tests in which the behaviour required for successful test performance is closely related to the particular skill she wishes to sample. Thus, not all of the sub-tests in a battery need necessarily be used.

5. The teacher should learn to look at reading tests critically in terms of her children's instructional needs and should use the sources of test information indicated in Chapter 5 to help her make informed choices. Above all, she should not be afraid of reading more about the uses of measurement in the assessment

of reading. There are numerous books which provide an introduction to this fascinating field. Its study is almost certain to lead to a more systematic observation of pupils' reading skills and attitudes and their instructional requirements. It is also likely to result in a more reliable and communicable evaluation of the efficacy with which the teacher's reading programme achieves its goals for her pupils.

The preceding comments are intended as a corrective to any tendency to over-simplistic interpretation of the many reading tests which give profiles for an individual. The assumption that the reading skills in a profile are functionally discrete rarely holds. The visually obvious differences between scores on any two sub-tests is often uncritically accepted as a real difference by test users unfamiliar with the ideas contained in this section. This can lead to unrealistic expectations by the teacher concerning the modification of the pattern of abilities identified, and to a subsequent and unjustified condemnation of the particular reading test. It can also lead to an unwarranted faith in the efficacy of a given teaching approach.

The observations apply particularly to standardised diagnostic reading tests. This is mainly because of the assumptions concerning normality of distribution of the abilities tested and the selection of items so as to maximise individual differences. If one chose to be more concerned with criterion-referenced profiles, the strictures *might* be less valid. However, as was pointed out earlier, every criterion-referenced test has a normative aspect and every normative test a criterion-referenced one.

There is a tremendous range of diagnostic reading tests available. Many of them give individual profiles of abilities. The majority are normative, a small number are criterion-reference constructed, and a few attempt to combine both aspects of measurement. They range from the pre-reading to the college level and measure a wide range of skills. Their use can be of great help to the teacher provided that no 'instant remediation' of children's reading difficulties is anticipated as a consequence of their use. To obtain the maximum return from any of these instruments requires a considerable investment of the teacher's time and effort. The effective interpretation of reading test scores is far from being an almost mechanical process.

Conclusion

The use of reading tests is a direct application of measurement theory to the assessment of reading abilities. Whilst such instruments as we have are far from completely satisfactory, developments in the measurement of reading abilities have extended our understanding of the reading process and our effectiveness in modifying it. Considerable progress in conceptualising the theoretical bases of the reading process and of test theory have taken place over the past twenty years. These developments are reflected in the measuring devices and approaches to the assessment of reading now available to the teacher.

Reading tests can help the teacher in any of the seven ways specified in Chapter 2 that are her particular concern. They can also help meet the needs and interests of other parties to the educational venture such as pupils, parents, administrators and researchers. In focusing attention on the effectiveness of a reading programme whether at the level of the individual, the group, the school or the nation, their effect is likely to be advantageous. Yet a word of warning is essential. The selection of specific reading tests for particular purposes requires that the points discussed in this book be considered before the teacher (or anyone) begins shopping in the bazaar of reading tests that are available.

References

BETTS, E. A. (1957) *Foundations of Reading Instruction*. New York, American Book Co.

BLOCK, J. H. (Ed.) (1971) *Mastery Learning : Theory and Practice*. New York, Holt, Rinehart and Winston.

BLOOM, B. S., ENGELHART, M. D., FURST, E. J., HILL, W. H. and KRATHWOHL, D. R. (Eds.) (1956) *Taxonomy of Educational Objectives, Handbook 1 : Cognitive Domain*. New York, McKay.

BLOOM, B. S., HASTINGS, J. T. and MADAUS, G. F. (1971) *Handbook of Formative and Summative Evaluation of Student Learning*. New York, McGraw-Hill.

BOOKBINDER, G. E. (1970) Variations in reading test norms. *Educational Research, 12*, 2, 99–105.

BUCHANAN, C. D. (1963) *Programmed Reading*. New York, McGraw-Hill.

CLARK, M. L. (1974) *Hierarchical Structure of Comprehension Skills*. Melbourne, Australian Council for Educational Research.

COOLEY, W. W. (1971) Techniques for Considering Multiple Measurements. In THORNDIKE, R. L. (Ed.) *Educational Measurement* (second edition). Washington, D.C., American Council on Education.

CRONBACH, L. J. (1970) *The Essentials of Psychological Measurement* (third edition). New York, Holt, Rinehart and Winston.

DALE, E. and CHALL, J. S. (1948) A formula for predicting readability. *Educational Research Bulletin, 27*, 11–20 and 37–54.

DANIELS, J. C. and DIACK, H. (1970) *The Standard Reading Tests*. London, Chatto and Windus.

DEAN, J. and NICHOLS, R. (1974) *Framework for Reading*. London, Evans.

Department of Education and Science (1975) *A Language for Life*. London, HMSO.

DIACK, H. (1975) *Literacy Tests for Schools*. London, Hart-Davis Educational.

DOLCH, E. W. (1942) *The Basic Sight Word Test*. Champaign, Garrard Press.

DURRELL, D. D. (1970) *Durrell Listening-Reading Series*. New York, Harcourt, Brace and Jovanovich.

EDWARDS, R. P. and GIBBON, V. (1964) *Words Your Children Use*. London, Burke.

ELLEY, W. B. (1969) The assessment of readability by noun frequency counts. *Reading Research Quarterly*, 4, 3, 411–26.

ELLEY, W. B. and REID, N. A. (1969) *Progressive Achievement Tests: Reading Comprehension and Vocabulary*. Wellington, New Zealand Council for Educational Research; London, Hodder and Stoughton.

ELLEY, W. B. and REID, N. A. (1971) *Progressive Achievement Tests: Listening Comprehension*. Wellington, New Zealand Council for Educational Research.

FLESCH, R. F. (1948) A new readability yardstick. *Journal of Applied Psychology*, 32, 221–33.

GEORGIADES, N. (1967) A Report of a Pilot Study on the Development of an Instrument to Investigate the Attitude of Children to Reading. In DOWNING, J. and BROWN, A. L. (Eds.) *The Second International Reading Symposium*. London, Cassell.

GILLILAND, J. (1972) *Readability*. London, Hodder and Stoughton.

GLENNON, J. V. (1975) The modification of language codes and their relation with reading attainments in adolescents. Unpublished M.Ed. thesis, University of Manchester Department of Education.

GOLDMAN, L. (1971) *The Use of Tests in Counselling*. New York, Appleton-Century-Crofts.

GOODACRE, E. J. (1972) *Hearing Children Read*. Centre for the Teaching of Reading, University of Reading, England.

GOODMAN, K. S. (1973) Analysis of Oral Reading Miscues: Applied Psycholinguistics. In SMITH, F. (Ed.) *Psycholinguistics and Reading*. New York, Holt, Rinehart and Winston.

GUNNING, R. (1952) *The Technique of Clear Writing*. New York, McGraw-Hill.

GUSZAK, F. J. (1972) *Diagnostic Reading Instruction in the Elementary School*. New York, Harper and Row.

HUNTER, E. and MERRITT, J. (1973) *Individual Progress in Reading*. Reading Development, Units 12 and 13, Milton Keynes, Open University Press.

Instructional Objectives Exchange (1976) *IOX Objectives-Based Tests*. Los Angeles, IOX.

JACKSON, S. (1971) *Phonic Skills (P.S.) Tests 1 to 11*. Glasgow, Robert Gibson.

KIRK, S. A. and KIRK, W. D. (1971) *Psycholinguistic Learning Disabilities: Diagnosis and Remediation*. Urbana, University of Illinois Press.

KLARE, G. R. (1963) *The Measurement of Readability*. Iowa, Iowa State University Press.

KRATHWOHL, D. R., BLOOM, B. S. and MASIA, B. B. (1964) *Taxonomy of Educational Objectives, Handbook 2: Affective Domain*. New York, McKay.

MAGNUSSON, D. (1967) *Test Theory*. London, Addison-Wesley.

MCLAUGHLIN, H. (1969) Smog Grading—a new readability formula. *Journal of Reading, 22*, 639–46.

MCNALLY, J. and MURRAY, W. (1962) *Key Words to Literacy*. London, Schoolmaster Publishing Co.

MELNIK, A. and MERRITT, J. (Eds.) (1972) *Reading: Today and Tomorrow*. London, Hodder and Stoughton.

MORRISS, E. C. and HALVERSON, D. (1938) Idea Analysis Technique. In GILLILAND, J. (1972) *Readability*. London, Hodder and Stoughton.

NEALE, M. D. (1958) *Neale Analysis of Reading Ability*. London, Macmillan.

NILES, O. S. (1969) Reading Skills Common to the Content Areas. In MELNIK, A. and MERRITT, J. (Eds.) *The Reading Curriculum*. London, Hodder and Stoughton.

OSGOOD, C. E., SUCI, G. J. and TANNENBAUM, P. H. (1957) *The Measurement of Meaning*. Urbana, University of Illinois Press.

PUMFREY, P. D. (1974) The Illinois Test of Psycholinguistic Abilities in the diagnosis and remediation of reading failure amongst eight-year-old children: some recent findings pertinent to the class teacher. Paper given at the UKRA 11th Annual Study Conference.

PUMFREY, P. D. (1976) *Reading: Tests and Assessment Techniques*. London, Hodder and Stoughton.

RANCE, P. (1971) *Record Keeping in the Progressive Primary School*. London, Ward Lock.

RANKIN, E. F. (1970) The Cloze Procedure—its validity and utility. In FARR, R. (Ed.) *Measurement and Evaluation of Reading*. New York, Harcourt, Brace and World.

SCHNEYER, J. W. (1965) Use of the Cloze Procedure for improving reading comprehension. *The Reading Teacher, 19*, 174–9.

SHEARER, E. (1974) Reading—2 New Words. *Times Educational Supplement*, 24th May, no. 3078, p. 34.

SPACHE, G. D. (1958) *Good Reading for Poor Readers*. Champaign, Illinois, Garrard Press.

SPACHE, G. D. (1976a) *Investigating the Issues of Reading Disabilities*. Boston, Allyn and Bacon.

SPACHE, G. D. (1976b) *Diagnosing and Correcting Reading Disabilities*. Boston, Allyn and Bacon.

SPACHE, G. D. and TAYLOR, S. E. (1963) *Reader's Inventory*. New York, Educational Developmental Laboratories.

SPOONCER, F. (1974) Hanging out the 'cloze' line. *Reading, 8*, 2, 19–26.

STOTT, D. H. (1971) *Programmed Reading Kit and Manual*. Edinburgh, Holmes McDougal.

THORNDIKE, R. L. and HAGEN, E. (1955) *Measurement and Evaluation in Psychology and Education*. New York, Wiley.

TURNER, B. and GILLILAND, J. (1972) The use of cloze procedures in the measurement of Schools Council Humanities Project materials. *Reading, 6*, 2, 4–13.

VARGAS, J. S. (1972) *Writing Worthwhile Behavioural Objectives*. London, Harper and Row.

WALKER, C. (1974) *Reading Development and Extension*. London, Ward Lock Educational.

WARD, J. (1970) On the concept of criterion-referenced measurement. *British Journal of Educational Psychology*, 40, 3, 314–23.

WILLIAMS, G. (1965) Williams' Reading Attitude Scale. Unpublished dissertation, University of Manchester Department of Education.

WOODCOCK, R. W. (1973) *Woodcock Reading Mastery Tests*. Circle Pines, American Guidance Services Inc.

YOUNG, G. D. (1968) *Group Reading Test*. London, Hodder and Stoughton.

YULE, W. (1973) Differential prognosis of reading backwardness and specific reading retardation. *British Journal of Educational Psychology*, 43, 3, 244–8.

Further reading

DELLA-PIANA, G. M. (1968) *Reading Diagnosis and Prescription*. New York, Holt, Rinehart and Winston.

MILLER, D. M. (1972) *Interpreting Test Scores*. New York, Wiley.

The firm Science Research Associates produces a series of pamphlets written for teachers and other personnel using tests. These pamphlets are available from:

SRA Testing and Measurement Extension Service,
SRA Inc., 259 E. Erie Street, Chicago, Illinois 60601, USA.

The series at present comprises the following eight pamphlets: Unit I: The Role of Standardised Testing; Unit II: The Language of Standardised Testing; Unit III: Basic Concepts in Standardised Test Construction; Unit IV: The School Testing Programme; Unit V: Interpreting Standardised Test Results; Unit VI: Teacher-Made Tests: Designing the Test; Unit VII: Teacher-Made Tests: Writing the Test; and Unit VIII: Evaluating and Reporting Student Progress. Though concerned with testing generally, it is easy to consider these topics in terms of the testing of reading.

Educational Testing Service (USA) will send teachers a 'Tests and Measurement Kit' comprising seven pamphlets concerned with testing in general. These too can readily be related to the testing of reading in particular: Selected References in Educational Measurement (an annotated booklist providing a guide to further reading at different levels of difficulty in the interpretation of test scores); Selecting an Achievement Test; Making the Classroom Test; Short-cut Statistics for Teacher-Made Tests; Multiple-choice Questions: A Close Look; ETS Publications; and Measurement Programmes, Special Services, Instructional Activities at ETS.

A selected list of word frequency counts (arranged chronologically)

THORNDIKE, E. L. (1921) *Teachers' Word Book.* New York, Columbia University.

The Child Study Committee of the International Kindergarten Union (1928) *A Study of the Vocabulary of Children before entering the First Grade.* Washington, D.C., International Kindergarten Union.

WHEELER, H. E. and HOWELL, E. A. (1930) A first-grade vocabulary study. *Elementary School Journal, 31,* 52–60, September.

THORNDIKE, E. L. (1932) *Teachers' Word Book of 20,000 Words.* New York, Columbia University.

BUCKINGHAM, B. R. and DOLCH, E. W. (1936) *A Combined Word List.* Boston, Ginn and Co.

GATES, A. I. (1937) *A Reading Vocabulary for the Primary Grades.* New York, Bureau of Publication, Columbia University, revised edition.

LANGSTON, R. G. (1941) A core vocabulary for the pre-primer reading. *Elementary School Journal, 61,* June.

STONE, C. R. (1941) *A Graded Vocabulary for Primary Reading.* St Louis, Webster.

DOLCH, E. W. (1942) *The Basic Sight Word Test.* Champaign, Garrard Press.

KYTE, G. C. (1943) A core vocabulary for the primary grades. *Elementary School Journal, 44,* 157–66, November.

THORNDIKE, E. I. and LORGE, I. (1944) *The Teachers' Word Book of 30,000 Words.* New York, Bureau of Publications, Columbia University.

RINSLAND, H. D. (1945) *A Basic Vocabulary of Elementary School Children.* New York, Macmillan.

VERNON, P. E. (1948a) A Preliminary Investigation of the Vocabulary of Scottish Children Entering School. In *Studies in Reading: Vol. 1.* London, University of London Press for Scottish Council for Research in Education.

VERNON, P. E. (1948b) Word Counts of Infant Readers. In *Studies in Reading: Vol. 1.* London, University of London Press for Scottish Council for Research in Education.

DOLCH, E. W. (1950) *Teaching Primary Reading.* Champaign, Garrard Press.

WEST, M. (1953) *General Service List of English Words.* London, Longman.

BURROUGHS, G. E. R. (1957) *A Study of the Vocabulary of Young Children.* University of Birmingham Institute of Education, Educational Monographs No. 1.

DALE, E. (Comp.) (1957) *Bibliography of Vocabulary Studies.* Columbus, Bureau of Educational Research, Ohio State University.

RADFORD, W. C. (1960) *A Word List for Australian Schools.* Melbourne, Australian Council for Educational Research.

ARVIDSON, G. L. (1961) *Alphabetical Spelling List.* Wellington, New Zealand Council for Educational Research.

MCNALLY, J. and MURRAY, W. (1962) *Key Words to Literacy.* London, The Schoolmaster Publishing Co.

EDWARDS, R. P. and GIBBON, V. (1964) *Words Your Children Use.* London, Burke.

WRIGHT, C. W. (1965) *An English Word Count.* South Africa, National
Bureau of Educational and Social Research.

CARROLL, J. B., DAVIES, R. and RICHMAN, B. (1971) *Word Frequency Book.*
Boston, Houghton Mifflin.

ELLEY, W. B. and REID, N. A. (1974) 2,000 Nouns Graded by Frequency of
Usage. In *Progressive Achievement Tests: UK Supplement to the Teacher's
Manual*, appendix 2. London, Hodder and Stoughton.

HILLERICH, R. L. (1974) Word Lists—Getting it all Together. *The Reading
Teacher*, January 1974, pp. 353–60.

HUNTER, D. L. (1975) Spoken and Written Word Lists: A Comparison. *The
Reading Teacher*, December 1975, pp. 250–3.

Appendix 1
Some useful addresses

American Psychological Association, Inc., 1200 Seventeenth Street N.W., Washington, D.C. 20036, USA.

Association for Special Education, General Secretary, 19 Hamilton Road, Wallasey, Cheshire.

British Psychological Society, St Andrew's House, 48 Princess Road, Leicester, LE1 7DQ.

Centre for Information and Advice on Educational Disadvantage, 11 Anson Road, Manchester, M14 5BY.

Centre for Information on Language Teaching and Research, State House, 63 High Holborn, London, WC1R 4TN.

Center for the Study of Evaluation, U.C.L.A. Graduate School of Education, Los Angeles, California, USA.

Centre for the Teaching of Reading, University of Reading, 29 Eastern Avenue, Reading, Berkshire, RG1 5RU.

Dyslexia Institute, 133 Gresham Road, Staines, Middlesex, TW18 2AJ.

Educational Resources Information Centre (ERIC) on Language and Linguistics, Centre for Applied Linguistics, 1611 N. Kent Street, Arlington, Virginia 22209, USA.

Educational Resources Information Centre (ERIC) on Reading and Communication Skills, National Council of Teachers of English, 1111 Kenyon Road, Urbana, Illinois 61801, USA.

Educational Resources Information Centre (ERIC) on Tests, Measurement and Evaluation, c/o Educational Testing Service (see below).

Educational Testing Service, Rosedale Road, Princeton, New Jersey 08540, USA.

Godfrey Thomson Unit for Academic Assessment, University of Edinburgh, 24 Buccleuch Place, Edinburgh, EH8 9JT, Scotland.

International Reading Association, 800 Barksdale Road, Newark, Delaware 19711, USA.

National Association for Remedial Education, General Secretary, 77 Chignall Road, Chelmsford, Essex CM1 2JA.

National Foundation for Educational Research in England and Wales (NFER), The Mere, Upton Park, Slough, Buckinghamshire, SL1 2DQ.

NFER Publishing Company Ltd,
Test Department,
Darville House,
92–3 Peascod Street,
Windsor, Berkshire, SL4 1DF.

New Zealand Council for
Educational Research,
Education House, P.O. Box 3237,
Wellington, New Zealand.

Right to Read Programme,
Room 2131, United States Office of
Education, 400 Maryland Avenue,
S.W. Washington, D.C. 20202,
USA.

United Kingdom Reading
Association,
Information Officer,
6 Barton Rise, Chilton Polden,
Bridgwater, Somerset.

Appendix 2
Further sources of information on measurement

The measurement of reading is but one application of measurement theory in education. The following sources of information are primarily concerned with general problems of mental measurement. The approaches discussed can be applied to the fields of reading and related skills, or to any aspect of education.

This is a selected list of current sources and supplements those referred to in the main text. It is divided into the following sections:
A. *Reference sources.*
B. *Books*   i. Theory and techniques of mental measurement,
              ii. Test construction, and
             iii. Critical discussions of mental measurement.
C. *Professional journals.*

A. Reference sources

The following reference books are secondary sources of measurement information, drawing on the primary sources such as theoretical or empirical articles in learned journals, published mental tests or books on measurement. They describe, summarise, review and evaluate the primary sources. Such secondary sources provide a valuable overview of the field, but in most cases should lead the reader to an examination of the primary source before any decisions are made or conclusions reached.

Annual Review of Psychology. Palo Alto, California, Annual Reviews, Inc.
This publication contains critical reviews by acknowledged authorities on some fifteen areas of psychology. The aim is to provide a complete coverage of significant new developments. Some topics are covered annually, others less frequently. At the end of each volume is a cumulative index of chapter titles for prescribed periods. Measurement and testing is discussed in chapters such as Scaling and Test Theory, Theory and Techniques of Assessment, Individual Differences and Learning and Motivation. The reviews are intended mainly for readers who have some knowledge of the area covered by the particular reviewer.

Dissertation Abstracts International. Ann Arbor, Michigan, University
   Microfilms.
About three hundred higher educational institutions submit abstracts of
doctoral dissertations and theses. Within each issue these are grouped
according to their content area. Abstracts bearing on mental measurement
appear in the Education, Psychology and Social Psychology sections. Copies
of the complete dissertations or theses can be bought either on microfilm or
on Xerographic paper. The abstracts are compiled monthly.

Education Index. New York, H. W. Wilson Company.
From a selected list of educational publications, a cumulative index is compiled. One section, Tests and Scales, is sub-divided into a large number of
sections listing articles on subjects such as Administration, Construction,
Criticism and Reviews of Tests. Cross-indexing enables measurement-
related articles under other subject headings to be readily located. It is
published monthly except in July and August.

Encyclopaedia of Educational Research. Ed. EBEL, R. L. (1969) New York,
   Macmillan, fourth edition.
A wide spectrum of topics in education and associated areas is discussed by
an acknowledged authority on each. The pertinent literature is discussed
and the implications of research findings for further studies and for current
educational practice is considered. The function of measurement in education
is considered in the following articles: Measurement in Education, Achievement Tests, Scores and Norms, Test Use, Measurement Theory, Scaling,
Prediction, and Marks and Marking Systems.

Psychological Abstracts. Washington, D.C., American Psychological Association.
Abstracts are classified according to areas of psychological interest. Work on
aptitude and achievement testing including reading is sub-classified under
the major area of Educational Psychology. Within the Personality and
Abilities category are sub-sections on New Tests, Test Construction, Test
Standardisation and Evaluation. Each issue is indexed by both author and
subject. This reference series is published monthly. Bound copies can be
found in the reference sections of most University libraries.

B. Books. i. Theory and techniques of mental measurement

ADAMS, G. S., in consultation with TORGERSON, T. L. (1964) *Measurement
   and Evaluation in Education, Psychology and Guidance.* New York, Holt,
   Rinehart and Winston.
This book emphasises measurement concepts rather than statistical procedures. It is a general textbook intended for undergraduate students but
containing sufficient in the way of footnotes and reference to other books
to be of value to teachers returning to further study after a period of teaching
experience. Consideration is given to Basic Principles and Procedures, The
Study of Individuals, The Improvement of Instruction and the Administrative, Supervisory and Guidance Aspects of Measurement and Evaluation.

AHMANN, J. S. and GLOCK, M. D. (1975) *Evaluating Pupil Growth* (fifth edition). Boston, Allyn and Bacon.
Readers of this book are expected to have no initial knowledge of statistics. A limited amount of such statistical procedures as are necessary to clarify certain points is introduced. The book stresses the importance of evaluation in education, informal methods of evaluating attainments, the evaluation of student's behaviour and the improvement of learning.

BAUERNFEIND, R. H. (1969) *Building a School Testing Programme*. Boston, Houghton Mifflin.
Intended as a basic text for undergraduate courses, the author reviews criticisms of current school testing programmes. The basic concepts in measurement are discussed. There is an interesting consideration of the criteria to be used in appraising the value of tests within the school programme.

BEGGS, D. L. and LEWIS, E. L. (1975) *Measurement and Evaluation in the Schools*. Boston, Houghton Mifflin.
This text assumes no statistical knowledge on the part of the reader. It is divided into four sections. The first comprises a discussion of evaluation in education, educational objectives and the functions of measurement. A consideration of measuring instruments developed outside the particular classroom, a comparison of norm-referenced and criterion-referenced measurement and criteria for appraising various measures forms the second section. The next discusses measurement techniques that can be developed and used in the classroom by the individual teacher. The book concludes with an examination of the importance and organisation of a testing programme for a school system, such as an LEA in Britain. This is a useful book for the reader who is interested in the concepts related to measurement but who has virtually no background in mathematics. This means that the text has, on other counts, some limitations in the precision with which some ideas can be discussed.

BROWN, F. G. (1976) *Principles of Educational and Psychological Testing*. New York, Holt, Rinehart and Winston.
It is interesting to note the changes over time in topics included in books on mental measurement. These changes reflect a growing awareness of the contribution that measurement and evaluation can make to conceptualising the nature of human abilities and attainments.
Brown's book provides a sound base for the reader who wants to understand the basic concepts in testing and mental measurement but who is also interested in topics of current concern. Thus the nature of norm-referenced, content-referenced and outcome-referenced measurement and their interrelationship is discussed. The measurement of both maximal and typical performance is extensively discussed in relation to various testing techniques. The final chapter is on the selection and evaluation of tests and on current issues, problems and trends.

DOWNIE, N. M. (1967) *Fundamentals of Measurement: Techniques and Practices* (second edition). New York, Oxford University Press.
This book is written for classroom teachers and school counsellors. While

covering practical problems associated with classroom assessments, it does
not deal in any technical detail with the theory underpinning particular
instruments described. After an introduction to elementary statistics, scores
and the uses of tests in education comes an examination of achievement tests,
intelligence tests, special aptitudes, adjustment and interests measurement
and their applications.

ELLEY, W. B. and LIVINGSTONE, I. D. (1972) *External Examinations and
   Internal Assessments*. Wellington, New Zealand Council for Educational
   Research. Distributed in the UK by Hodder and Stoughton.
The problems of evaluation in the secondary school considered in this book
are presented in the context of the New Zealand school system. Despite this,
the analysis made of the nature of the problems involved and the discussion
of the advantages and disadvantages of seven important methods of moderat-
ing teachers' assessments of pupil attainments are pertinent to all countries
having a well-developed secondary school system.
   A number of alternative ways of reforming the New Zealand secondary
school examination system so as to ensure more valid institutional decision
making are presented. The authors achieve their goals of informing this
continuing educational debate, of spelling out the implications of various
courses of action and also specifying areas in which further information can
and should be obtained in order to help policy makers reach sound decisions.

FINDLEY, W. G. (Ed.) (1963) *The Impact and Improvement of School Testing
   Programmes*. The sixty-second Yearbook of the National Society for the
   Study of Education, Chicago. Distributed by the University of Chicago
   Press.
For anyone interested in evaluating the effectiveness of an educational system,
the above book is essential reading. The twelve chapters written by eighteen
experts are, in the main, as valid now as when they were originally written.
In so far as Britain is concerned it is a matter of some regret that such school
testing programmes as we have retain inadequacies which could and should
be eradicated. An awareness of the issues discussed in this book, by both
teachers and administrators, is overdue.

GHISELLI, E. E. (1964) *Theory of Psychological Measurement*. New York,
   McGraw-Hill.
This book is intended for students taking an initial course in mental measure-
ment. It covers the statistical techniques and theoretical concepts of testing.
The use of mathematical models in mental measurement is described,
together with a discussion of the limitations.

GRONLUND, N. E. (Ed.) (1968) *Readings in Measurement and Evaluation :
   Education and Psychology*. New York, Macmillan.
This is a very readable introductory book for students interested in measurement. It covers consideration of the measurement and evaluation process,
the construction of classroom tests, interpreting test scores and norms,
validity and reliability, the selection of standardised tests, standardised
testing, the use of the results of measurement, new developments and current
controversies in the field.

GRONLUND, N. E. (1976) *Measurement and Evaluation in Teaching* (third edition). New York, Macmillan.
In this extensive revision of a deservedly popular text, in which classroom assessment and evaluation are presented as central to the teaching process, the author has incorporated sections on criterion-referenced measurement, on mastery learning and on the implications for the individualisation of instruction. The book is in five major sections. These cover the role of evaluation in teaching and its relationship with the establishment of educational objectives, the construction of classroom tests, the uses of normative tests, observational techniques, peer assessments and self-report procedures, and some uses of evaluation in improving learning and teaching.

The book is written for use by both primary and secondary school teachers as well as by undergraduates interested in understanding the contribution that measurement can make to the improvement of education. Gronlund writes in a commendably lucid style and provides many practical examples to illustrate the points that he makes.

GULLIKSEN, H. (1950) *Theory of Mental Tests*. New York, Wiley.
The material in this book is generally of a technical nature suitable for specialists in mental measurement. It was one of the earliest attempts to summarise the results of fifty years of technical progress in the extension of test theory. The derivations of numerous widely used measurement formulae are presented.

HEDGES, W. D. (1969) *Evaluation in the Elementary School*. New York, Holt, Rinehart and Winston.
Dr Hedges has written a very practical book. It explains how the teacher can construct her own tests, how the observation of children's behaviour can be organised so as to yield valuable information that might otherwise be overlooked and how to discuss a child's progress with his parents (amongst other interesting topics). The arithmetical ability needed to cope with the examples presented is minimal.

INGENKAMP, K. (Ed.) (1969) *Developments in Educational Testing* (two volumes). London, Hodder and Stoughton.
This publication was one outcome of an international conference on the uses of tests in education. Contributions by seventy-nine authorities from six continents provide informative and fascinating glimpses of testing practices and developments throughout the world.

Volume 1 is in two major sections. The first comprises twenty articles outlining the uses of tests in institutions such as schools, universities and clinics in different countries. The second part contains eighteen papers grouped under the following areas: educational objectives of testing; tests of scholastic achievement, of creativity, of social behaviour, interests and attitudes, of culture-fair tests and of recent developments in test construction and automated scoring.

Volume 2 begins with five articles on tests in the primary school. It continues with ten related to secondary schools and nine concerned with uses in universities. A further six sections are devoted to the following: tests and the learning process; teachers and testing; presentation and interpretation of test results; assessment of teaching methods; technical problems concerning test validities and also the relationship between testing and curriculum development.

The sheer breadth of the two volumes makes them well worth a place in the reference section of a library, despite the almost inevitable variability in the quality of the contributions.

LEWIS, D. G. (1974) *Assessment in Education*. London, Hodder and Stoughton. The author presents an overview of assessment in education with particular emphasis on the later stages. Thus tests of intelligence, attainments, scholastic aptitude, divergent thinking and attitude are described and discussed. Dr Lewis also considers examinations and the assessment of teaching, two topics of considerable current interest. A very helpful chapter on reliability and validity is provided. This helps to make the discussion of the strengths and limitations of the various procedures described of more value to the reader.

The summaries presented at the end of each chapter, together with the glossary of technical terms provided at the end of the book, contribute towards making this a very valuable publication to the teacher who wishes to get an overview of the testing 'scene'.

LINDVALL, C. M. (1975) *Measuring Pupil Achievement and Aptitude* (second edition). New York, Harcourt, Brace and World.
This is an introductory text on the principles of mental testing and evaluation written specially for teachers in training and for interested qualified teachers. After discussing the role of testing in education come discussions on the need for specific objectives, criteria determining the suitability of tests for given purposes and descriptions of various kinds of tests. Examples are given of the practical applications of measurement techniques in a school testing programme.

LORD, F. M. and NOVICK, M. R. (1968) *Statistical Theories of Mental Test Scores*. Reading, Addison-Wesley.
This is a major publication in the field of test theory. The relationships between test theories and the associated mathematical models form the core of the book. The authors' intention is to help the reader to interpret the data from mental tests and also to use mental tests as tools of psychological theory rather than allowing the mathematical 'tail' to wag the psychological 'dog'. It is intended for statistically sophisticated readers.

MCFARLAND, S. J. and HEREFORD, C. F. (Eds.) (1971) *Statistics and Measurement in the Classroom*. Dubuque, Brown.
This book is addressed to the question 'Why should teachers study statistics?' Having provided an answer, the editors have brought together articles by eminent authorities on various important topics in measurement. The articles are generally written at a level appropriate to the mathematical background of their intended audience. The authors have also contributed themselves. The book is in three sections, Basic Statistical Concepts, Classroom Testing and Standardised Testing.

MEHRENS, W. A. (Ed.) (1976) *Readings in Educational and Psychological Measurement and Evaluation.* New York, Holt, Rinehart and Winston.
Mehrens has brought together an admirable collection of up-to-date descriptions and discussions of important aspects of the theory, practice and ethics of applying measurement techniques in education and psychology. The book is particularly helpful to the reader who has not studied statistics in depth. The central points in most of the chapters can be readily grasped without such a background, although a knowledge of statistics perhaps allows a deeper understanding of the material in certain of the chapters. The book is divided into six units. These are concerned with the role of measurement and evaluation, basic principles of measurement, constructing and using tests, standardised evaluation procedures, reporting and using results, and a final unit on trends and issues in evaluation. Some of the social consequences of the application of measurement are discussed in the sixth unit. The consideration of the confidentiality of test results in the light of the American 'Family Educational Right and Privacy Act, 1974' will be of interest to anyone concerned with the current deliberations on these points taking place in England.

MEHRENS, W. A. and LEHMANN, I. J. (1969) *Standardised Tests in Education.* New York, Holt, Rinehart and Winston.
This book provides information on the selection, administration and interpretation of tests. Both cognitive and non-cognitive tests available at that time are classified and evaluated. The establishment of a school testing programme is discussed in some detail.

MORONEY, M. J. (1956) *Facts from Figures* (third edition). Harmondsworth, Penguin.
Various editions of this book have been in Penguin's List since 1951. In many ways Moroney's claim that the book is a layman's introduction to statistics is justified. Although the author moves fairly rapidly into some complex mathematical considerations, he tries to avoid giving 'symbol shock' to the reader by lucidly explaining each symbol and principle as it is introduced.

NUNNALLY, J. C. (1964) *Educational Measurement and Evaluation.* New York, McGraw-Hill.
Intended for prospective teachers, this book concentrates on the use of mental tests in improving educational decision-making. It covers basic principles of measurement and evaluation, the construction and use of teacher-made tests, the uses and limitations of standardised achievement tests, prediction and trait measurement in relation to both cognitive and non-cognitive characteristics, and the development of school testing programmes.

NUTTALL, D. L. and WILMOTT, A. S. (1972) *British Examinations: Techniques of Analysis.* Slough, NFER.
This book is focused on examination methodology, and in particular on reliability and question analysis. The research techniques are outlined in the context of both GCE and CSE examinations. The extent to which our examinations are able to do the job that is required of them is explored. Suggestions for improving current practices are made.

REMMERS, H. H., GAGE, N. L. and RUMMEL, J. F. (1966) *A Practical Intro-
    duction to Measurement and Evaluation.* New York, Harper and Row.
Intended as an initial text for teachers and educational administrators,
statistical concepts are presented and explained. The classification of educational objectives and the evaluation of the effectiveness of instruction is
covered at an appropriate level. Criticisms of the uses of tests are discussed.

SCANNELL, D. and TRACY, R. (1975) *Testing and Measurement in the Class-
    room.* Boston, Houghton Mifflin.
The authors discuss measurement as an integral part of teaching, giving
particular emphasis to classroom applications. Various types of measuring
instrument are described and their uses in both the cognitive and affective
fields discussed. A section on grading and reports is included.

STANLEY, J. C. and HOPKINS, K. D. (1972) *Educational and Psychological
    Measurement* (fifth edition). Englewood Cliffs, Prentice-Hall.
This is a revision of a popular book by Stanley entitled *Measurement in
Today's Schools* (1964). The authors assume that their readers have no
formal training in psychology or statistics, and have produced a basic textbook for measurement and evaluation courses at the undergraduate level.

STODOLA, Q. and STORDAHL, K. (1967) *Basic Educational Tests and Measure-
    ment.* Chicago, Science Research Associates.
This is an introductory text covering the theoretical and applied concepts
essential to the understanding of educational measurement. The statistical
bases of the various instruments are not examined in depth. This book
contains eighteen self-tests to help the reader assess his understanding of
the material covered. Among the aspects of measurement discussed are
measurement theory, classroom tests, standardised tests and the applications
of educational measurement.

STRUENING, E. L. and GUTTENTAT, M. (Eds.) (1976) *Handbook of Evaluation
    Research,* Vols 1 and 2. London, Sage.
Articles by forty-five experts have produced a valuable reference book
offering guidance on the theoretical and practical problems of evaluation in the
social sciences.

TENBRINK, T. D. (1974) *Evaluation : A Practical Guide for Teachers.* Maiden-
    head, McGraw-Hill (UK).
This volume considers the function of evaluation in education with particular
reference to the work of the teacher. It requires no initial knowledge of
statistics. The collection and interpretation of information in the service of
effective decision-making is explored. Each chapter begins with specific
behavioural objectives and contains exercises that allow the reader to determine whether or not, from his point of view, they have been achieved. The
planning and construction of norm-referenced and criterion-referenced tests
is dealt with, as is the development of questionnaires, interview schedules
and sociometric measures.

THORNDIKE, R. L. (Ed.) (1971) *Educational Measurement* (second edition).
    Washington, D.C., American Council on Education.
This is a leading reference book and text for post-graduate study in the

theory and practice of educational measurement. Twenty foremost experts under Thorndike's editorship have produced a book worthy of the tradition of its illustrious predecessor. In four sections it covers Test Design, Construction, Administration and Processing, Special Types of Tests, Measurement Theory and The Application of Tests to Educational Problems.

THORNDIKE, R. L. and HAGEN, E. (1976) *Measurement and Evaluation in Psychology and Education* (fourth edition). New York, Wiley.
In this very popular introductory textbook the authors have stressed the practical uses of measurement by teachers, guidance personnel and educational psychologists. The authors explain basic concepts and describe various types of instruments. Examples are given of the selection, administration and interpretation of several types of assessment procedures in the school setting.

THYNE, J. M. (1974) *Principles of Examining*. London, Hodder and Stoughton.
This book provides practical guidance on the techniques necessary for the production of valid examinations. Chapters 8 and 9 give a helpful consideration of the relative strengths and weaknesses of criterion-referenced and norm-referenced tests.

TRIANDIS, H. C. (1971) *Attitudes and Attitude Change*. New York, Wiley.
The author presents a survey of recent developments in the theory and measurement of attitudes and attitude change. Some important current controversies are discussed and suggestions for research projects are put forward.

TYLER, R. W. (Ed.) (1969) *Educational Evaluation: New Roles, New Means*. Sixty-eighth Yearbook of the National Society for the Study of Education, Chicago, Part 2. Distributed by the University of Chicago Press.
Seventeen specialists consider developments in evaluation that have taken place over the past thirty years. The book is intended as supplementary reading for teachers, curriculum specialists and administrators. Topics discussed include theoretical issues, evaluation in relation to guidance, group and individualised instruction, the impact of machines on measurement and a consideration of the ways in which full use might be made of the potential of evaluation in improving education.

B. Books. ii. Test Construction

ANSTEY, E. (1966) *Psychological Tests*. London, Nelson.
Dr Anstey provides a clear account of some of the procedures currently available for constructing psychological tests and for evaluating the results obtained from them. The major part of the book is concerned with the design and construction of a test for a specific purpose. It is a great pity that, at present, this book is out of print.

BEGGS, D. L. and LEWIS, E. L. (1975) *Measurement and Evaluation in the Schools.* Boston, Houghton Mifflin.
The authors take a pragmatic approach to the uses of measurement and evaluation. The statistical aspect is minimised. The inter-relationship between educational objectives and the development of a school testing programme is considered. A discussion of the strengths and weaknesses of both normative and criterion-referenced tests is presented, the development of standardised tests being given quite detailed treatment. Each of the book's ten chapters commences with a list of concerns and concludes with reflections plus a set of exercises.

BORMUTH, J. R. (1970) *On the Theory of Achievement Test Items.* Chicago, University of Chicago Press.
In this book Bormuth questions the validity of certain approaches to the writing of items for use in conventional achievement tests. His major argument is that test items written in the traditional manner are based on intuition rather than through a process open to public inspection, despite the statistical operations that are then performed on the items. Bormuth suggests that a theory of achievement test items can be developed on the basis of linguistics. An appendix by Peter Menzel considers this proposition in some detail. The implications of this work for test construction are considerable.

EDWARDS, A. L. (1957) *Techniques of Attitude Scale Construction.* New York, Appleton-Century-Crofts.
This book is extremely helpful to anyone interested in measuring attitudes. Six methods are described and their weaknesses and strengths discussed. Examples of how the scales are constructed are given in sufficient simplicity and detail that anyone with minimal mathematical knowledge should be able to follow them.

EVANS, K. M. (1965) *Attitudes and Interests in Education.* London, Routledge and Kegan Paul.
This is an introduction to the study of attitudes and interests built up by children. It includes a brief consideration of the instruments used in the assessment of attitudes and interests at an elementary level but with ample indications to the reader of where more advanced material may be found.

FURST, E. J. (1961) *Constructing Evaluation Instruments.* New York, Longmans, Green and Co.
This book is in two sections. The first presents a consideration of such basic problems as Determining What to Evaluate, Defining the Behaviour, Selecting Appropriate Situations, Getting a Record and Summarising the Evidence. The second section presents an account of the construction of achievement tests.

MCINTOSH, D. M., WALKER, D. A. and MACKAY, D. (1962) *The Scaling of Teachers' Marks and Estimates.* London, Oliver and Boyd.
The authors explain how classroom marks and estimates of children's relative performances in various tasks can be turned into acceptably valid measures on a standard scale. The fundamental principle in scaling is to make the

mean and dispersions of one set of marks comparable to that of another. The ways in which this can be done in various practical situations are discussed and illustrated.

NUTTALL, D. L. and SKURNIK, L. S. (1969) *Examinations and Item Analysis Manual.* Slough, NFER.
The authors present a method of analysing the results of tests or examinations in which all questions are compulsory, considerable in number and able to be marked correct or incorrect with high reliability. A multiple-choice sentence completion test of reading comprehension would be an example. The concept of 'measuremetre' as a practical index of reliability is introduced. This is a very helpful handbook for teachers considering constructing an objective type test in any subject area.

OPPENHEIM, A. N. (1972) *Questionnaire Design and Attitude Measurement.* London, Heinemann.
This book has proved popular with research students requiring an introduction to the field. It is an Open University set book.

PAYNE, D. A. and MCMORRIS, R. F. (Eds.) (1974) *Educational and Psychological Measurement: Contributions to Theory and Practice.* New York, General Learning Press.
The series of readings comprising this book spell out all the stages and considerations involved in the development of a psychological test. The chapters have themselves been rated by student readers for readability, clarity of exposition and relevance to professional needs. The final chapter gives an interesting treatment of the social perspective of educational and psychological testing.

SCHOER, L. A. (1970) *Test Construction: A Programmed Guide.* Boston, Allyn and Bacon.
This programmed text is intended for use in test and measurement courses at the undergraduate level. The functions of testing in the teaching programme are considered. Readers are taken through all the steps involved in constructing a classroom test and in validating it.

B. Books. iii. Critical discussions of mental measurement

BLACK, H. (1963) *They Shall Not Pass: The World of School Testing from Kindergarten IQs to College Entrance Exams.* New York, Morrow.
The author's aim is to encourage a more sceptical yet informed attitude towards the use of standardised testing in educational programmes. It is addressed to the general public rather than to professionals working in education.

GOLDMAN, L. (1971) *Using Tests in Counselling* (second edition). New York, Appleton-Century-Crofts.
For the teacher wanting an informed and balanced assessment of the

contribution of psychological tests in helping individuals to understand themselves, their abilities, aptitudes and interests, this book is excellent. It aims to
answer the question: 'How can a counsellor/teacher help her students to use
a wide variety of psychological test information to plan and live their lives as
effectively as possible?' Goldman does not overstate his case. He shows a
caution not always found when the uses and limitations of testing are considered. The concluding sentence of his book vividly demonstrates his
moderation: 'Used properly and intelligently, tests should be able to make
a small but noticeable contribution to individuals who are seeking to find
themselves and their place in the world' (p. 446).

GROSS, M. L. (1962) *The Brain Watchers*. New York, Random House.
This book is an attack on the use of mental tests, with particular reference to
abuses relating to the testing of personality in both business and industry.
The book is polemic in style. Chapter 7 is called 'Brain Watching in Our
Schools'.

HOFFMANN, B. (1962) *The Tyranny of Testing*. New York, Crowell-Collier.
Hoffmann is a distinguished scientist and mathematician, formerly a co-
worker of Einstein and a member of the Princeton Institute for Advanced
Studies. For many years a test consultant of the Westinghouse Annual
Science Talent Search, Professor Hoffmann questions some of the assumptions and practices of 'objective-test' constructors. The book is non-technical,
written in a popular style and attempts to be very controversial. His more
balanced conclusions tend to be lost within the strong presentation of the
case against testing. Despite this, his point of view is one which anyone
interested in mental measurement should consider.

LUMSDEN, J. (1976) Test theory. In ROSENZWEIG, M. R. and PORTER,
    L. W. (Eds.) *Annual Review of Psychology, Vol. 27*. Palo Alto, Annual
    Reviews Inc.
An up-to-date and cogent criticism, presented with humour, of aspects of the
theory and practice of mental testing.

REICHMANN, W. J. (1964) *Use and Abuse of Statistics*. Harmondsworth,
    Penguin.
This is not a textbook. It is intended for the non-mathematician who would
like to know something about the nature of statistics, and when and how they
should or should not be used. No particular mathematical ability is required
to cope with the many topics considered, although some calculations are
included. The more difficult ones are assigned to an appendix. In all cases
the author's aim is not to solve particular problems but to illuminate the
principles involved. This book is very useful preliminary reading for anyone
venturing into the field of mental measurement yet lacking a background in
mathematics.

C. Professional journals

The British Journal of Educational Psychology, London, British Psychological Society. Issued three times yearly: February, June and November.

The British Journal of Mathematical and Statistical Psychology, London, British Psychological Society. Issued twice yearly in May and November.

Educational and Psychological Measurement, Durham, North Carolina. Issued quarterly.

Evaluation in Education : International Progress, Pergamon Press, Headington Hall, Oxford, OX3 0BW. Issued quarterly (vol. 1 will appear in 1977).

Journal of Educational Measurement, East Lansing, Michigan, National Council of Measurement in Education. Issued quarterly.

Measurement and Evaluation in Guidance, Washington, D.C., American Personnel and Guidance Association. Issued four times yearly: January, April, July and October.

Psychometrika, Richmond, Virginia, Psychometric Society. Issued four times yearly: March, June, September and December.

Index